FRIED WALLEYE & CHERRY PIE

AT TABLE

Fried Walleye & Cherry Pie

MIDWESTERN WRITERS ON FOOD

Edited and with an Introduction by Peggy Wolff

UNIVERSITY OF NEBRASKA PRESS
LINCOLN AND LONDON

Acknowledgment for the use of
copyrighted material appears on
pp. 257–58, which constitutes an
extension of the copyright page.
Manufactured in the United
States of America

∞

Library of Congress
Cataloging-in-Publication Data
Fried walleye and cherry pie:
midwestern writers on food /
edited by Peggy Wolff.
pages cm — (At table)
ISBN 978-0-8032-3645-5
(pbk.: alk. paper);
978-0-8032-4855-7 (pdf web)
1. Cooking, American—Midwestern
style. 2. Cooking—Middle West.
3. International cooking—
Anecdotes. 4. Food habits—Middle
West—Anecdotes. 5. Authors,
American—Middle West—
Miscellanea. 6. Middle
West—Social life and customs—
Anecdotes. I. Wolff, Peggy,
editor of compilation. II. Title:
Midwestern writers on food.
TX715.2.M53F85 2013
641.5977—dc23   2013022747

Set in Minion by Laura Wellington.
Designed by Nathan Putens.

In memory of my father

Growing up, my favorite hot dog was the one at Wrigley Field, home of the Chicago Cubs. "It's just a ballpark hot dog," my dad would say. But no other Vienna Beef dog anywhere else was the same. That's because we waited in line together, the thick smoke from the vendor's cart seeping into our noses, our hair, and our mitts, while we watched our red hots stuffed into a poppy-seed bun. This was where I learned that food is not just food. It's the experience that counts — where you are, whom you are with, and, if you're lucky, a win for the home team. Thanks, Dad.

Contents

Holidays, Fairs, and Events

A Full Belly

The Midwestern Sweet Tooth

Acknowledgments

Thanks to Harriet Bell for green-lighting a collection of food stories and being a wonderful ally; Lisa Ekus for being completely thorough and steering me through this; and farmers David and Susan Cleverdon for teaching me the ways of an organic micro farm.

This project would have been a lot more difficult without the support of in-house editors Heather Lundine and Bridget Barry at UNP; also my summer intern Allison Grover, for a hundred helpful things; and my children, Jordan, for tech support and formatting, and Zoe, for all illustrations.

Thanks also to the "Tuesdays" at the Wesley Writers Workshop and to leaders Sharon and Steve Fiffer for giving generously of their time; and to so many friends for recipe testing: Sonja and Eric Anderson, Ellen Barreto, Claudia Fariello Bolnick, Pat Hitchens-Bonow, Meri Clement, Laura Friedman, Linda Gartz, Elise Kapnick, Holly Raider, Lauren Taslitz, and Lindy Waldman.

Thank you Glencoe Roast Coffee and Park City's Silver Star Café, because working at home is never any fun.

And I embrace longtime writing pals Pamela and Pat, for giving real meaning to the word "write-in." Lastly, to Sam, for any measure you want to apply, especially for enjoying the pleasures of the table with me.

Introduction

When I was eleven years old I wrote a hate letter to Betty Crocker. The chocolate chip cookies I baked from Betty's *Picture Cookbook* didn't look at all like the ones in the book's photo. Those cookies could transport you, lacy yet chewy looking, studded with chocolate chunks folded into the dough, piled four high on a pristine white plate. Mine were soggy in the middle, lacking crispy brown edges, a flop. It was all her fault and I thought she should know.

Betty wrote me back! I imagined the most popular American woman, second only to Eleanor Roosevelt for a time (according to *Fortune* magazine), sitting at her desk up there in Minnesota at General Mills, rolling up her sleeves, and typing *me* a letter.

I don't have the letter today, but the way I remember it, she was truly sorry my cookies didn't come out right, and she meant it. She suggested that I measure the ingredients carefully because they test all their recipes in the Betty Crocker kitchen. To show her regret, she sent me a consolation prize: a hardcover book full of cooking basics, tips, and food preparation terms *and* a set of colored measuring spoons. They were *mine*. They came from Betty.

I was flattered beyond words, rubbing elbows with celebrity. My package was from the queen of the Midwest, the Martha Stewart of the twentieth century, and her image said, "I am competent. I don't burn the roast."

With my new book and measuring spoons, I was in business, wonderfully armed with the first tools of my kitchen. Though I now know the cheery all-American Betty to be a myth, a fictitious character invented to pen a warm, friendly signature to all those letters giving advice to home cooks, still, opening such a package kick-started a lifelong love of cooking and eating.

I grew up in the Midwest and live there now. Of all the collections of contemporary food writing that have appeared in recent years, none have come from the heartland, the region where *the whole food industry began*!

Alongside the innovative mechanical staples — cast-steel plows, tractors, reapers designed to satisfy the needs of the average U.S. family farmer — the Midwest gave the nation the food giants and the whole industrial processing of grains, which amounts to nearly everything we grew up eating. Quaker Oats, Post Grape-Nuts, Wheaties, Rice Krispies, Jiffy, Bisquick, Crisco, and Spam. Swanson's gave us frozen TV dinners; Kraft gave us the ultimate childhood food in a box, mac 'n' cheese. Also from the heartland, the Weber grill, the Reuben sandwich, Oreos, Cracker Jack, the hot dog bun, Good Humors, Hostess Twinkies, and sloppy joes. Midwestern entrepreneurs gave the country fast-food chains such as Pizza Hut, Domino's, Wendy's, Arby's, and White Castle. And the franchise that set its headquarters here, McDonald's.

I felt that it was time to build a collection of heartland food stories from the region's most talented authors. I asked them to recall the times when food triggered a memory, raised a question, or was a starting place for a meditation on the times when growing or cooking or eating became an unforgettable experience. Stories told around and about the table with midwestern foods in the starring role.

As much as *Fried Walleye and Cherry Pie: Midwestern Writers on Food* is memoir — a voyeuristic peek into a life — it's also informational. Who knew about Japanese Mirai corn in Illinois? The Iowa skinny? That gourmet tamale? The top-selling cake pan in the world . . . from Minnesota?

To see this region, get inside a speeding car on the interstate. Start at the eastern border in Ohio where the Midwest region begins, farmed by people like the Amish who use no electricity or modern farm machinery and don't stretch the seasons but adhere to the notion of the ticking of the seasonal clock. Drive west from there and you will see large-scale postmodern agribusinesses that don't feel the slightest quickening at the sign of cold weather because technology has smoothed the boundaries between seasons.

Make your way through the Corn Belt in the three "I" states: Indiana, Illinois, and Iowa. Corn, wheat, soybeans, corn, exit ramp, corn, and every few miles a herd of pigs or sheep way off on a reach in the distance, a house, a tree with a tire swing, a barn, a satellite dish. You will see America's pastoral face. Grain silos are the only skyline.

Some of this land is flat as a cracker, a rural crossroads where corn is king. There is a hot breeze and, in the wipe of blue sky, a wedge of birds. Piercingly loud and soaring like gulls with extended wings, killdeer throw the boomerang of their song across the ripening fields. Zigzagging along the sides of roads are fields of green, like tiles of colored dominoes laid end to end, the green tint of the Mongolian garlic matching that of the Siberian garlic chive; the very rare Japanese shallot butted up against crookneck squash. French Batavia lettuce next to Winter Density.

Now head north. You think the Midwest is landlocked? Stand on the rocky northern bluffs of Wisconsin with Lake Michigan to the east, Sturgeon Bay to the south, Green Bay to the west, and Death's Door with its smattering of islands to the north.

Head back south through the dense forests of the northern Midwest, its wide and fertile river valleys and broad expanses of grasslands, into Nebraska and Kansas. Here, in America's middle ground, are ranchers letting herds of cattle roam in open pastures, fattening on grass, not corn, just the way livestock was meant to be raised. A fog hangs just over the fields even though it is over eighty degrees and climbing. Later on, the skies can turn green with tornado-warning storms, and at night lightning can run magnificent and terrible from the horizons.

Need some refreshment? Get off the striped pavement and pull over at a farm. Coming up the long drive, the farm and all the outbuildings look like rising bread against a backdrop of folded countryside. The farmer will get you to the right road and the road will get you to the diner. If you're lucky, and there's still pie, the most agreeable food a farmer's family can make, go ahead, explore the boundaries of *sweet*. It will sustain your hunger until dinnertime.

In *Fried Walleye and Cherry Pie: Midwestern Writers on Food* this wonderful group of authors write about food so simply and exuberantly that I cannot help thinking that I missed out on something by not having farm roots, or not crossing the country in search of pie.

Writing from a culinary lens, Sue Hubbell explains that good pie cannot be found within one mile of an interstate. After reading her overland pie quest, you'll want to search too at an independent truck stop for apple pie that is every bit as good as that served in the United States Senate Family Dining Room.

In "Midwestern Staples," you'll get a mouthful of our iconic foods — beef, corn, cheese, grains, and pork. Here you can follow Robert Olmstead's digressions into the Aztec civilization when he delves into all the variations of Cincinnati chili. Also, there's a lively memoir from Stuart Dybek about a school field trip to a slaughtering house and from Elizabeth Berg a nostalgic look back at her aunt's meatloaf and her longing for the ritual of family dinnertime that has all but vanished today. In Peter Sagal's essay the city made infamous by Upton Sinclair's meatpacking exposé grapples with fattened duck liver, and it does so the Chicago way.

"Distant Cultures" is a section offering up tales of the Midwest as culinary melting pot. Because so many churches in the middle of the country have sponsored refugees, great ethnic food is no longer confined to the country's perimeters or our urban centers. As Carol Mighton Haddix will show you, their foods have gone beyond the boundaries of their original neighborhoods. For many immigrants who need to earn a living, daily life often means the food business, whether lunch stand or food truck, diner or deli. Greek author Harry Mark Petrakis brings us an elegiac and pensive story as he remembers the redeeming aspects of what was for him at the time an exhausting experience owning a south side Chicago lunchroom.

In "Holidays, Fairs, and Events" you'll find a vivid memoir from comedy writer John Markus about wandering the midway at his Ohio county fair and lusting after much more than fried foods-on-a-stick.

And while we're on the road, unplugged from all the servers, databases, and webmasters that rule our daily lives, we can spend a day with Lorna Landvik at the Minnesota State Fair, nibbling on every calorie-laden food.

In "A Full Belly" you'll find essays on memorable experiences from lives centered around food. Molly O'Neill, whose culinary path all over America has taken her to the best addresses for food, traveled back to her Ohio hometown and found that the heart of the country was rapidly becoming the center of the second wave of the gourmet revolution. Douglas Bauer concentrates on the midday farm dinner, his mother's ambitious preparations from the moment of first field work in spring to the end of the harvest, and how he, as a young boy, saw that the kitchen routine was harder than the laborer's work out in the field.

In "The Midwestern Sweet Tooth," a section devoted to our rich, sugary foods, Bonnie Jo Campbell deconstructs a homemade fudge recipe from an old *Joy of Cooking*. Along the way she serves up thoughts about candy making as a means toward a more meaningful life.

These stories and nineteen more follow the authors' passions and appetites, at times focusing on the uncelebrated, homely, traditional foods that were at the time completely off the radar of almost everyone who made a living caring or writing about food. And they bring us into the present by showing us how to live a locavore's life in the upper Midwest or how gene splicing the DNA of sweet corn gave us a hybrid that has, well, everything.

I offer this collection for armchair road trippers and foodies and those who want to peer into the nooks and crannies of the region and make hunger-induced pit stops in the culinary middle ground. Pull up a chair and help yourself. I hope you find enough to satisfy your appetite.

FRIED WALLEYE & CHERRY PIE

Midwestern Staples

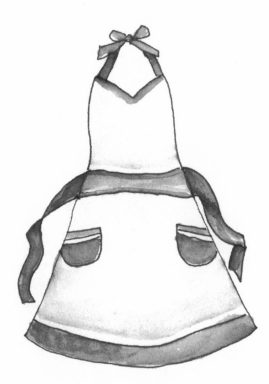

Where has all the meatloaf gone? Where is the meatloaf of yesteryear? Sometime during the seventies we became food snobs. No more casseroles with cream of mushroom soup. No more meatloaf from the recipe on the side of an oatmeal box. And everyone too busy for the shared family dinnertime experience. This is the heartfelt concern of an author who reaches into her memory and comes up with the dish that restores her.

In the Midwest, It's Meatloaf

Elizabeth Berg

I was raised an Army brat. That meant I was jerked irregularly from one location to the next. I lived overseas in Germany; I lived on a farm in Indiana; I lived in Oklahoma and Texas and Missouri. But my home state was Minnesota, smack dab in the Midwest. And so, naturally, I love meatloaf.

Meatloaf may very well be a descendent of European pâté. The first recipe was published around 1900. The ingredients can vary widely, but the taste is always the same: truly satisfying. The usual method is to use a mix of beef, pork, and veal; one or two eggs; a liquid such as tomato juice or milk; an "extender" such as oatmeal, crackers, or bread crumbs; and spices ranging from salt and pepper to mint and marjoram. You mix the ingredients with a spoon if you're a wimp or by hand if you know how to have fun, and when everything hangs together, you put it in a loaf pan and bake it for about an hour and a half.

Growing up, my favorite meatloaf was my Aunt Lala's. "It's only from the recipe on the box of Quaker Oats," she would say modestly. But if you followed that recipe to the letter, it would not be the same. That is because the recipe says nothing about washing up before dinner

---

Elizabeth Berg is the author of many bestselling novels. *Open House* was an Oprah's Book Club pick, and both *Durable Goods* and *Joy School* were chosen as the American Library Association's Best Book of the Year. She is at work on her next novel. She has also written two short story collections, two works of nonfiction, and one play. Her website is elizabeth-berg.net, which features her popular blog, and she also chimes in frequently on Facebook. She lives and eats near Chicago.

in Lala's kitchen sink with Ivory soap and drying off with a towel that smelled pleasantly of laundry detergent. Nor does it say anything about preparing the table with a well-worn embroidered tablecloth. Or serving mashed potatoes and Blue Lake green beans as accompaniments in pastel-colored bowls — pink or green or yellow. That is what you must have with meatloaf. You also must have apple pie for dessert, made from scratch, the crust rolled out on the kitchen table to the sound of great music, preferably big bands like Tommy Dorsey and Glen Miller.

There used to be a lot of support for serving meatloaf. I'm sure the Stones and the Cleavers had it all the time. Probably Ed Sullivan, too, although you never got to see him eat. Every time I saw a cowboy movie where the handsome lead would stay to dinner after having mended the fence, I was sure that meatloaf was what he'd eaten. "Thanks for the meal, ma'am," he would say, looking up from his empty plate and untucking his blue-and-white-checked napkin from the front of his shirt. "That was mighty good." The heroine, bosom heaving, would tell him that he was very welcome and suggest that perhaps he should . . . stay awhile. She would come closer, ostensibly to pick up his plate, but really to let him smell her perfume. And on that plate would be the telltale signs of meatloaf, I was sure of it. Aunt Lala's rolled-oat recipe, served on a blue-speckled tin plate. I mean, really, what else *would* it have been? Eggplant stuffed with goat cheese? Baby vegetables? Pasta?? No. It was meatloaf.

Of course it's not just the taste of meatloaf that I love. It's the memory of the whole dinnertime experience that particular dish represents. You remember this: You'd be lying on your belly in your striped shirt watching *The Mickey Mouse Club*. Your mother would be in the kitchen wearing an apron and making dinner. You'd hear a few bangs and clangs, drawers sliding in and out, the thunka-THUNKA-thunka of the knife against the chopping board. And pretty soon, seductive finger-like waves of smell would come from the kitchen out into the living room to find you. They would float under your nose and past you, then curl around for another go-by. It would be getting harder and harder to pay attention to Spin and Marty. You would feel very close to being levitated, like the cartoon figures who floated in the air, seeming to body surf on currents of smell alone. Eventually you would have to do the inevitable: leave *The Mickey Mouse Club* to announce to your mother that unless you ate instantly, you would die.

"Pretty soon," she would say, her back to you, and you would know she was lie, lie, lying because there she was at the sink, *peeling potatoes.* They were not boiling and almost done. They weren't even in the pot! "Pretty soon" my eye! You'd be in another geologic age before you ate! You would explain some of this to your mother. You would ask for a bite of the meatloaf in the oven; surely the ends were done. You would be given a piece of raw potato (this chosen over the alternative, a stupid carrot) and you would sulk a little, stomp your feet a little if you thought you could get away with it, and then salt the potato piece and viciously eat it. Then you would go and finish watching television.

At last it would be time. Your father would come home, a tidy stack of white bread would be put on the table next to his plate (because he ate the most of it), and everyone would wash up and sit down. You would put butter on your potatoes and catsup on your meatloaf and eat the green beans first because, although they were good, they weren't the best. Probably after dinner you had to help with the dishes, and if you were the younger sibling you were stuck with the dreaded task of drying. It occurs to me now that there is still a part of me that believes everyone grew up this way, that I could say "meatloaf" to any passing stranger and the same rich and familiar imagery that comes to me would come to them. What a wonderfully secure and narrow-minded sensibility I had! For years, my kaleidoscope was fixed in one position: All fathers worked. All mothers stayed home with their children. Though you weren't rich, you didn't worry about money. And everyone had meatloaf once a week.

Well. My worldview may have widened, but I still love meatloaf and I still make it, though certainly not once a week. For one thing, it is RED MEAT. For another, it is no longer stylish, unless it is gourmet meatloaf, in which case it is not meatloaf. In fact, I'm a little shy about admitting my love of meatloaf to anyone I don't know well. But I've got a lot of recipes for meatloaf, and I make them, including a potato-frosted one, which is my favorite. The thing about meatloaf is how good it is cold, too. Better than turkey, oh yes. What you do is you put mayonnaise *and* mustard on. Don't mess with lettuce because anything crunchy interferes with the comfort food factor. And use icky white bread because it *enhances* the comfort food factor.

The biggest reason I don't make meatloaf a lot, though, is that I don't cook very much anymore. This bothers me. Because I believe that cooking is about more than taking care of a certain unrelenting biological need. I believe it is spiritual, and calming, and centering. I believe that making something with your own hands and feeding it to the ones you love is communicating something that can't be communicated any other way. As families, we need the time required for preparing and eating dinner to just be together, to see what comes up for conversation, to look around the table and see the faces of those we live with. We need to save this stuff, store it in some vital compartment, because we will need it later. It will sustain and support us, keep us from feeling bad when some stranger is yelling at us, when we lose a job, when our honeys break our hearts.

But times have changed, irrevocably, I suppose. It's hard to have time to make old-fashioned meals. People eat instant mashed potatoes, take-out food, microwaved meals (low cal, low fat, low everything but price). Schedules are crazy — it's a rare thing for all members of a family to sit down together. I'm sad for the loss of that; I'm scared it will never come back; and I make meatloaf every now and then to pretend it's still possible to live the way we used to.

Not long ago, I found myself cracking up a little — snapping at my husband and the kids, lying in bed at night staring at the wall and sighing. This can and does happen to all of us, I suppose — I mean, we *do* live in the nineties. I took a little vacation by myself so I could heal. I went to an ocean-side town and stopped first at the local grocery store. The place I was staying at had a little kitchenette, and I needed to stock up. I wasn't interested in eating in restaurants; I was interested in holing up, lying around in my underwear, and reading.

I bought some designer water. I got some nice-looking fruit and cheese, some eggs. And then, over at the deli counter, I spotted some meatloaf. There were several fat slices, all on white Styrofoam trays, covered rather sickly with plastic wrap. It wasn't like my aunt Lala's and it wasn't like mine, you could tell. The truth is, it sort of looked like dog food. But it was meatloaf, symbol of too much to pass up. I bought it all. And when I got to my little place, I made a meatloaf sandwich. As soon as I ate it, I felt better. Honest. Not everything changes.

Although the Chicago stockyards were dismantled and have been gone for over thirty years, the author got a firsthand view of the city's legendary meat-packing plant.

Field Trips

Stuart Dybek

We took two field trips in grade school. The first was a tour of the
Bridewell House of Corrections and the Cook County jail. The
next year the nuns avoided the jail and instead took us to the stockyards,
a trip that required a bus. A rented yellow school bus was already waiting
when we got to school that morning, and we filed on, boys sitting on
the left side of the aisle, girls on the right. I sat next to a new kid, Joseph
Bonnamo. Usually, new kids were quiet and withdrawn, but Bonnamo,
who'd only been at St. Roman for a couple weeks, was already the most
popular boy in class. Everyone called him Joey B. His father had been
a Marine lifer and Joey B. was used to moving around, he said. He'd
moved around so much that he was a grade behind, a year older than
everyone else, but he didn't seem ashamed of it. He was a good athlete,
and all the girls had crushes on him. That included Sylvie Perez, who
over the summer had suddenly, to use my mother's word, "developed."
Exploded into bloom was closer to the truth. Along with the rest of the
boys, I pretended as best I could not to notice — it was too intimidating
to those of us who'd been her classmates for years. But not to Joey B.

Stuart Dybek is the author of three books of fiction, *Childhood and Other Neighborhoods*, *The Coast of Chicago*, and *I Sailed with Magellan*, and two collections of poetry, *Brass Knuckles* and *Streets in Their Own Ink*. His poetry, fiction, and nonfiction have appeared regularly in magazines such as the *New Yorker*, the *Atlantic*, *Tin House*, and *Poetry* and in numerous anthologies, including both *Best American Fiction* and *Best American Poetry*. Among the many prizes he has received for his work are a Guggenheim Fellowship, a Lannan Writers Award, the Rea Prize for the short story, and an award from the MacArthur Foundation.

"Like my old man says, tits that size have a mind of their own," he confided to me on the way to the Yards, "and hers are thinking, 'Feel me up Joey B.'"

"How do you know?"

His hand dropped down and he clutched his crotch. "Telepathy."

"Class," Sister Bull Moose asked, "do you know our tradition when riding a bus on a field trip?"

"A round pound?" Joey B. whispered to me.

No one raised a hand. We didn't know we had a tradition — as far as we knew we were the first class from St. Roman ever to take a bus on a field trip.

Sister Bull Moose's real name was Sister Amabilia, but she had a heft to her that meant business, and she wielded the baton she used to conduct choir practice not unlike the guard we'd seen wielding a nightstick at Bridewell a year before, so my friend Rafael had come up with the nickname. From within her habit, a garment that appeared to have infinite storage capacity, she produced the pitch pipe also used in choir practice and sustained a note. "Girls start, and boys come in on 'Merrily merrily merrily . . .'"

Joey B. sang in my ear, "Row row row your boner . . ."

At the Yards there was a regular tour. First stop was the Armour packing plant, where the meat was packaged into bacon and sausage. I think that the entire class was relieved that the smell wasn't as bad as we worried it might be. We knew we had traveled to the source of what in the neighborhood was called "the brown wind" or "the glue pee-ew factory," a stench that settled over the south side of Chicago at least once a week. My father said it was the smell of boiling hooves, hair, and bone rendered to make soap. I'd once dissected a bar of Ivory on which I'd noticed what appeared to be animal hair to see if there were also fragments of bone and if beneath the soap smell I could detect the reek of the Yards.

We left the processing plant for the slaughterhouse and from a metal catwalk looked upon the scene below, where workmen wearing yellow hard hats and white coats smeared with gore heaved sledgehammers down on the skulls of the steers that, urged by electric prods, filed obediently through wooden chutes.

Every time the hammer connected, my friend Rafael would go, "Ka-boom!"

The steer would drop, folding at the knees.

"That has to smart," Joey B. said.

For the finale they took us to where the hogs were slaughtered. A man with hairy, thick, spattered forearms, wearing rubber boots and a black rubber apron shiny with blood, stood holding a butcher knife before a vat of water: An assembly line of huge, squealing hogs, suspended by their hind legs, swung past him, and as each hog went by, the line would pause long enough for the man to slit the hog's throat. He did it with a practiced, effortless motion, and I wondered how long he'd had the job, what it had been like on his first day, and if it was a job I could ever be desperate enough to do. Up to then, my idea of the worst job one could have was bus driver. I didn't think I could drive through rush-hour traffic down the same street over and over while making change, as bus drivers had to do in those days. But watching the man kill hogs, I began to think that driving a bus might not be so bad.

With each hog there was the same terrified squeal, but louder than a squeal, more like a shriek that became a grunting gurgle of blood. A Niagara of blood splashed to the tile and into a flowing gutter of water, where it rushed frothing away. The man would plunge the knife into the vat of water before him, and the water clouded pink; then he'd withdraw the shining blade just as the next squealing hog arrived. Meanwhile, the hogs who'd just cranked by, still alive, their mouths, nostrils, and slit throats pumping dark red gouts, were swung into a bundle of hanging bodies to bleed. Each new carcass slammed into the others, causing a few weak squeals and a fresh gush of blood.

The tour guide apologized that we couldn't see the sheep slaughtered. He said that some people thought the sheep sounded human, like children, and that bothered some people, so they didn't include it on the tour.

It made me wonder who killed the sheep. We'd seen the men with sledgehammers and the man with a knife. How were the sheep slaughtered? Was it a promotion to work with the sheep — someplace they sent only the most expert slaughterers — or was it the job that nobody at the Yards wanted?

"Just like the goddamn electric chair," Rafael complained.

"How's that?" Joey B. asked.

"They wouldn't let us see the chair when we went to the jail last year."

At the end of the tour, on our way out of the processing plant, they gave each of us a souvenir hot dog. Not a hot dog Chicago-style: poppy-seed bun, mustard — never ketchup — onion, relish, tomato, pickle, peppers, celery salt. This was a cold hot dog wrapped in a napkin. We hadn't had lunch and everyone was starving. We rode back on the bus eating our hot dogs, singing "Frère Jacques."

I was sitting by the window, Joey B. beside me, and right across the aisle from him — no accident, probably — was Sylvie Perez. I realized it was a great opportunity, but I could never think of anything to say to girls in a situation like that.

"Sylvie," Joey B. said, "you liking that hot dog?"

"It's okay," Sylvie said.

"You look good eating it," he told her.

It sounded like the stupidest thing I'd ever heard, but all she did was blush, smile at him, and take another demure nibble.

I knew it was against the rules, but I cracked open the window of the bus and tried to flick my balled-up hot dog napkin into a passing convertible. Sister Bull Moose saw me do it.

"Why does there always have to be one who's not mature enough to take on trips?" she asked, rhetorically. For punishment I had to give up my seat and stand in the aisle, which I did to an indifference on the part of Sylvie Perez that was the worst kind of scorn.

"Since you obviously need special attention, Stuart, you can sing us a round," Sister said. Once, during our weekly music hour, looking in my direction, she'd inquired, "Who is singing like an off-key foghorn?" When I'd shut up, still moving my mouth but only pretending to sing, she'd said, "That's better."

"I don't know the words," I said.

"Oh, I think you do. *Dor-mez-vous, dor-mez-vous, Bim Bam Boon.* They're easy."

Joey B. patted the now empty seat beside him as if to say to Sylvie, "Now you can sit here."

Sylvie rolled her pretty eyes toward Sister Bull Moose and smiled, and Joey B. nodded that he understood and smiled back, and they rode like that in silence, communicating telepathically while I sang.

This essay is from an ex-boxer and former night custodian in a high school who turned short story writer and won awards every writer dreams of. Here, Jones offers a sharp and humorous memoir about working inside a General Mills industrial food factory outside of Chicago during the sixties.

Easter Island Almondine

Thom Jones

I grew up in a factory town, Aurora, Illinois, some forty miles west of Chicago. There were so many factories in Aurora that you could get fired from one in the morning and be spot-welding or running a punch press in another by early afternoon. When I landed a production line job at General Mills in West Chicago, the work was go, go, go, but the bosses were okay. They drove around the plant in two-seater white golf carts wearing white coveralls. None of them growled or yelled or threatened to kill you. If something went wrong they would say, "How can I help you out here?"

I worked the cake-mix line. Machines did most of the packaging. They shaped and folded spring-fed cardboard, forming it into boxes, inserted wax-paper envelopes, then passed them on to a conveyer belt that dropped eighteen ounces of cake mix from gleaming chutes, weighing the boxes — shunting the partially filled ones along a dead-end rail — as the filled and fitted boxes were sealed and sent rolling along on the express line at breakneck speed. At the end of the line production workers such as myself stood at the ready grabbing six boxes at a time (heavy little mothers) that seemed especially dense on days when you showed up sick or hungover, or on shifts when your back might be sore

Thom Jones is the author of three short story collections, *The Pugilist at Rest*, a National Book Award finalist; *Cold Snap*, and *Sonny Liston Was a Friend of Mine*. His stories have been published in the *New Yorker*, *Playboy*, *Esquire*, *Harper's*, and many other publications. His stories have been widely anthologized, and one appeared in *The Best Short Stories of the 20th Century*, edited by John Updike. Jones is a native of Aurora, Illinois, and currently lives in Olympia, Washington.

and all that repetitive weight cantilevered away from your spine. Six at a time they came at you, a blizzard of flour when boxes of lemon poppy-seed cake mix emerged from machines like clowns from a Volkswagen, pi squared only more so. Pi squared to infinity.

The next worker taped the boxes shut and stacked them on pallets. There was lemon poppy-seed flour in the air; it got in your eyes and nose. You could skip lunch and still gain weight on the cake-mix line. All you had to do was breathe. I imagine that you swallowed it, too. If you let something like that throw you, there was a pile of cake boxes on the floor and the whole line had to be shut down. If you wanted your days to go by at a slower clip you could go to the heavy industry factories of Aurora where school lockers, earth-moving equipment, vending machines, and power tools were made. A day could last a century. A week, a millennium. A year could start in the Jurassic Age and go backwards rather than forwards in time. A year was forever.

At GM, time could actually fly and space could move into new dimensions. It was utterly fantastic, everywhere except on the New Country Corn Flakes line. It was not a punishment or a disciplinary assignment, but packing monstrous boxes of cornflakes required unnatural strength and stamina. They hit you harder than the defensive line of the Chicago Bears. Cornflakes could break the human spirit. I was witness to dazed men staggering from the back of the plant drenched in sweat who, if they could speak at all, said things like, "Who the fuck needs this god-damn motherfucking shit, anyhow? I am gone!"

As I saw it, New Country Corn Flakes was the maker of men. An Olympic event. Neck, shoulders, and arms turned to steel. Backs, obliques, and abdomens molded to flexible iron. Hearts developed the sleek splendor of racing steeds. And lastly, it was mind over matter, as is the case with life's most difficult challenges. If you could make it back there, nothing in the everyday world was impossible.

In truth, when a manager pulled over to the cake line and politely requested my services back in cornflakes, my knees tended to buckle, my throat became dry, my palms moist but, like a soldier in the mob, I went into the belly of the beast without complaint. The workers made all this easier, and if not easy, at least fun. Many of them were college students who could earn enough in a summer to get them through a year at undemanding state schools like Northern Illinois U in DeKalb or Southern Illinois U, where you partied, got drunk on your ass and laid every weekend.

The Betty Crocker Noodles Almondine line was a beauty. Two production workers dropped small packets of cracked almonds into the colorful boxes that shuttled past on their way into a machine that filled them with light, crispy noodles. A pal, Bobby, handled them like a card shark. He could backhand them in and juggle with them. ("Four in the air, can he do five? Oh *yeah!*") Bobby coordinated doo-wop songfests with the "B"-operator running the machine. It was a lot of fun but things spun out of control.

Bobby took me aside with alarm on his face. "Some woman wrote executive management about a handwritten note in a box of Almondine. HELP! SLAVE CHAINED TO THE CORNFLAKES LINE. CALL THE NATIONAL GUARD. She said someone carved almonds into little Easter Island heads!"

You would think they'd found a dead mouse in a bottle of Coke. What was the big deal over a few carved almonds?

Word spread around. Any moment the hammer would come down, hard and fast. The plant worked three shifts: days, swing, and graveyard. Every two weeks day-shift workers moved to swing and so on. No one on my shift had any notion of who was writing the notes. And the men on the adjoining shifts, whom we knew peripherally, sorely lacked imagination.

Our guys looked at one another inquisitively. They lay in bed at night and pondered. When you were with a buddy working a line together, eating lunch together, taking breaks side by side in the naivety of youth, you trusted them. And now, suddenly, there was a sociopath among us with the steel-trap mind of an East German spy. I was the guy jabbering on about writing a great novel. I could just see it: *Novel my ass! Jones hasn't penned a line other than those Typhoid Mary fucking notes he stuffs in the noodles almondine.*

But it wasn't me. I was being framed!

When I found myself back out in cornflakes I knew it was only a matter of time. It's hard to box New Country Corn Flakes when you keep looking over your shoulder. You sweat extra.

It was no better the next week when I was head to toe in Strawberry Swirl cake mix. Since people were assigned here or there, I realized it could have been anyone. Trusted friends, well, you just had to wonder. None of my pals were talking to me. The plant buzzed along as always. It remained fastidiously clean as always. Anything that hit the floor went into offal containers. There were times when the cornflakes oven overflowed and it would snow cornflakes from three stories on high. The "B"-operator on the line would immediately shut down the machine and run pell-mell to various portals to prevent jams in a notoriously difficult machine. The cornflakes were an inch and a half deep.

One night during a corn storm a relief team was on level one shoveling New Country Corn Flakes into huge waste barrels. In 1965 cornflakes cost a half cent per box and printed cardboard boxes, a quarter. The plant facilities, overhead, payroll, etc. Take this into account the next time you buy a nine-dollar box of breakfast cereal. The storm grew worse and I went upstairs to investigate. Throughout the plant were vertical escalators. A worker could place a foot on a step, grab the pole, and ride up. You would pass through a hole on the second level and step off there or continue your ride to level three. You could also reverse the procedure and come down, meeting people in either direction, firing off a Beetle Bailey salute, anything, just so you didn't fall off.

That night I saw the ovens backing up and extra help dashing forth to control the problem on level three while I just watched in a detached fashion and rode up and down. What great evil had befallen us? On level two an oven was baking a new snack product, Bugles corn chips. They were made of the same corn that was snowing. Things were going like clockwork. The workers moved methodically with neutral expressions. It reminded me of the pod-loading scene in *Invasion of the Body Snatchers*. Oh, my God! I knew this was going to happen. Are there any *actual* people left or is it just me?

There was an enormous thunderstorm going on outside. The lights flared on and off. Thunder boomed. On and off and then it was just off.

Bobby and I were handed flashlights and sent to dispose of discarded barrels of cornflakes.

"With all this flavorful, nutritious food," Bobby said as he scooped up flakes, "you could feed half of Africa."

The plant had a huge furnace and its flames provided light. Throughout the plant, workers began to revel in the darkness. They sat in small groups and talked Cubs and White Sox.

"Hey, now, kick back, brother. We are getting paid for this shit. Paid overtime!"

"Yeah, man. Paid in spades."

Bobby and I passed a group of layabouts who handed us a large sack of Bugles, still warm from the oven. They were delicious. Bobby and I sat on a pallet of flattened cardboard boxes in the furnace room eating Bugles.

Billy Pierce threw a two-hit shutout the night before. Two outs into the bottom of the ninth, the Indians' pitcher tossed a ball to second to hold Aparicio to the bag when "Jungle" Jim Rivera shot for home like a streak of blue lightning. He made a patented headfirst dive at the plate, won the game, and Comiskey Park almost exploded.

Bobby started laughing. His body was jiggling as he fought to restrain it. His merriment overflowed in waves.

"What's so funny?" I said. "I'm the one headed for Stateville Penitentiary. They think I did it." He laughed all the more.

"Tell me, what in the fuck is so goddamn funny; what in the fuck is the matter with you?"

Bobby straightened up, twisting his neck side to side, making loud cracks. He said, "There was no note."

"What?"

"How many times do I have explain *no*? What is it about *no* that you don't get? There was *no* note, all right? It's all a big hoax. A joke. Nobody wrote a note. Noodles almondine are germ-free. Every box is cleaner than an operating room."

"Well, okay, but who tossed the miniature Easter Island heads in the noodles almondine?"

"No one! Nobody! It was all a joke, dipstick."

It took me a few seconds to drink this information in. I said, "You fucker! It was you! You did this to me! I'll kill you!"

Bobby leaped from the cardboard and ran off into the dark night, baying like a hound: "*Bah rah hahaha ha.*"

I saw his flashlight beam cut through the darkness. It was Bobby's last night. He was driving down to Carbondale the next morning in his MG Midget. Registration for fall semester classes began early Monday morning. The last fleeting words from his mouth were "Suck-*ah!*"

I was too stuffed with Bugles to give chase. In fact, I had to laugh. What a clever motherfucker, Bobby.

They still make Bugles, but forty-four years and counting I have touched nary a one. Too much of a good thing. For all I care you can toss in a box of noodles almondine and send them all to Somalia.

Food has never taken a backseat in Michael Stern's life. He is the true roadfood warrior, best known for spending hours in a car, crisscrossing America to discover barbecue joints, small-town diners, truly local menus, even places that make a specialty of the lesser parts of an animal's anatomy. Circling back to Chicago, Stern's essay on his beloved beef sandwich (no skinny supermarket flap of beef) proves that in his hometown it is still very possible for a traveler to stand up and eat well.

The Sandwich That Is Chicago

Michael Stern

In the years Jane and I have traveled around America looking for authentic regional food, we have learned one surefire way to find it. We think of someone who used to live in the place we are about to explore but doesn't live there anymore. We ask that person what they miss the most. What's the first thing they would eat when they went back home and where would they go to eat it? Almost always, the reply leads to a unique dish and to a restaurant that does something other than reflect national common denominator taste.

I know this trick works because it was only after I moved away from my hometown of Chicago at the age of seventeen that I recognized the importance of the sandwich known as Italian beef: a heap of thin-sliced roast beef soaked with brothy gravy piled into a length of sturdy Italian bread and garlanded with spicy vegetable giardiniera or roasted peppers. I enjoyed plenty of Italian beef growing up but never thought of it as a rarity. Why would I? It is everywhere throughout Chicagoland, served by countless places in the city and suburbs. When I moved to

Born in Chicago and educated at Johns Hopkins, the University of Michigan, Yale, and Columbia, **Michael Stern** is the author, with Jane Stern, of more than forty books about American food and popular culture. After coining the term *Roadfood* for their original guidebook to regional restaurants, the Sterns created Roadfood. com, which originated internet food reporting and inspired countless other media to follow its path. Since 2005 Roadfood.com has hosted gastronomic tours of Chicago, Milwaukee, Austin, Nashville, New England, New York, and New Mexico and annually sponsors the New Orleans Roadfood Festival. The Sterns currently are contributing editors for *Saveur* magazine and regular contributors to *Parade*.

Baltimore to attend school, I was dazzled by new and exciting dishes to eat around the Chesapeake Bay: luxurious crab cakes like nothing I'd ever tasted, oysters and rockfish and country ham and biscuits. One evening in the autumn of my freshman year, my appetite casually drifted toward the pleasant thought of an Italian beef. Maybe double-dipped (sopped with gravy), hot and sweet (with giardiniera and peppers). How nice it would be to have one. None of my classmates knew what I was talking about, and as I browsed the dining choices in and around Baltimore, it became clear that there was no way I would be eating Italian beef until I went back home.

At that moment I finally realized that Italian beef is not something to be taken for granted. It is a distinct regional specialty, as fundamental a marker of Chicago's culinary character as Frango mints, deep-dish pizza, shrimp de Jonghe, chicken Vesuvio, and red hots dragged through the garden in a poppy-seed bun. Indeed, I have come to think of it as the signature dish that embodies Chicago's personality better than any other. It is brawny, intense, symphonic, and, for all its apparent disarray, audaciously composed. As sandwiches go, it is brash and impertinent, but it demands savoir faire in its ordering and eating. In the broadest sense of the expression, it is a taste of Chicago, but to me it is more than that. It is the alpha and omega of American street food.

Italian beef has kin around the country, among them the cheese-steak of Philadelphia, the roast beef po'boy of New Orleans, beef on weck in Buffalo, and the French dip that once was unique to southern California but is now universal. I can say with the certainty of one who has taste-tested the best of them all that no other sandwich is as grand as a fully dressed Italian beef. Even the New Orleans po'boy, when its beef is augmented by a heap of crisp-fried oysters, glorious as the improbable surf-n-turf duet may be, doesn't bear the majesty of an Italian beef combo in which sirloin shares space with a length of fennel-spiked, charcoal-cooked Italian pork sausage in the absorbent maw of a chewy loaf from Gonnella or Turano Bakery.

When Chicagoans casually talk about Italian beef sandwiches, the word Italian frequently is dropped. Like the Corn Belt's favorite sandwich, the tenderloin (pounded-tender pork, crisp fried and bunned), Italian beef is so essential a part of local culinary identity that no explanatory modifier is needed. If the word *beef* is singular, everybody knows it means one thing: an Italian beef sandwich. In most places that make a worthy one, it is not merely a single item on a list of various sandwiches. It is the headliner. Indeed, it is part of the name of many of its stand-out sources: Mr. Beef, Tony's Italian Beef, Carm's Beef & Snack Shop, and the king of them all: Al's #1 Italian Beef.

Prior to *Chicago* magazine naming it the best beef in the city some thirty years ago, Al's #1 Italian Beef used to be named Al's Bar-B-Q. Located on the Near West Side in what was once Little Italy, Al's is to Italian beef what Nick's Cafe of Huntington, Indiana, is to the tenderloin: arguably, the original source. As told to us by Al's co-owner Chris Pacelli Jr., it was his grandfather, Tony Ferreri, who conceived the sandwich during the Great Depression. "He and my uncle Al were doodlers," Chris remembered.

> Forever trying something new. Tony used to drive a carriage along the streets and sell his sandwiches in the hospitals. All the doctors knew him. So one day he decides to shave his beef — thin as you could cut it with a knife — and with a little gravy to soften the bread, everybody wanted some. In 1938 my uncle and my father opened a beef stand to sell it on the sidewalk. They sold beef in its juices in sandwiches and they cooked sausages over charcoal. There were no tables, no place to sit down; people ate all along the street. In those times in this neighborhood, every day was a food festival.

When Al Ferreri's friends and associates saw how well his enterprise was doing, they opened their own beef eateries in and around Little Italy, and during the years after World War II Italian beef stands became part of the Chicago landscape.

Some Italian beef restaurants roast their own meat and brew the gravy (a thin stock like au jus), but for decades now, a large number of places have procured provisions from the Scala Packing Company. Scala has its own story of the sandwich's origin. As Pat Scala explained it to Rich Bowen and Dick Fay, authors of the seminal guidebook *Hot*

Dog Chicago (Chicago Review Press, 1983), his grandfather Pasquale introduced Italian beef during the lean years of the Roosevelt era as a way to help customers of his butcher shop stretch their food dollar. Italian beef always is sliced very thin, and its long, slow cooking procedure is well suited to less-expensive cuts of meat. Pasquale suggested that thin-sliced beef and natural gravy on good Italian rolls was a thrifty way to give people something special for weddings and saints' day banquets.

Whatever its exact beginnings, beef always has been neighborhood food — virtually nonexistent in the linen-tablecloth, knife-and-fork restaurants of the all-business Loop but abundant in the wards where people live. Many of the old-time places began as open-air establishments that served as ad hoc community centers, and nearly all appended their beef sandwich menu with sausage cooked over charcoal that sent inviting smells curling up to third-floor windows of adjacent apartment buildings. When Al's moved to its current location in 1966, it added glass walls and doors to become an actual indoor restaurant, complete with modern stainless steel counters around the perimeter for stand-up dining. True to Chicago street-food custom, it has no tables and chairs.

On a pleasant day, a majority of Al's customers eat al fresco, on the sidewalk or in the parking lot leaning on their cars. One afternoon in April we shared the parking-lot dining facilities with clusters of Italian-speaking men eating off their truck's hood, city cops on lunch break with sandwiches and French fries strewn across the roof of their cruisers, a Polish-speaking girl celebrating her Sweet Sixteen birthday party with family and friends, a nonagenarian in suit and tie pushed in a wheelchair by his equally ancient wife, neighborhood teens escorting their cousins from Portland, Oregon, to show them what real beef is all about, raucous hoards of Bulls devotees in full fan attire, and a small coterie of hundred-dollar-haircut executives with their neckties thrown back over their shoulders to escape beef juice leakage.

Inside the little cement-floored shed that is Al's, every available eating surface was elbow to elbow with beef aficionados, their hands glistening with juice, their eyes riveted on their sandwiches. The far end of the order counter has room for about ten stand-up eaters, where the scenery is a vista of sausages sputtering over charcoal. On two sides of the rectangular eat shop the gleaming silver counters offer picture-window views of the parking lot and the sidewalk. The little bit of wall space available for decoration features a picture of old-time singer-comedian Jimmy Durante standing with his arm around Al Ferreri, inscribed by The Schnozzola, "To Al's and Baba [Al's nickname]: Jink-a-dink-a-doo. What a beef sandwich!"

While franchised offshoots of Al's offer sit-down dining, when you look around the original place on Taylor Street it becomes clear why standing up actually makes more sense than sitting down when you confront an Italian beef sandwich. If you position yourself the way you're supposed to, you can walk away from lunch as unsullied as you arrived. Chris Pacelli pointed out that nearly all the experienced customers in his dining room were leaning forward at the counter as they ate — a posture he has dubbed The Stance. He demonstrated, lining up to face the counter with his feet spread and planted far apart. "Like you are going to be frisked," he explained. "Put your two elbows on the counter and put your both hands on the sandwich, thumbs underneath." Standing in this position with his mitts enveloping an Al's big beef sandwich, he looked like a giddy strangler with his fingers wrapped around a neck. "Now, bring it to your face," he said, pausing a delicious moment when the sandwich was close enough to smell its warm, beefy bouquet. His elbows never left the counter as he opened wide to yank off a juicy chaw then pulled what was left away to a nice viewing distance, relishing the sight of it and the savor in his mouth. "See how all the juice drips on the counter, not on your shoes or shirt!" he exulted. "That's because of The Stance!"

The din inside Al's can be deafening: customers calling out orders and the staff behind the counter calling back at them. While not blatantly rude, most countermen in Italian beef establishments do not suffer indecision or dilly-dallying. It behooves the greenhorn to known these terms for efficient order placing:

Big beef: An extra-large sandwich.

Double-dipped: Once assembled, the sandwich gets reimmersed in a pan of natural gravy so the bread is soaked through.

Dry: The sandwich maker plucks a heap of beef from its pan with the serving tongs and lets excess juice drip away before inserting it in the bread.

With hot: A request for the relish known as giardiniera, an eye-opening garden mélange of finely chopped celery, capers, and spice that is roast beef's perfect complement.

Sweet: The popular alternative (or companion) to giardiniera, sweet is a call for roasted peppers. Some customers order double hot or double sweet; some get their sandwich sweet and hot.

Combo: Also known as half-and-half, a combo is a sandwich that contains not only beef but also a length of Italian sausage, preferably cooked over charcoal. Newer restaurants must use a gas grill because of clean-air regulations, but several of the old places, including Al's, are grandfathered in. The coal fire gives their taut-skinned tubes of peppery, coarse-ground pork a sharp, smoky flavor. Succulent and well-spiced, the sausage is itself a major lure for some customers who sidestep beef altogether and order double-sausage sandwiches, hot or sweet, dipped or dry.

Soaker: Bread dunked in beef gravy, hold the beef.

Cheesy: Although heretical, and to serious beef connoisseurs a nearly mortal sin, mozzarella or provolone cheese melted on the beef is offered by a few misguided Italian beef shops.

The stealth element of a beef sandwich, the one essential ingredient that brings everything together but generally goes underappreciated, is the bread. Chicago's Gonnella Bakery, the motto of which is "We Bake to Differ," supplies Al's and many of the city's beef stands with long, buff loaves ideally suited for the critical job of absorbing massive amounts of meat juice while remaining intact and appealingly bready. Rugged-crusted but not brittle, with none of the fragility of French loaves used to make a New Orleans po'boy, this Italian bread has an earthy interior that softens as the gravy infuses it but remains intact and does not lose its character. A great loaf from Gonnella or Turano Bakery doesn't taste quite right if it's totally dry. At least a quick dip in beef juice, or a long double-dip to attain maximum lusciousness, makes its flavor blossom.

Just as there is a proper way to ingest an Italian beef sandwich, there is a code of etiquette in the dining room. As at most beef-focused eateries, Al's provides stacks of napkins with each order but no knives, forks, or plates. Trash receptacles are positioned throughout the parking lot and the restaurant's interior. When one is finished eating, it is the polite custom to gather crumbs and detritus in the sandwich wrapper and heave everything into a can on the way out.

At its best, Italian beef is a good example of culinary transcendence: cheap ingredients made into something regal. But it isn't always at its best. After all, to slice a tough top sirloin or top or bottom round paper thin and to keep the slices in a pan of gravy is an invitation to disaster if the beef isn't lean and extraordinarily supple and if the gravy is anything but pure. Even good beef can be undermined by sissy bread or bread that is stale. Overcooked sweet peppers can be bitter; old ones turn flabby; and a giardiniera that doesn't snap with garlicky zest is just plain sad.

While gravy makes any beef sandwich moist, the beef itself must be cooked right or no amount of juice will revivify it. "Anywhere you bite into a sandwich made with Al's beef, you get hot juices," Chris Pacelli exulted, showing a slice of beef that was about to be thrown into the gravy pan of Al's open kitchen. "Look at how smooth and tender it is," he said, stroking the limp, dark shred as if it was rare silk. "There's no fat, no gristle, and when it's cut thin like this, it wants to suck in all the juice it can get. That's how come a good sandwich drips, even if you don't double-dip it."

To create its exquisite beef, Al's puts sirloin butts in the oven layered in a pot full of spices including several whole crushed bulbs of garlic. When they have cooked at least three hours, they are retrieved from their spicy cooking juices, which are poured through a superfine strainer, yielding an unclouded mahogany broth. The broth is diluted and simmered atop the stove, gradually becoming the precious dipping juice in which beef is immersed just before serving and into which some whole sandwiches are plunged. After the slabs of beef have cooled and settled overnight, all their fat is cut away and they are sliced extremely thin. Without the juice added back, these slices are dry, albeit high-flavored and butter-tender. At this point in the preparation, a condition of supreme purity has been attained. On the cutting board is a pile of impeccable lean beef and on the stove is a pot of clear beef essence. The challenge now is to combine the two in such a way that the beef sops up maximum amounts of savory liquid just before it gets piled into a sandwich.

Many Italian beef restaurants sell their beef by the pound and even mail-order it around the country to homesick Chicagoans. From these facts I deduce that there are people who sit down at the dinner table at home and eat the beef from a plate, using knife and fork, like it was meat cut from an ordinary roast. But such amenities are anathema to most of us Chicagoans, for whom Italian beef means just one thing: a paper-wrapped sandwich at a curbside stand where we can assume The Stance and savor a perfect harmony of meat and gravy, bakery-fresh bread, and the company of fellow connoisseurs.

Chili is a fine bowl of heartland comfort, often a cold-weather dish and one of the most satisfying lunches made on a stove. But for this author, who is given to far-flung digressions, it's a classic example of familiar American ingredients coalescing into a most peculiar composition.

Cincinnati Five-Way Chili

STILL LEGAL

Robert Olmstead

On the table before me are three coney dogs, each topped with a slurry of chili and a mound of shredded orange cheese. It's a chili-dog, staple of the midway, and nothing out of the ordinary aside from the super-sized top hat of mild Cheddar — old-fashioned American graffiti. But wait. Beside that plate is another, a plate of spaghetti topped with that same slurry of redolent chili, this time masquerading as marinara, and there's that same mound of shredded orange cheese. A food experience of familiar constituents in a most peculiar composition. A house of mirrors, a culinary tabletop where I suspect nothing will be quite what it seems.

I pause in anticipatory confusion, my shirtfront unstained, my taste buds primed but unsure of what direction to turn, unsure of what valves to turn: sweet, salty, sour, bitter, the upstart umami? I inject hot sauce because it's on the table and because it's one of my several vices, one I depend upon to bring a familiar voice to a strange land, hot sauce the

Robert Olmstead is the author of *River Dogs*, *A Trail of Heart's Blood Wherever We Go*, *Soft Water*, *America by Land*, *Stay Here with Me*, and the best seller *Coal Black Horse*. *Far Bright Star* is a 2010 Western Writers of America Spur Award winner and *Coal Black Horse* is the winner of the Heartland Prize for fiction and the Ohioana Book Award as well as a 2011 Choose to Read Ohio selection. Olmstead has earned senior arts awards from the states of Pennsylvania and Ohio, an Apex Award in journalism, and an Idaho Press Club Award. His reputation is international, with translation in both Europe and Asia. He is the recipient of a Guggenheim Fellowship and a grant from the National Endowment for the Arts. He is currently a professor at Ohio Wesleyan University who teaches widely throughout America, Europe, and Russia.

temporizer, the great equalizer. For some the reach is salt or pepper, or catsup. For me it's hot sauce. Actually it's a vice that bridges to the shore of addiction. I love hot sauce and always carry a bottle with me whenever I travel: hot sauce, Advil, tooth paste, quinine . . .

I am, as they say, a man with an appetite. I must eat. I lift a fork and dig in with gusto. A pitch and a twirl and lofted into my mouth is a swirl of Cincinnati five-way goodness, Cincinnati five-way chili, a dish and a city inseparable.

Hmmmmm. That's different. The texture is that of fast food, not unlike baby food. One does not need too many teeth to eat this food. This must explain the many families who are present and their over-burden of self-regarding children decorating themselves with food.

As to the flavor, it's not necessarily good or complex but still intriguing, intentional and elusive, like slow food, the culinary movement that promises better eating through chemistry. I give it another go and then another after that and suddenly there is something here that demands to be eaten. My gosh. What is that? The transept of an experience crossing the nave of life. It is nothing like marinara, but it's not like anything I've ever called chili either. There is an ingredient I am trying to catch in the melding of flavor and the soothing texture and it is fleeting and so I eat faster and faster to catch what I caught before, but it has already changed and yet is the same, like the spinning of a circus ride.

I want to know and the only way of knowing is to eat more and more and again and again and faster and faster. I am trying to slow down, but it seems rather impossible. I am reaching for something I cannot name.

Then I have it, the experience, or more appropriately, it has me. There comes a strange narcotic-like effect. My breathing slows and I encounter tranquility. I am stupefied. I am suffused. I am spread through and over. I glow. I am transcended. I am as if opiated. I recognize the otherness that resides within me. I feel so good eating this food I think I must be breaking a law.

So, what is this concoction, this Cincinnati chili? To begin, the ways of the chili are thus: A "one-way" is a bowl of chili. A "two-way" is spaghetti topped with chili. A "three-way" is spaghetti, chili, and cheese. Unlike a more traditional chili, beans and onions are not essential until the fourth and fifth editions. Thus a "four-way" is spaghetti, chili, cheese, and red kidney beans. A "five-way" is spaghetti, chili, cheese, red kidney beans, and onions. "Inverted" is the cheese under the chili and "wet" is extra chili over the spaghetti. It's all a bit like a game.

And the chili itself? No less than a chaos of flavor ingredients: ground beef, minced garlic, chili powder, allspice, cinnamon, cumin, cayenne pepper, salt, unsweetened cocoa, tomato sauce, cloves, beef broth, cider vinegar, coriander, turmeric, cardamom, Worcestershire sauce. The list seems to be endlessly tapping cultures and climates, ranging by latitudes and longitudes, finding histories and holidays.

How strange the faint shadowy flavor hunch that unsweetened cocoa is one of the secret ingredients. Eyes closed and mouth full and suddenly I have the feeling I am not in Cincinnati anymore. The chili powder, cinnamon, and cocoa step forward, repeat: *chili powder, cinnamon, and cocoa* and I imagine Montezuma, the emperor of Mexico, handing a goblet of liquid to Hernán Cortés, the boy conquistador newly arrived from Spain, predation on his mind. The date is sometime in 1519 and the drink is *xocolatl*. It is revered by the Aztecs as an aphrodisiac as well as an offering to the gods, and Montezuma in his luxury drinks as many as fifty goblets a day.

Cortés will take it to Europe and in time it will become sugared chocolate powder and then sugared chocolate bars. In the meantime, the Aztecs won't just drink away all their chocolate and chilies. Having not yet encountered the concept of too much of a good thing, they'll add the garlic, cumin, salt, tomato, and meat, along with a few other ingredients, and voila! We will name it *mole*!

It will be several civilizations later, say about 1920 (thank you, Wikipedia) when a cast of nostalgic food-tinkering Greeks and Macedonians immigrate into the Cincinnati area. They bring with them flavor memories and family recipes and no doubt the need to connect where they are with where they've come from, a flavor from home so home will not seem so far away. And they need to earn a living and for so many immigrants this traditionally means the food business, whether pushcart or lunch wagon, diner or deli, a new family with recipes and ambition can make a go of it in this new world where so many opportunities beyond the kitchen are indeed not theirs for the taking.

Stirring and stirring, measuring and weighing, tasting, tasting, tasting from the so many pots on the so many iron stoves. What burbled in those pots and baked in the black maws of those ovens must have been ridiculous medleys, gallimaufries, salmagundis, bricolages, the cooks fiddling and tweaking, the clack of wooden spoons and the chop of sharpened knives, the eye straining to measure an eighth of a teaspoon here, a pinch there, a shake, a dollop, the heart willing, the dream of making alive, the memory of home in a sip from a spoon. Changing and changing and changing until finally finding the signature flavor that would never be changed again. Such pattern and joy these kitchen chemists must have experienced and for some few the bounty derived from American appetites.

And how strange the ground beef, more matter and medium than food and flavor. Now I don't know about other folks, but I can't say that I have ever boiled meat other than to cook a hot dog when the grill can't be lit. Where I'm from meat is generally grilled or fried or ovened and even when added to a soup or stew it is first browned, but the beef in this chili is BOILED! Recipes insist the ground beef be finely chopped in a food processor and BOILED!

Harold McGee in his definitive book *On Food and Cooking: The Science and Lore of the Kitchen* tells us the flavor in meat is shaped and developed when it is cooked, a process called the Maillard reactions, after Louis Camille Maillard, who identified such in 1912. When heat is applied to meat, carbohydrate molecules and amino acids form an intermediate structure that produces hundreds of different by-products. At three hundred to five hundred degrees Fahrenheit, the denatured proteins on the surface of the meat recombine with the sugars present. This creates the meaty flavor we are so fond of. As many as six hundred components have been identified in the aroma of beef and that is the problem. To develop a signature flavor, ingredients must be highly controlled and to do this one must not activate flavors with volatile natures.

So the meat is chopped and boiled. There is no magic here, no nostalgia, just hardnosed food making. The meat is chopped for texture and boiled for control — a modern and American fast-food concept. You must control the flavor. You control flavor by removing it, or in this case, by not activating it. Then you add back the flavor that is your signature, the flavor that is your brand, the flavor that you own coast to coast and whether the beef was raised in Iowa or Argentina, it all tastes the same and not at all. It's hard to explain to someone younger than forty how a beefsteak, a chicken, a pork chop, these all tasted different and their flavors depended upon their age, feed, and breed. Their flavor did not come from a sauce or rub. It did not pour from a bottle. It was not applied with a brush. Forty years ago these meats were not homogenous but brought their flavor with them.

But I digress and perhaps overstate. We should not forget the extraordinary and transformative and violent histories of salt and pepper, two ingredients we take for granted.

All around me are masticating jaws and bulging cheek pouches. Huge men wear plastic bibs to keep their shirtfronts unstained. What intoxicated the Aztec emperors intoxicates us today. Tongues like rudders usher a viscous lava flow to the throat passage. Chili and cocoa — the coastlines of my mouth begin to sing. The hot sauce wants of itself, calls for another injection. For some reason my neck hurts. Hot sauce vapor issues from cheesy fumaroles. I intuit a sudden plume of smoke and a quiet rumble, a gastronomic event of volcanic proportions. I reach for a strand of thought of mind, but it isn't there. Comprehensible order has been shattered. I am euphoric. I am blissful. I am crushed by mystery and overwhelmed by the unknown. My shoulders ache. I am one with the five-way.

I stand as if rising from wreckage, tip generously, settle my bill, and stagger into the light. I have chili legs and chili arms and chili face. My shirtfront is speckled red. This must be what it's like to enter a carwash on foot and emerge water-beaten, brush-battered, and naked. I wonder if I should I get behind the wheel. I am satiated. I am exhausted. I feel like I ate a baseball. I want to sleep for a very long time. I never want to go back, but I know I will.

During the midsummer harvest Mitchard gives her heart to Mirai sweet corn and praises the Illinois farmers whose genetic tinkering bred the centerpiece of the summer season.

Corn in Heaven

Jacquelyn Mitchard

For a midwestern girl, it's like a tribal memory. I don't remember the first time I ate sweet corn. I was with my family, my uncles and cousins and my little brother. People were laughing, standing up to use the tin shaker of salt that hung from a tree branch over the campfire. Where was I? What woodland clearing or picnic meadow or lakeshore? I remember that it was nighttime and the sky was a crystal blast of stars. And the corn. I remember the corn. It had been thrown in a fire, and the kernels were crisped and browned at the edges. Now I'd walk a mile for an ear. I'm a fanatic. In shepherd's pie and baked pudding, in bread with peppers but . . . mostly, on its own, the centerpiece of the season. How sweet it is.

Sweet corn.

For its glories, many have driven hundreds of miles and stood in line under the hot sun. It has inspired statues, tears, at least one book of verse, a few wagers, and some shouting matches. Prairie bard Garrison Keillor has called it "better than sex."

There are a few things almost everyone agrees on: In heaven, the time is about four on an afternoon in July. In heaven, the soundtrack is a child's laugh over the crack of a bat on a ball. In heaven, there's a banquet every night, of the simplest things — plain fresh things with

Jacquelyn Mitchard is the author of nine novels for adults, including *The Deep End of the Ocean* and the upcoming *Second Nature: A Love Story*, and ten books for children and young adults. A contributing editor for *Parade* magazine, she lives south of Madison, Wisconsin, across from a cornfield.

nary a blizzard of this or a reduction of that. Every night, the center of the feast at the banquet of the gods is sweet corn.

It's not just corn, it's . . . well, it's regional corn.

There are only two regions, and one is mine.

People say that the best sweet corn on earth is not the one you grow in your yard. They only say that to make you feel better. It's just not true. It's the corn grown in the back yard of my life. You don't have to believe me. You can ask the haute corn-tiers, such as William Sertl, the former travel editor of *Gourmet* magazine. "There's simply nothing else like it," he says. "Nothing tastes as fresh. It's like opening night at the opera, except it's the opening night of summer. When July comes, my whole menu changes. Whatever it is, I'm going to incorporate corn. I'm going to throw it on the grill with a little olive oil and salt." He adds, "For my money, it's corn grown in upstate New York, and then in Wisconsin, Illinois, and a little bit of Indiana. And that is it."

Corn has . . . well, roots.

There really are only three kinds of sweet corn, according to Professor Jerald (he asks you to call him "Snook") Pataky of the University of Illinois at Urbana-Champaign. Thomas Jefferson wrote of eating the original "white maize," or sugary corn. Genetic tinkering led to "sugary-enhanced." The third, says Pataky, is supersweet. In simplest terms, the conversion from sugar to starch is somewhat slower in the newer varieties so that the old saw about boiling the water before you pick the corn is no longer true. (Supersweet can hold up for two weeks in a refrigerator.) But as for varieties (white, yellow, white-and-yellow, bigger or smaller ears), that's all up to you. There is, however, enough subjectivity to inspire about two hundred different brands, including "Kiss and Tell," "Divinity," "Lancelot," "Bodacious," and, yes, "Sugar Buns."

Says Snook, sweet corn also is the only truly American food, first given to European settlers by the Iroquois around three hundred years ago, but until about ten years ago, sweet corn was also *solely* American. Disdained in Europe as livestock feed, it was prized in the United States as the ultimate picnic food and in South America, the everything ingredient, folded into everything from tortillas to tamale pie. Sweet corn inspires not only passion but (like those battling Brothers Peck) territoriality. "Those big beefsteak tomatoes from New Jersey? They may be great," Sertl says. "But when they start in about their corn, and they do? I'm not giving them that."

In Madison, Wisconsin, there's Peck's Farm Stand on Highway 14, where Richard Peck sells corn on the original family plat. "I've had ten years longer to make mistakes and I guess I think I know a little more about how to do it. Timing's everything." Great corn, he adds, is just a little brown around the tassels and when you strip back the skin, the kernel should be so plump it bursts at the touch of a fingertip. Brad Peck, of Peck's Farm Stand on Highway 14, agrees. He's Richard's baby brother and they get along fine, except during corn-growing and -selling season, a mere six months of the year.

"You're thinking of an older fella, a little bit on the heavy side? That's my brother. People will drive right past his stand to get to mine," says Peck the younger.

For a while, Janet Heck worked for Peck's during college summers. She decided to start her own stand, which is next door to the original Peck's. Says Richard Peck, "People say, I thought you were Heck's. I say, heck no, we're Peck's."

Corn is grown in places other than New York state, Highway 14, and across the street from my house. To be fair, they say it's good. In Taber, Alberta, Canada, the sweet corn is so prized (because it's too far to drive to Wisconsin) that growers there have to obtain a license to prove they're truly selling the genuine Taber-grown product. Olivia, Minnesota, boasts the world's largest ear-of-corn sculpture. It stands (high) above corn festivities that include a Corn Maze, a Corn Toss and a Corn-lympics. There are corny hijinks in Arizona, California, Illinois, Indiana, Ohio, Pennsylvania, and Iowa. (And in Iowa, they could drive to Wisconsin, so what's their . . . well, let me not put salt on the wound.) You can buy corn by any other name (and it should be under another name), frozen or from Florida, nearly year-round at the supermarket, sort-of fresh. The whole idea makes me squeamish, like going to Belgium and walking past five generations of chocolatiers to buy a Dove bar at the airport. No offense to a Dove bar, but you don't order champagne at the Mobile station, do you? It's just a disgrace, is what it is. There's a power and a glory that inspired poet James Stevenson to write,

"WHY AM I HAPPY
THAT I WAS BORN?
THE REASON (IN SEASON)
SWEET CORN!"

Perhaps the best corn I've ever eaten as an adult was grown, and I just have to say it, grown in Illinois. My name is Jackie. I was born in Chicago, but now I come from Wisconsin. And I gave my heart to corn from Illinois. My pulse quickens here, with the shame of stepping out on my own corn sweetie and also with lust. Tim Pack (Do you notice the similarity of these names? I do, but I can't connect the dots . . .) in Harvard, Illinois, hit the trifecta. It's the marvelous Mirai. In Japanese, Mirai is a common name for a beloved child. Or a beloved plant. It means "the future." Bred by Pack, working with corn scientist David McKenzie, who came up with the hybrid that has everything, the plumpness, the sweetness, and the longevity. Perfected by Japanese farmers planting five kernels in a single hill of soil. Mirai now, quite frankly, rules. The Mick Jagger of corn growers, Pack can perhaps be forgiven his cockiness: "When someone says, my cousin says there's better in Nebraska, I love those words. I say, have your cousin ship some and if you win that contest double your money back." Corn lovers drive hundreds of miles for their two bags of Mirai. "It's intense. These people are crazy! I wait for it all year. I just love selling a dozen ears of corn in a mesh bag for three bucks."

And why wouldn't he?

Heaven at three dollars a bag is a pretty good bargain.

Of course, it was no bargain for me. Last summer I bought Mirai corn for my family — of eleven, and a couple of good friends. Two cookouts' worth. The first night I set thirty-six ears on two platters and glanced up again ten seconds later. One was left, and my oldest son said, "If nobody's going to eat that . . . " Everyone laughed. Mist glistened on the pitcher that held the lemonade. The children were buttery and sleepy and replete. And so was I. It was sort of the way I imagine heaven, a reunion that goes on and on. When you have sweet corn, it's always summer, and you never grow old. And I'll think that when I don't even have the teeth left to eat it.

By the way, those eight bags, for three dollars each, plus Fed-Exing, cost about the same as a minute of commercial time during the Super Bowl. It was worth every cent.

Chicagoans can feast on foie gras once more. The Chicago City Council repealed the ban, which was a source of embarrassment for the city as residents accused officials of trying to micromanage people's lives.

Let Them Eat Pâté

Peter Sagal

In April 2006 Chicago — not Berkeley, not Santa Fe, not Northampton, Massachusetts — became the first city in the United States to ban the sale of foie gras. How, in the name of Upton Sinclair, could that have happened? This is a city that grew up, and grew rich, by being cheerfully cruel to animals on an industrial scale. This is a city with a vast and varied and hungry immigrant population, meaning they're cutting the heads off live ducks in Chinatown and doing things to the inside of a pig out in the Polish butcheries on Archer Avenue that you wouldn't wish on, well, a pig. But a French delicacy of fattened goose liver or duck liver? That offends our sensibilities? Makes you want to weep for a once-great city, it does. Why, time was, you couldn't claim to have thrown a real Chicago shindig if you hadn't force-fed some animal through a metal tube and then butchered it to harvest its distended organs. Or, if no goose were handy, we'd do it to the guests. And, dammit, they liked it.

"Our city is better for taking a stance against the cruelty of foie gras," said Alderman Joe Moore, the city politician behind the measure.

"This is the silliest ordinance the City Council has ever passed," said Mayor Richard M. Daley.

"What about my hamburger?" said my wife, Beth, who just wanted her hamburger.

Specifically, the seventeen-dollar hamburger at Sweets & Savories on Fullerton Avenue, which the menu describes as "Strube Ranch American

---

Peter Sagal is the host of NPR's weekly news-based quiz show *Wait Wait . . . Don't Tell Me!* and author of a perfect guide to sinful behavior, *The Book of Vice*.

Kobe beef with foie gras paté and truffled mayonnaise and toasted brioche roll" and which, when served with a side of duck-fat fries, is the kind of meal God would cook for houseguests if God were a twelve-year-old kid.

Seventeen dollars is a lot to pay for a hamburger, especially one that does not come with a toy in the bag, but a couple of things you should know are, first, that it is enormous, the size you remember your first Big Macs being when you finally convinced your parents that you were old enough to graduate from McNuggets, and second, that the heat from the beef melts the paté, just a little bit, so it seems to absorb the truffle mayo above it and then ineluctably swirls into both the beef and the bread, infecting them with glory, the way Agent Smith converted everybody into himself in those awful *Matrix* sequels. The result inspires guttural grunts of pleasure as you realize you must put the burger down, because if you don't, it will fall apart, but instead you take another bite, *mmmph mmmph mmmph.*

As Beth says, "It's yummy."

We went down to Sweets & Savories recently, about half a year after the ban went into effect. The restaurant is a converted storefront run by chef-owner David Richards, who is always visible by the stove in the back, cooking exactly what he wants, and what he wants to cook is foie gras, city of Chicago be damned. Or so we hoped.

"We came for the burger," I said to the waiter, trying to adopt the knowing manner of a gentleman knocking on the door of a speakeasy.

"Of course," he said.

"Is it still, you know . . . *the burger*?"

"It comes with all its . . . *accessories*," he said. It is possible he laid his index finger along the side of his nose.

He didn't have to be coy. There it is, right there on the menu. Like most chefs in Chicago, Richards thinks the foie gras ban is insane. His method of protest is simply to continue serving it, both on the hamburger and by itself, as "Seared Hudson Valley Foie Gras" — as stark and plain an act of civil disobedience as Gandhi's march to the sea. By contrast, the anti–foie gras protester's method of protest is to actually protest, right outside the restaurant, with poster-size photos of tormented geese and custom-composed chants.

"It's the Animal Defense League," says Richards. "They showed up on weekends for over a month. Last Friday, my tenant upstairs started throwing water balloons at them. Then I think they decided to take the summer off."

He has not yet suffered the wrath of city hall for defying the ban. A complaint to the city occasions a visit from a health inspector, and the first time she came, Richards says, they ended up having a "spirited discussion of the ban and other interesting political issues" while she poked about the kitchen, looking for contraband liver. One gets the sense that the inspector would rather have spent her time inspecting restaurants for less delicious violations, like rats. But it was one of the few days when there was no foie to be found, so Richards escaped a possible $500 fine.

It is hard not to be sympathetic to the protesters — even compared with the other routine degradations involved in factory farming, force-feeding poultry is pretty harsh. And one wants to feel for the aldermen of Chicago, who, knowing their city is neither the entertainment capital nor the financial capital of the country, hoped to get some headlines by being the City Most Friendly to Poultry. But my feelings, and my allegiance, have been bought by a mere hamburger. Long live the *résistance*! But not, please, the goose.

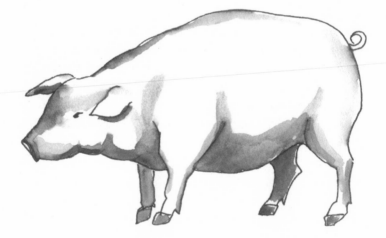

Iowans prefer plain, simple food and they stick with something they like. In this memoir, a Hawkeye state transplant ponders his love for the infamous breaded, fried pork tenderloin sandwich.

High on the Hog

Jon Yates

I started working in the rough-and-tumble grocer's world three days after my sixteenth birthday. As a part-time employee at the local Hy-Vee, I was tasked with bagging groceries, mopping up all manner of spills, and schlepping a seemingly endless supply of Milwaukee's Best twelve-packs to the store's beer cooler in an effort to quench the insatiable thirst of young, party-loving college students from the nearby Iowa State University campus.

The hours were long, the pay was paltry, and perhaps worst of all, I was required to wear a tie. I might have quit after just a few weeks if it hadn't been for the store's one saving grace — the Hy-Vee deli.

It was there, at the tender age of sixteen, that I ate my first breaded pork tenderloin sandwich. It would be several more years before I lost my virginity, but that first bite of hot, juicy, delectably fried pork was a similarly religious experience.

For the next six years of my life I toiled as a bagger-stocker-checkout boy for the Hy-Vee chain, often working long, soul-crushing shifts

---

Jon Yates is a columnist at the *Chicago Tribune* and author of the self-help book *What's Your Problem?* He grew up in Ames, Iowa, home to the Iowa Pork Industry Center, the Pork Profit Network, and the Ames Straw Poll, which culls Republican presidential candidates from the herd. After graduating from the University of Iowa, he started his journalism career at the *Press-Citizen* in Iowa City, a mere ten-minute drive from the biggest pork tenderloin sandwich in Iowa. He briefly covered Sonny Bono for the *Desert Sun* in Palm Springs, California, then was a police reporter for the *Tennessean* in Nashville. He lives in Oak Park, Illinois, with his wife and two young children, who have yet to develop a taste for Iowa skinnies.

punctuated by a glorious thirty-five-minute lunch break. Each break, I would belly up to the deli counter, peer under the glass shield separating the food from the customers, and pick out the largest, most delicious-looking breaded pork tenderloin sandwich available.

You've heard of the "freshman fifteen"? Over the years I've packed on the tenderloin twenty, but it's been worth it. Each bite has been like a little taste of heaven (and undoubtedly brought me a little bit closer to actually visiting there). Pork tenderloins are not, by any definition, a health food, but then this is not the *Midwest Journal of Medicine*. Besides, if the National Institutes of Health funded a major study of the pork tenderloin, I'm convinced they could find some medicinal benefit. After all, the pork tenderloin sandwich is nature's most perfect food.

For the uninitiated (i.e., those of you not from middle America), the breaded pork tenderloin sandwich is a delicacy found in small-town restaurants and diners throughout the Midwest, a culinary marker that helps separate the region from other areas of the country. The sandwiches are, in many ways, the embodiment of midwestern values — nothing fancy, but considerably more complicated than they initially appear.

A perfectly constructed breaded pork sandwich begins with a carefully butchered piece of pork loin, which is then pounded into a large, thin, amoeba-like shape. It is a delicate process. Pound the loin too thin and you risk overcooking the meat, zapping it of its juiciness. Leave the pork too thick and it will cook unevenly. Tenderloin enthusiasts strive for a thickness of about three-eighths of an inch, although consensus is fleeting.

Although pork loin needs no seasoning, the best tenderloins are marinated in buttermilk to soften the meat and infuse flavor, then coated with breading. Finally, the pork is plunged into a bubbling deep fryer, heated between 350 and 360 degrees Fahrenheit, for exactly three minutes.

When executed correctly, the results are nothing short of spectacular: moist, succulent white pork encased in a crispy breading, fried to a golden brown, a massive portion of meat spilling out from beneath a preposterously tiny-looking bun like a rapturous porcine explosion.

Because of the way the pork is pounded, no two breaded pork tenderloin sandwiches are exactly the same. They are the road food equivalent of snowflakes.

Quality pork tenderloin sandwiches are a point of pride in my home-town of Ames, as they are for Iowans in general. People often mistake Iowa for a corn state, no doubt swayed by Hollywood's image of baseball players fading softly into an endless field of cornstalks. In reality, Iowa is all about the pigs. According to the Iowa Pork Producers Association, at any one time there are roughly nineteen million pigs living in Iowa. The human population of the state is just over three million. At some point, the pigs will do the math and stage a bloody coup, but until then Iowans will continue to produce more pork than any other state in the country. The *National Hog Farmer*, a publication that bills itself as "the pork business authority," says that in 2008 Iowa accounted for almost 30 percent of the entire U.S. hog market.

Not that Iowa's pork production is all about volume. La Quercia, an artisan pork producer based in Norwalk, ships cured meats that are among the finest in the world. Chef Mario Batali called La Quercia's prosciutto "the best American prosciutto on the market." And pork from Becker Lane Organic Farm in Dyersville graces the tables of some of the best restaurants in the Midwest.

But for most Iowans, myself included, the breaded pork tenderloin remains king, a sandwich so ubiquitous it can be found in virtually any roadside diner, restaurant, or grocery store deli.

I once asked pork tenderloin blogger Allen Bukoff, who grew up in Coon Rapids, Iowa, about why we Iowans have such reverence for the sandwiches. "We grew up in a richer environment because we had breaded pork tenderloin in our community," he said, and I wholeheart-edly agree. "Think of all the children of the world who grew up without that."

It boggles the mind.

Not that Iowa has the pork tenderloin market cornered. In fact, while some will argue that the pork tenderloin sandwich was invented in the Czech neighborhoods of Cedar Rapids, evidence suggests the sand-wich was born in 1904, created by a pushcart operator named Nicholas

Freinstein — in Huntington, Indiana. The idea was to bring the German Wiener schnitzel to the masses. Pork tenderloin connoisseur and historian David Stovall said the Wiener schnitzel had several things working against it: It was generally served on a plate without a bun and covered in gravy, which made it less portable. And although it was breaded and fried, the meat inside was veal, which didn't play particularly well with Hoosiers. "When it translated to America, you couldn't sell veal to a working man, so pork was substituted in the Midwest," Stovall said.

Freinstein's pork tenderloin proved so popular, he opened a restaurant in 1908, called Nick's Kitchen. "As far as I can tell, there is no written record of a pork tenderloin sandwich that predates Nick's Kitchen," Stovall said.

Over the next century, the sandwich gained popularity in small-town diners and restaurants along a swath of the Midwest, from Indiana through Illinois and into Iowa, an area sometimes referred to as the "pork tenderloin corridor." The farther you stray from Interstate 80, the less likely you are to find pork tenderloin nirvana.

Throughout the years, each restaurant placed its own stamp on the recipe, some pounding the pork so thin that the sandwich became almost crispy, a style sometimes referred to as an Iowa Skinny or an elephant ear. Restaurants prided themselves on producing the biggest sandwich and hungry farmers gobbled them up.

When I attended college at the University of Iowa many eons ago, my buddies and I would occasionally skip class to drive the eleven miles up Highway 1 to nearby Solon, Iowa, home to a small diner called Joensy's, a Mecca of sorts for pork tenderloin enthusiasts. Solon, it should be noted, holds an annual town celebration called Beef Days, but it is best known for Joensy's, which sports a sign above its front door proudly proclaiming it to be "Home of the Biggest and Best Pork Tenderloin in Iowa."

The sandwiches are comically large, more the size and shape of an elephant footprint than an elephant ear. But Iowans pride themselves on thriftiness, and a Joensy's tenderloin is nothing if not a good value. One sandwich can probably feed a family of four, but I've never seen anyone split one.

The concept of massive, artery-clogging sandwiches has not played so well with consumers outside the tenderloin corridor, perhaps because pork is not as revered in other parts of the country. Texans have been serving up chicken-fried steak since the nineteenth century, with pounded, breaded cube steak as the star. The Georgia-based Chick-fil-A, established in the 1960s, has created a near cult-like following with its fried chicken sandwiches. Neither incarnation can hold a candle to the pork tenderloin.

There have been attempts by some fast-food chains to mass market a breaded pork tenderloin sandwich, most of which have ended in abject failure. Burger King test marketed a breaded pork sandwich called the Country Pork Sandwich in midwestern restaurants. I tried one once. It had the consistency of a hockey puck and tasted like breaded sawdust. It was, in a word, unworthy.

As a birthday gift several years ago, my wife bought me frozen pork tenderloin sandwiches from an Iowa-based online retailer. It was an incredibly sweet gesture and a very thoughtful present, but the tenderloins were unspectacular. Because we do not own a deep fryer, the pork wound up tough, the breading overcooked, and much of the flavor was lost. I ate them anyway because they were, after all, pork tenderloins. But it just wasn't the same.

Part of the problem, I now realize, is me. I'm older now and my palate is more mature. I realize the sandwiches I ate as an impressionable young grocery store employee weren't the finest examples of the craft. Still, it made me nostalgic when I heard that my beloved Hy-Vee chain, in a show of support for local pork producers, purchased one million pork tenderloins in January 2010 and planned to sell their Jumbo Breaded Pork Tenderloin Sandwiches for just $2.88 apiece. I now live in Chicago, where breaded pork tenderloins do not fall from passing pigs like they do in my home state. The nearest Hy-Vee is more than an hour's drive away, perhaps longer depending on traffic.

Not that I'm left completely high and dry in the big city. Recently, the Wisconsin-based fast-food burger chain Culver's opened a restaurant exactly 1.3 miles from my house. As luck would have it, Culver's offers a pork tenderloin sandwich, which it hails as "inspired by an Iowa farmland specialty," made with "premium center-cut pork loin."

A couple of weeks ago, I drove to Culver's, waited in an insufferably long line at the drive-thru, then placed my order: one breaded pork tenderloin with lettuce, tomatoes, onions, and mayonnaise.

As I sat there waiting for my sandwich to be delivered, I heard the driver behind me place his order: a double Cheddar burger with bacon. I chuckled. What a sucker, I thought. Burgers are for losers.

Moments later, a Culver's employee handed me my bag and I drove back home. I opened the bag to find . . . a double Cheddar burger with bacon. I reluctantly choked down the burger but vowed to never let it happen again.

Next time, I'll go the extra mile. I'll drive to Hy-Vee.

While each region of the United States draws from its *terroir*—the climate, soil, and sun—the rolling hills of southern Indiana offer the perfect environment for a working dairy farm. In this essay, a pastry chef takes a break from her restaurant kitchen and forges a relationship with a trusted dairy farmer whose cheeses rival those of the French. She gets back much more than a small, creamy round of aged cheese soaked in the local moonshine, Kentucky bourbon.

The Chef and the Farmer

Gale Gand

A fter I read that Wabash Cannonball won best of show at a national cheese competition in 1995, I decided I needed to make a trip to Capriole, Judy Schad's goat farm, to see the level of devotion needed to produce goat cheese the right way. It was something American cheese makers hadn't generally mastered at that point. Most goat cheese at that time tended to be very fresh and plain tasting with the creaminess of ricotta, lacking the complex flavor and texture that distinguished the aged French goat cheeses.

The names still tumble through my mind. Mont St. Francis, O'Banon, Chantal Aperitifs. And no, not from France. *Indiana.*

Over the past thirty years Capriole has become much more than a farm to food journalists, chefs, mixologists, restaurant managers, or other cheese makers needing a retreat. When we feel burned out, lost, disillusioned, or just plain tired, in one visit Judy and her husband, Larry, can reenergize us with their hospitality and warmth.

Gale Gand is the founding executive pastry chef and a partner of the restaurant TRU in Chicago, which received a AAA Five Diamond Award, four stars, and one Michelin star. She was also awarded pastry chef of the year by the James Beard Foundation and *Bon Appétit* magazine in 2001. Gand has hosted the Food Network's and the Cooking Channel's *Sweet Dreams*, judged Bravo's *Top Chef*, and appeared on *Iron Chef America, Martha Stewart, Baking with Julia* (Child), and *Oprah*. She has authored seven cookbooks and makes and sells root beer through her own company, Gale's Root Beer. After finishing her BFA from Rochester Institute of Technology, she attended culinary school at La Varenne in Paris. Gale is married to an environmentalist, Jimmy Seidita, and has three children.

You can run down to the stream and search for tadpoles, hang out with the baby goats, sit around the kitchen counter while Judy makes breakfast. The farm offers a chance to breathe and realign yourself and be surrounded by the kind of food you wish you had all the time.

Judy is a stunning salt-and-pepper-haired woman with farm hands, yet she has a casual, even elegant, southern relaxed way even when she's on foot in her acres of alfalfa or hay-filled goat stalls. I remember the time when she and another cheese maker from New York State came into my Chicago restaurant. I thought she'd be this bumpkin farmer coming to lunch. She walked in wearing a starched linen blouse and a strand of white pearls. At work, I wear practically no jewelry except for pearls, even with my chef's coat. Although she's chosen this rustic farm life and I'm back in a hot, sweaty kitchen piping a thousand truffles, our pearls help us feel like we're a little cleaned up.

Judy and her husband, Larry's skill for hospitality on the farm is peerless. While they're hosting you, there's time to help you sort through whatever needs sorting. Though I was interested in the farm, her extensive vegetable garden, and her exacting methods for making such delicious goat cheese, I also needed to sort out a few things in my life.

It was a time when I was considering separating from my lifelong culinary partner. We were married, built careers together, had a three-year-old son, and owned a four-star, five-diamond restaurant, TRU. Because of the passion of the farm's owners and the whole idyllic farmstead setting, Capriole offered me a chance to think about my marriage and make the tough decision to break up the band.

One of the times I went there to restore myself (that's where the word *restaurant* comes from), we harvested okra from Judy's garden and ate it raw. We gathered eggs from her dozen chickens and fed them kitchen scraps. We picked blackberries that she baked into a completely dreamy pie. Coming from me, a pastry chef, that's a huge compliment. I'm a fourth-generation pie baker and still carry around my great-grandmother's rolling pin.

On another visit, I just remember bacon, lots and lots of thick, chewy, smoky bacon, fresh chicken eggs, crusty sourdough bread, and a wheel of well-aged Old Kentucky Tomme. She was doing a riff on a traditional French cheese with a thick, rough and tough rind and a slightly mushroom-y tasting interior pate, somewhere between an American Jack and a classic French Tomme du Savoie in texture.

You can see why I keep going back. If I wasn't a pastry chef, I'd be a cheese maker.

There are three types of cheese making: industrial, where the milk can come from anywhere and cheese is produced with the use of heavy machinery; artisanal, where all the milk comes from the same controlled area and the cheese is somewhat hand produced; and *fermier* or farmstead, where milk comes from the cheese maker's own farm and herds and is hand produced. This is Schad's method, and it is the most careful, consuming, and expensive way to make cheese. But she exceeds the farmstead standards by growing twenty acres of alfalfa for her herd of 500 goats: 450–480 females and the remainder males. This way she knows exactly what the herd eats and how that feed was grown.

Standing outside her cheese-making facility, you would never suspect that alchemy of the most delicious sort was going on. It is filled with stainless steel, looking a bit like a surgical suite, with workers in sterile white lab coats and hairnets. They are controlling the process of harnessing beneficial bacteria. Introducing it into the milk makes the curds ripen, developing flavor and texture.

Beginning with the goat milk from the morning milking, Schad adds rennet, an enzyme, to coagulate the curds and separate them from the whey. Salt is added for flavor and to encourage moisture release. The whey gets drained off and fed back to the animals, or me, as I like to sneak a sip of it when I'm there. It is super high in nutrients.

Finally, there's the aging process, called *affinage* or *affiner*, the finishing school for cheese. As the cheese rests, dries, and ripens, it's rotated at a very cool and controlled temperature. This helps the cheese develop a protective rind that seals in the beneficial bacteria, giving the cheese its flavor. The rind also keeps out any foreign things floating in the air that might infiltrate the cheese, causing a change in the intended flavor.

Capriole cheeses cover a range of textures and styles. Some are fresh, straightforward, and light, others rich, earthy, and complex. There are twelve to fifteen varieties, which take between seven days and eight months to age. Young ones such as Blue River Buttons and Chantal Aperitifs come in logs or rounds, either straight up or seasoned with dry herbs or wasabi, green Japanese horseradish. If I'm looking for surface-ripened cheeses, I'll ask for Crocodile Tears, Piper's Pyramid, Wabash Cannonball, or Sofia, which is one of my favorites. It's a barquette-shaped loaf with layers of vegetable ash running through that look a bit like veins. The ash helps dry out the cheese's interior and gives it a distinctive look while allowing it to develop the creamiest of textures.

If I have a taste for her aged, raw-milk specialty cheeses, I like Juli-anna, Mont St. Francis, Old Kentucky Tomme, and O'Banon, which is wrapped in chestnut leaves and soaked in Woodford Reserve Bourbon for two months. Everything going on in Louisville, Kentucky (Churchill Downs racetrack is fifteen miles south) influences the farm. So Schad bathes her cheese in bourbon, the local moonshine.

I love that Judy names all her goats. It's not easy to keep track of five hundred names but her system is to start the names with the same letter each year. One spring when I was visiting, five to eight new babies were born in the barn overnight. It was the year of the Gs. How perfect for me.

As a pastry chef cooking at my fancy-pants restaurant, TRU, the ingredients in my arsenal to make even one night's worth of desserts number in the hundreds. But cheese? Cheese is made from just three things: milk, rennet, and salt. I have great respect for something so delicious that relies on only three ingredients for its flavor and texture.

At TRU, goat cheese ends up in just about every course; in the *amuse-bouche*, a two-bite portion to tickle the taste buds served before the meal commences; in gnocchi with shaved white truffles; in petit tarts garnished with dried fruit compote; in ice cream or on the cheese cart that follows the meal. Our extensive nightly selection of fifteen to twenty-five cheeses is divided between sheep's milk, cow's milk, and goat's milk.

Next comes the dessert *amuse*, which might be a little lemongrass panna cotta or some strawberry-rhubarb soup with sour cream sherbet that helps diners transition to a plated dessert from the menu. The final treat is the petit four cart with ten to fifteen tiny items, such as lavender lollipops, chocolates filled with salted caramel, black pepper shortbread, or passion fruit gelée. Finally there's a little wrapped goodie like an apricot *financier* or a chocolate-pistachio madeleine for customers to enjoy at home the next morning.

Most chefs love cheese as an ingredient and a course unto itself. But for me it's a much deeper experience. Because of my relationship with Judy, Larry, and the goats, my appreciation for the cheese is woven in with my experience on the farm holding the baby goats, watching them nurse from their mothers, picking vegetables from the garden, feeding the chickens, looking out at the whole herd in the sprawling barn, and sitting, just sitting, in that wonderful, warm, healing farm kitchen.

Goat Cheese Panna Cotta with Caramelized Figs

Makes 6 to 8 servings

2 teaspoons unflavored gelatin

4 teaspoons cold water

2 cups heavy cream

1/2 cup sugar

1 cup fresh Capriole goat cheese, softened

1 1/2 teaspoons pure vanilla extract

1 cup buttermilk

Sprinkle the gelatin over the 4 teaspoons of water to soften. Meanwhile, in a large saucepan, combine the heavy cream and sugar. Bring cream to a simmer over medium heat but do not let it boil, then turn off the heat and whisk in the softened goat cheese, whisking until the pieces of cheese are totally incorporated and the mixture is smooth. Add vanilla and softened gelatin and whisk again to dissolve gelatin and then whisk in the buttermilk. Strain the hot mixture through a fine sieve into a pitcher with a pour spout.

Pour into 6 to 8 ramekins or custard cups and refrigerate covered in plastic wrap for at least 3 hours, or up to 2 days. To unmold and serve, briefly and carefully dip the bottom of each ramekin in a baking pan of hot water. Run a thin knife around the edge of the mold to loosen the panna cotta. Wipe the bottom of the mold dry and invert the mold onto an individual, chilled dessert plate. Or serve in the ramekin. Garnish with caramelized figs.

FIGS

4 ripe figs, cut in half

1/4 cup coarse sugar

Dip the cut faces of the figs into the sugar and caramelize them with a blowtorch or by placing them under a broiler.

Distant Cultures

In the 1940s, for a brief period of time, the author and his business partner owned a lunchroom in an urban factory and railroad neighborhood. Petrakis now calls it "the year of the plague" and humorously reveals what men will do when their survival is at stake.

Art's Lunch

Harry Mark Petrakis

In the first years following my marriage in 1945 to my childhood sweet-heart, Diana, I worked a variety of jobs. These included scheduling mill production at the South Works of U.S. Steel, handling baggage at the railway express, loading and unloading cases of Schlitz on a beer truck, pressing clothing for a cleaner (an onerous occupation), and clerking in a liquor store. And in 1948, for about a year, I was co-owner of a small lunchroom in a railroad and factory district of Chicago.

My partner in the lunchroom was a childhood friend who before his discharge several years earlier had served in the U.S. Air Force as a navigator on a B-29 during the Second World War. He had survived thirty missions over Japan without a scratch. A postscript about his invincibility will come later.

The summer of 1948, Ted and I, embracing the dream of becoming

---

Harry Mark Petrakis's parents, Rev. Mark and Stella Petrakis came to America from the island of Crete in 1916. Harry grew up in a Greek immigrant community in Chicago that he has used as a locale for many of his stories. A high school dropout, he worked numerous jobs to survive. His first story, "Pericles on 31st Street," was published in the *Atlantic Monthly* in 1957. He has since published twenty-four books and has been nominated twice for the National Book Award in fiction. His novel *A Dream of Kings*, a national best seller, was made into a movie starring Anthony Quinn and Irene Papas. He has lectured extensively as a storyteller and teacher. He holds honorary degrees from a number of universities including the University of Illinois, the University of Indiana and the American College of Greece. He is married to the former Diana Perparos and they have three sons. After living forty-four years in Chicago, they have now lived the last forty-four years on the southern shore of Lake Michigan in northwest Indiana.

entrepreneurs, discussed entering business together. We explored a coffee dealership (we knew nothing about coffee), a bakery (neither of us were bakers), and finally moved toward restaurants. We had no experience in that business either but it seemed that restaurants and Greeks were a natural blend. We figured, smugly, how smart did one have to be to make a ham sandwich, mix a salad, and collect a check?

We inspected one restaurant owned by three brothers looking for additional partners. They were a troika of unsmiling and unfriendly men from the Mani, a mountainous, rock-strewn, and inhospitable region of Greece. We might have risked it if the sides were even but their numbers gave them an edge in any vote.

Our funds were limited and we could not afford many of the restaurants we inspected. Those we could afford were no more than greasy spoons.

We had been searching for months and were resigned to finding nothing suitable when, one afternoon in early November, we stumbled on ART'S LUNCH.

There was a flourishing restaurant on the busy corner of Thirteenth and Michigan, an elegant establishment with tiled booths, murals of Greece on the walls, and linen tablecloths. Ted and I ate lunch in that restaurant and then walked east down Thirteenth Street to where we had parked our car. For the first time we noticed this small, unimposing lunchroom with a shabby wooden sign, ART'S LUNCH, hanging above the door. What impressed us was a steady stream of customers entering and departing the small lunchroom.

We entered and spoke to the owner, a gracious older Greek man who in response to our query told us he was actually considering retirement and had plans to sell. He told us we'd have to wait to speak to him until the lunch rush was over and he set two chairs for us in a corner of the restaurant and brought us coffee.

The lunchroom was a small one with only four tables and about fifteen stools. Counter, stools, and tables all showed signs of excessive wear. The walls were shoddy with patches of peeling paint. Yet every stool and chair was taken and as soon as a seat was relinquished it was occupied again. The customers appeared to be blue-collar workers and, we learned later, were workers from nearby businesses: a potato warehouse, an armature factory, and the busy railroad yards a few blocks away.

The owner and two waitresses kept hurrying back and forth from the kitchen. In the small aperture between lunchroom and kitchen, the face of the cook appeared and disappeared. Occasionally I heard him respond with a snarl to one of the waitresses shouting for her order.

The owner also waited on customers but most of his time was spent at the register taking cash. Every time the register bell rang, it sounded to Ted and me as heartwarming as a Christmas carol.

For the following hour we watched in amazement the onslaught of customers that never seemed to end. Ted whispered, "We've found a gold mine!"

With his waitresses handling the dwindling number of customers, the owner joined us.

He had been in business at that location for about twelve years, the fourth owner of the lunchroom since the original Art. He had relatives still living in Greece and his plan was to retire and go home to join them. He was willing to sell at a price we could afford. At the same time he issued us a warning.

"Don't let your judgment be swayed by the amount of traffic you see coming in and out here today," he said. "We're very busy now because the armature and potato factories and the railroads are swollen with holiday help." His voice turned somber. "After Christmas you must be prepared for business to fall abruptly. Then you must take care in what you buy and in how you use any food left over."

We heard his warning but, bedazzled by the sheer volume of customers that kept filling the lunchroom, we overlooked the stark reality that the stove in the kitchen was a huge coal-burning behemoth that had to be loaded with coal and stoked in the middle of the night to be ready for breakfast. The icebox was a battered, three-tiered, six-compartment monster that looked as if it might have first seen service in the Civil War.

We met the chef, a stocky Swede with a forlorn chef's cap perched on his head and the stub of a dead cigar clenched between his teeth.

The sinks were two great iron tubs that were the domain of an older black man named George who, the owner told us, had served as a fifteen-year-old bugler in the Spanish-American War. He was a wiry man with alert eyes, strong arms, and shoulders stooped from years of bending over the tubs.

"George has been here since Art opened the lunchroom forty years ago," the owner said. "He sleeps in the storeroom back of the kitchen and gets up at four to load coal in the stove. All day long he washes dishes, cuts the meat, scrapes vegetables, scours pots and pans. He is worth three men in the kitchen."

In the following few weeks we worked out the details of the sale. The price we paid was $5,000, with Ted and I putting in $1,000 each as a down payment. The remaining $3,000 was taken back by the owner as a mortgage. We'd need to make monthly payments on his loan and pay a monthly rent to a city realtor as well.

By the first week in December, Ted and I had become the proud owners of ART'S LUNCH. We briefly discussed changing the name to TED AND HARRY'S CAFÉ (I generously conceded to putting Ted's name first) but when we learned how costly taking down the old sign and putting up a new one would be, we postponed any change. I suspected that might have been the same reason the sign had remained unchanged since Art first opened.

At the end of our first two weeks, after all expenses were paid, there remained $300 profit for each of us. Ted and I were elated that we'd have our down payment back in a few weeks. We complimented one another on our good fortune in finding the place as well as the business acumen we had shown by moving quickly to its purchase.

The first intimation of trouble came almost immediately after the first of January. Except for a coffee and doughnut crowd filling the lunchroom at breakfast and a modest surge of customers at lunch, the stools and tables remained unoccupied most of the day. At week's end we threw away a considerable amount of spoiled meat and wilted produce.

The trickle of business continued through January. By the last week in that month we had started losing money and Ted and I were forced to borrow from family and friends to meet our bills.

A major problem was that we lacked experience in how to reduce our purchases to match the dwindling number of customers. Despite a few suggestions from our cook, we also lacked the ability to utilize leftovers for making soups and stews.

There were in this gathering gloom a few pleasant experiences during our tenure. At dawn when we first opened, the lunchroom would become crowded with truck drivers and railway workers coming in for coffee, a doughnut, or a sweet roll. As they came to know Ted and me the teasing banter became lively.

"Hey, Harry, I remember this doughnut from last week!"

"I broke my tooth on one just like it!" another man said.

"How come so many Greeks go into the restaurant business?" a third man asked.

"To poison as many non-Greeks as possible," a trucker named Noodles responded. "That way they'll be the only hombres left on the planet."

In the beginning Ted and I had to endure the teasing and the jibes with what patience we could muster. As we got to know the customers better, we teased them back.

"These doughnuts are specially made for us in a Highland Park bakery serving the city's finest restaurants," I told Noodles. "We should be charging you extra."

When another trucker complained loudly for several days that the oatmeal was too watery, I poured a half box more Cream of Wheat into his bowl. "Stir it up good now," I advised.

From time to time the ribbing took on a meaner edge and Ted, more short-tempered than I was, found it hard to take.

One morning a truck driver named Bungo ordered a piece of blueberry pie. When Ted brought him the pie, Bungo shook his head.

"I ordered peach," he said.

"You ordered blueberry," Ted said.

Bungo appealed to his mates seated on either side of him.

"Did you hear me order?" he asked. "What did I ask for?"

"Peach," one said and others nodded in agreement. "Definitely peach."

I saw Ted's surging temper as he returned to the kitchen for a piece of peach pie.

"Stay calm," I warned him.

When Ted carried the piece of peach pie back to Bungo, he was greeted with disdain.

"I asked for lemon cream!" Bungo said indignantly.

"Lemon cream," one of his mates said gravely. "I heard him clear as day."

"Lemon cream," his second friend added, trying to conceal his smirk.

From the kitchen I could see Ted bristling in anger. Instead of standing and arguing he carried the piece of peach pie back to the kitchen and quietly cut a large piece of lemon cream pie.

"Let me take him the pie this time," I said, sensing danger.

Ted brushed by me. When he reached the men, their taunting began again.

"I didn't say lemon cream! I said apple!" Bungo cried. He looked to his buddies for confirmation. "Didn't I say apple?"

"He said apple! I heard him!"

Feeling a sudden panic at what might be about to happen, I started quickly from the kitchen through the swinging door. I got to Ted and the men on the adjoining stools just in time to hear Ted say, "You asked for lemon cream! By God, you're getting lemon cream!"

I witnessed Ted's arm draw back and then arc forward like a quarterback hurling a football. I recall Bungo's shocked face with lemon cream and meringue dripping down his cheeks.

I cannot remember what happened then. There were some shouts and curses but these were overwhelmed by the clamor of laughter that rolled across the crowded lunchroom.

From the beginning of our tenure, when a homeless man or one of the hoboes off the freights from the nearby yards entered our lunchroom, whether he could pay or not, George made sure he had a bowl of soup and a sandwich.

"We been doin' that since Art," George said firmly. "Long as I'm here, we ain' never goin' to turn a hungry man away."

Ted and I did not feel any compulsion to overturn George's edict and we agreed to feed the hoboes off the freight cars. As word of our bounty spread the number of hoboes stopping in increased. The alley exit of our lunchroom had prominently displayed a scrawled circle with an X within, denoting our place as good for a handout.

That winter, with the wind howling against the stained glass and the battered sign of the old lunchroom, at times as many as a score of hoboes clustered around the great coal-burning stove in the kitchen.

They were often remarkable storytellers, whether their tales of the road were enhanced or not. What I came to understand was that riding the rails was dangerous. The bulls, or railroad policemen, would mercilessly kick hoboes off the trains, so the hoboes would have to take care when boarding. They would hide along the tracks outside the yard until a train was being formed. They'd wait until it started up and then run alongside the cars, grab hold, and pull themselves up into the boxcars. Sometimes men missed and fell below the wheels. I saw a number of hoboes who had lost one or both legs in train accidents.

There were journalists and teachers, businessmen and ex-convicts among the hoboes, men often fleeing devils like alcohol and gambling, riding the freights, and all telling their stories.

Men spoke of the 1930s, the years of the Great Depression, when great crowds of hoboes rode the rails seeking new places where they might find work. The hobo jungles where they camped were small cities with a hundred campfires. In that time of travail, many hoboes were good about sharing what food they had with others.

Since those Depression years hobo traffic across the country had diminished, but for a submerged population of the country without money for fare, it was still the way to travel.

During those nights around the stove in our kitchen I picked up a smattering of the hobo language. *Bulls* were the brakemen who drove them off the cars, *harness bulls* were uniformed policemen, *high iron* was the main line of the railroads, *horstile* a town unfriendly to hoboes. The *Big O* was a train conductor, a *hobo special* a freight train of empty cars. Men spoke of *the highball whistle*, one short and one long whistle signaling a train was about to leave the yards.

The hoboes spoke of trains rushing through mountains and deserts, of notorious railroad brakemen, like Oklahoma Charley and Matt the Mug, remembered for their cruelty, or of fellow hoboes they met in their travels.

There were also hobo names for the various railroads: High Line, the old Great Northern running through the Dakotas and Montana; High Yaller Line, the Savannah & Atlanta Railroad; Horned Toad, the extension of the Chicago, Burlington, and Quincy Railroad; and the Apple Butter Route, the Norfolk and Western Railroad.

At the beginning of February, after one of our waitresses quit, we let go our cook. Ted and our remaining waitress, a sturdy veteran of eateries named Maude, handled the front. After trimming our menu to match my unexceptional skills as a chef, I retreated to the kitchen to handle the cooking. As I stumbled from stove to icebox, trying to make a salad while endeavoring to keep bacon and eggs from burning, George watched me with what I could only assume was pity. Often, shaking his head at my culinary ineptitude, he left the sinks and came to my aid.

In this time, coming to realize that the restaurant could not sustain two of us, Ted and I decided that only one of us could remain. From the beginning he had been more antagonistic to the environment of the restaurant than I had. Despite his period of dangerous service in wartime, he found the environment of the lunchroom more stressful. While I wanted desperately to be the partner who was liberated, I was the one we decided would stay.

Bracing myself for a final offensive against imminent catastrophe, I was sustained by Maude working the stools and tables and George in the kitchen. From time to time, to relieve Maude, my wife, Diana, pregnant then, and my sister, Irene, came in to help me as waitresses.

In this critical period I would never have survived if it were not for George. He worked double shifts that began at 4:00 a.m. when he first stoked the coal-burning stove. For the following sixteen hours he never ceased working at assorted tasks. I survived as long as I did only because of his Herculean labors.

Predating McDonald's and Burger King, I devised a meal called "Burger in a Basket," which consisted of a burger, a few French fries, and a slice of pickle. To provide an aesthetic flourish I added a sprig of parsley. Our customers responded with enthusiasm but burgers alone couldn't pay our bills.

Desperate times required desperate measures. Ted and I had been approached in the past by a scurrilous meat salesman we knew only as Sam. His rock-bottom prices and the wretched appearance of his products suggested a slippery slope to food poisoning. (Once when we asked Sam why his poultry appeared so dark, he reassured us that the chickens had been bred on a farm in Florida.) Our own somber assumption was that his creatures had died a natural death.

Frantic as I was, for the first time I bought a crate of turkeys from Sam at fifteen cents a pound. I boiled those turkeys all that night and part of the following day. When customers complained about the foul smell I told them a gas main had broken.

I served the turkeys all that week, varying the menu slightly each day. Monday: Roast young tom turkey. Tuesday: Turkey and noodles. Wednesday: Hot turkey sandwich. Thursday: Turkey croquettes. Friday: Turkey hash. Saturday: Chicken a la king.

Despite showing a profit that week for the first time in months, I could not stave off my collapse. In the early spring, after a futile effort to sell the lunchroom came to nothing, I had the fixtures, china, and silverware sold to an auction house that specialized in equipment from small lunchrooms. The few hundred dollars I received was barely enough to cover the hospital bill my wife and I incurred when our first son, Mark, was born.

In the decades that have passed since then, whenever I enter a restaurant owned by a Greek, I watch closely to determine whether the owner exhibits any of the anguish my own experience produced. They all seem untroubled while spending an uncommon amount of time at the cash register.

So many decades ago, my failure in the restaurant business seemed an unhappy augury of future calamities to come. As I began to write, I found myself drawing upon that year of the plague. Some of my first stories were based in lunchrooms similar to ART'S LUNCH. Many of the truckers, drivers, and hoboes I met in the restaurant as well as their stories found their way into my novels. Even when I wrote of much more elegant emporiums than our own shabby establishment, I still drew on memories of ART'S LUNCH, the kitchen blending assorted smells, the sounds of customers eating, the quiet interludes before and after lunch, and the countless people who came just for a cup of coffee and to talk. Like a bartender, a small lunchroom owner can become the recipient of a hundred sad and lonely tales.

If Greeks and restaurants belonged naturally together, my own experience proved I might have been simply the wrong Greek.

Yet through the years that have passed since then, I have come to appreciate and be grateful for the cauldron of fire I went through that year and for the fruitful repository on life and human beings the experience provided me.

The open-air market of Maxwell Street became known as the Ellis Island of the Midwest, a port of entry into Chicago for immigrants arriving from all over Europe, Latin America, and the southern states.

A Tale of Two Tamales

Carol Mighton Haddix

The tamale was too hot, wrapped in its husk of corn, so I had to wait. I sat down on the nearby bench under a tree, settling my bag of produce beside me. It had been a brisk but sunny morning at Chicago Green City Market, a sustainable food market at the southern end of the city's Lincoln Park, not far from the zoo and the beaches of Lake Michigan.

I was pleased with the long stalks of rhubarb and fat spears of asparagus sticking out from my canvas bag. It was my first visit to the market this season. I had hovered over the purple, red, and green lettuces and the baby leeks and green garlic stalks. I had dodged the baby strollers and dogs on leashes. Now I was hungry.

At one end of the market, just opposite the stand selling grass-fed Piedmontese beef, was Las Manas Tamales. I had read about the tamales

Carol Mighton Haddix recently retired as food editor of the *Chicago Tribune*, a post she held for thirty-one years. Under her direction, Good Eating, the *Tribune's* food section, won yearly best-section awards and nominations from the Association of Food Journalists and writing awards from the James Beard Foundation. Haddix is a board member and past president of Les Dames d'Escoffier Chicago, a professional food society. She is a founding member of the Culinary Historians of Chicago. She also is a member of the James Beard Foundation, where she was former chairman of the Beard Book Awards committee. She has edited many *Tribune* cookbooks, including *Good Eating's Best of the Best: Great Recipes of the Past Decade from the "Chicago Tribune" Test Kitchen*. She has judged national and local food competitions and given lectures on Chicago food history. Haddix divides her time between Chicago and the Leelanau Peninsula in Michigan.

on a local online food newsletter that raved about their unusual fillings, so I headed over and bought one of few remaining tamales. Owner Amber Romo Wojcinski was apologizing to other customers about running out of one flavor. "I'm sorry, we're almost sold out again," she said. It was only 11:00 a.m.

Sampling my tamale, I understood why. Invaded by a fork, it released a fresh fragrance of corn and the cooked masa dough fell apart easily into airy, tender pieces. Inside, a filling of shredded brisket, spinach, and smoked Muenster cheese lay waiting. The slow-cooked beef was perfectly seasoned and well matched with the smoky goodness of the cheese and a few leaves of fresh spinach. It was gone in five minutes. I looked around at the bucolic scene, full and happy, watching the trendy Lincoln Park crowd go by. Maybe a tamale to go for dinner? But I realized Amber no doubt had sold her last one by now.

The popularity of Las Manas Tamales is understandable. Handmade and fresh, the products are a far cry from the typical frozen tamales you find at the supermarket. Amber, a Kendall College culinary school grad, has help from her husband, Jeff, and her sisters (the company name was taken from *las hermanas*, the sisters) in running the new business.

Amber's father hails from a small town in Jalisco, Mexico, and she grew up eating tamales. But now, she is turning those traditional tamales into artisanal creations. She uses products from the market, so her fillings change from week to week, depending on what's in season. One week it's shredded brisket with tart cherry compote, another it's pulled pork shoulder with rhubarb. She always makes a vegetarian option such as peaches with basil and goat cheese or summer squash with grilled onions and Cheddar.

Four miles south and one week later, I strolled through a very different kind of market and sampled another unique tamale. The Maxwell Street Market has been in operation since the late 1800s. Though the location of the market has changed twice due to urban renewal, its long history reflects the changing groups of immigrants that have arrived and made their homes in the Windy City.

The Irish first settled the area near Halsted and Maxwell Streets, where the market began. Later came the Greeks, Bohemians, Russians, Germans, Italians, African Americans, and Mexicans. Russian Jews dominated the market from the 1880s to the 1920s. It featured all kinds of goods, from clothing to food, and served as the neighborhood's social nexus. The market began to draw Chicagoans from all over the city in search of bargains. Gradually, the Jews and other immigrant merchants moved on to the suburbs and other city neighborhoods. They were replaced by African Americans who were part of the Great Migration from the South in the early 1900s. Then Mexicans arrived, settling mainly in the nearby Pilsen neighborhood and farther west in what is now called Little Village.

Today Maxwell Street Market stretches for about four blocks down Desplaines Street, located across I-94 and north of the original location. It's filled with a hodgepodge of goods: CDs, perfumes, socks, underwear, shirts, dresses, shoes, purses, electronics, mattresses, and tools. And lots of food, mostly Mexican.

On this sunny morning I wandered past the many booths and watched families carrying off crates of peaches and bags of avocados from the produce stands. Others were seated at picnic tables under canopies, pouring hot sauce over freshly made tacos of tongue or zucchini flowers at stands with names such as Manolo's, Rubi's, and Tito's Tacos. A long line formed at the blue churros truck where shoppers ordered just-pulled-from-the-fat sticks of dough filled with vanilla custard, better than any coffee-shop éclairs.

But I was after the Oaxacan tamales. It took a while to find them at a small unnamed stand with only a few tables and a handwritten sign listing *Oaxacan tamales: verde o roso*. A smiling woman took my order.

"Con crema?" she asked.

"Si. Un poco." A huge dollop of the Mexican tangy sour cream fell next to the tamale that the cook had pulled from a steamer, unwrapping its banana-leaf covering. I took my purchase to one of the tables nearby. A giant plastic squeeze bottle of green salsa sat in front of me, and I timidly squeezed a glob next to the tamale.

The masa dough was fragrant as I dug into the center of the tamale with a fork. Shreds of chicken — white and dark meat — tasted as if they came from a stewed hen, perhaps cooked with onions. The flavor was mild and comforting, but after I dipped the next forkful into the tomatillo salsa and the *crema*, the whole mouthful burst with a tangy, earthy flavor that quickly needed a follow-up. And then more. All I needed, I thought, was a Bohemia beer. But I was already too full. As I left, I asked the woman for the name of the stand. "Oh, no," she said, shaking her head. "No name!"

The Chicago region is home to one of the largest populations of Mexican Americans in the United States, with about 1.4 million. The Pilsen and Little Village neighborhoods are dotted with their restaurants, bakeries, and supermarkets. The walls of the buildings provide a canvas for their colorful murals. Street vendors nearby sell equally colorful *aguas frescas*, fresh-fruit drinks made from mango, watermelon, or lime. Some offer *elote*, corn on the cob that's slathered with mayonnaise, cheese, and chili powder.

Mexican foods also have spread far from those neighborhoods. Mom-and-pop taco stands or small Mexican cafes can be found in almost all neighborhoods of the city. Chicagoans love the now-familiar street foods such as tacos, *sopes*, quesadillas and tamales as well as the more sophisticated stews and moles. Mexican food has gone mainstream and become a culinary success story in Chicago.

But those from Mexico are not the only ones with a success story in this city of immigrants. The Italians came in the late 1800s, settling on and around Taylor Street, just south of today's ever-sprawling University of Illinois–Chicago campus and not far from Maxwell Street Market. They brought their love of pasta, robust sauces, and herbs. And through the years, enterprising cooks created new Italian American dishes unique to Chicago: a garlicky roast chicken with potato wedges called chicken Vesuvio, for example. Italian restaurants around town serve it still sizzling from the oven and aromatic with herbs, garlic, and wine. They also contributed the iconic Chicago street food, the Italian beef sandwich. Made from long-simmered, lean beef roast dosed with healthy amounts of oregano, basil, garlic, and crushed red pepper flakes, this sandwich is known for its messy, juicy goodness and its traditional spicy topping of pickled sport peppers (or sweet bell peppers, if you must). Devoted fans debate the merits of popular sandwich stands such as Mr. Beef and Al's Beef in Chicago and Johnnie's Beef in Elmwood Park.

Equally debated are the best places in town to try German, Polish, Irish, Greek, Chinese, Korean, Thai, Japanese, Ukrainian, Pakistani, Indian, Lithuanian, Czech, and Puerto Rican food and many others. Today, Chicagoland has the third-largest immigrant population in the country. When it comes to restaurants serving their food, the variety is mind-boggling.

Devon Avenue, for example, stretches for miles on Chicago's far north side, presenting a lively mix of Pakistani, Indian, Jewish, and Russian markets, bakeries, butchers, and restaurants. Names such as Patel, Hema, Bhabi, and The Bagel appear on the colorful signs that stretch up and down the avenue. The aromas of freshly ground coriander, cumin, and fennel seeds seep from the doorways.

Harlem Avenue on the west side of town offers different aromas. Numerous Italian delis, pasta shops, markets, and restaurants line the street, giving off wafts of garlic and pork sausage. As Italian immigrants moved from the Taylor Street area to the near west suburbs such as Elmwood Park, they opened their small stores and cafes nearby on Harlem, north and south of Irving Park Road.

A similar tale repeats this shifting population. Once, the small Chinatown area, around Cermak Road on the south side, was home to most Chinese immigrants here. But now many have moved north. Chinese storefront shops now mix with Thai and Vietnamese shops on Argyle Street on the north side to form a new Asian area.

Most of these neighborhood cooks still continue to cook according to the traditions of their homelands — to the pleasure of appreciative Chicagoans. Oh, there may be a tweak or two to appeal to the American palate, a tamer spice profile in certain dishes, perhaps, or simply not offering offal or ingredients that are too expensive or not even available in Chicago. As long these cooks keep stirring their *pho*, curries, and *caldos*, area foodies will flock to ethnic neighborhoods.

Meanwhile, the children, grandchildren, and great-grandchildren of immigrants embrace our fast-food culture, learning the joys of Vienna hot dogs with yellow mustard or Quarter Pounders with crispy fries. Many observers fear the eventual loss of their traditional ways of cooking. They see a gradual eroding of classic ethnic recipes, discarded like so many worn shoes.

After all, the rest of us love to take their ethnic dishes and fuse them into Americanized versions. Pad thai becomes sweetened up and watered down. A dish of Italian seafood pasta gets an unorthodox coating of cheese. Spicy Szechuan beef becomes meek. And tamales turn from a humble holiday food to trendy market fare.

Adventuresome Midwest cooks switch imported ingredients for local products in ethnic dishes. A locally made artisan cheese, for example, brings a new flavor to the classic Polish pierogi. Grass-fed beef from Wisconsin adds its own unique flavor to a Korean *bulgogi*. Chefs mix direct-from-the-farm ingredients of the Midwest with Asian, French, Italian, and other culinary traditions, as they look to a time when farmers were always local, not part of America's large agricultural conglomerates.

But one lure of the city is in the excitement of trying these new things. In food, as in technology, the new is so much more interesting. Tweak those recipes, some say. Let Nonna turn over in her grave. As long as it tastes good, let's switch things up.

Will the new generations, the sons and daughters of immigrants now embracing American food, lose their culinary pasts? Will there be a constant evolution of ethnic dishes? New sensibilities beget new tastes and the process is perhaps inevitable in a city like Chicago, where we are exposed to so many new foods. World trade now brings us ingredients that never before have been available in markets, from exotic condiments and spices to tropical fruits.

Traditionalists may worry, but young chefs applaud. One food culture melds with another. It's a give and take that has been going on for centuries. As long as someone keeps count, keeps a record of the originals. And is willing to teach and share the older culinary traditions, so they are not lost forever.

In the meantime, let's go ahead and savor foods like Amber Wojcinski's new Midwest tamales of brisket with cherries and chilies, and please, pass the napkins.

Beef Brisket, Savory Cherry Compote, and Jalapeño Cheese Tamales

Makes about 24 tamales

Amber makes her own masa, a long process of grinding non-genetically modified corn that she buys from the Three Sisters Farm in Kankakee, Illinois, treating it with limewater, grinding it, and adding butter and vegetable oil (not the traditional lard) to turn the meal into a dough. The result is a more tender, flavorful corn wrapping for her fillings. The whole tamale is wrapped in corn husks and steamed. Cooks at home can use a prepared masa dough, if they live near a *tortilleria* that sells it. Commercial dry masa harina (found in most large supermarkets) also will work, once reconstituted. The brisket is cooked the day before and allowed to chill overnight in the liquid. The cherry compote also can be made ahead. Use drained canned tart cherries if no fresh cherries are available. Freeze any leftover filling and use later for tacos or barbecue sandwiches.

BEEF BRISKET

1 1/2 pounds beef brisket
Sea salt
2 tablespoons sunflower oil
2 cloves garlic, peeled, smashed
1 medium yellow onion, halved, sliced
1 teaspoon each: dried oregano, ground cumin
1 tablespoon each: cider vinegar, honey, molasses
1 1/2 cups water

SAVORY CHERRY COMPOTE

1 tablespoon sunflower oil
1 shallot, finely chopped
3 serrano chilies, minced
Braising liquid from beef brisket, cooled, strained
1 pound sour cherries, pitted
1 tablespoon plus 1 teaspoon sugar
1 tablespoon masa harina

For tamales and filling:

8 ounces grated jalapeño or pepper Jack cheese
24 dried corn husks, plus 8 extra for lining the pot, soaked 2 hours,
patted dry
Prepared masa dough for 24 tamales

Heat oven to 275 degrees. Season the beef generously with salt to taste. Heat a large Dutch oven over medium-high heat. Add the oil; heat just until beginning to smoke. Add the meat; cook, turning once, until browned on both sides, about 10 minutes total. Transfer the meat to a plate.

Add garlic, onion, oregano, and cumin to drippings in the Dutch oven; stir until fragrant, about 1 minute. Add vinegar, honey, and molasses, scraping the bottom of the pan with a wooden spoon. Stir in water; heat to a boil. Return the brisket to the Dutch oven. Cover; place in the oven. Cook the brisket until it pulls apart easily with a fork, about 5 to 6 hours. Let beef cool in its braising liquid; refrigerate overnight.

For the compote, heat a saucepan over medium heat; add the oil. Cook the shallot until translucent, about 2 minutes. Add the serrano chilies; cook, stirring, 1 minute. Add the reserved braising liquid; heat to a boil. Cook until liquid is reduced by half, about 10 minutes. Add the cherries and sugar; heat to a boil. Cook, stirring often, until reduced by half, about 15 minutes. Stir in masa harina; cook, stirring, until thickened, 2 minutes. Adjust seasoning; let cool. Puree half of the compote in a food processor until almost smooth; return to saucepan. Stir. Set aside or refrigerate overnight.

Cut the beef brisket, against the grain, in 1-inch-thick pieces; shred into a large bowl. Fold in the cherry compote and grated cheese. Adjust the seasoning.

For tamales, place a corn husk pointed side toward you on a working surface. Evenly spread about ¼ cup of prepared masa dough in the middle of the corn husk, leaving a large border of husk at the bottom and smaller borders on each side. Place about 2 tablespoons of the filling down the center of the masa dough. Carefully fold over the edges of the corn husks toward the center until the masa dough encloses the filling, overlapping the edges. Fold up the bottom of the corn husk toward the middle; tie tamale closed with kitchen string. Repeat with remaining corn husks.

Line a steamer rack with extra corn husks in a steamer or Dutch oven over water, leaving small spaces between husks for the steam. Place tamales upright, folded side down, on the rack. Cover with more corn husks; cover pan. Heat water to a boil; reduce heat to medium. Steam until cooked through, about 1 hour, 15 minutes, adding more boiling water if necessary. Masa dough is cooked when it easily pulls away from the corn husk after opening. Let tamales cool to firm up, 5 to 10 minutes, before serving. Tamales can be refrigerated or frozen and re-steamed until hot.

From the take-out window of his food cart, a Hungarian born on the Danube now finds enjoyment and meaning by feeding a revolving menu to the crowds in a Big Ten university town. Hungarian paprikash? Pheasant under Styrofoam? Lobster bisque? From a gourmet hot dog stand?

Le Dog, Ann Arbor, Michigan

Jules Van Dyck-Dobos

Imagine a midwestern town with a renowned university. The population of about 114,000 is diverse, with many foreign-born students, faculty, researchers, and staff. Family-friendly and rich with cultural offerings, the town often ranks high on lists of the best places to live. A few steps from Division Street, so named because it separates the town from the university campus, is a small, red hot dog stand called Le Dog, best known today for its lobster bisque and over 240 soups that revolve on the ever-changing menu. Only two hundred square feet in size, Le Dog is an Ann Arbor landmark.

Soups were not even on the menu in 1979 when Le Dog began. That summer, while in town visiting my parents, I noticed a boarded-up refreshment stand called Karamel Korn Kastle and suddenly had a vision of the University of Michigan campus covered with hot dog carts — forty thousand students enjoying "tube steaks"! Not long after, my first cart arrived from New York, and with the little refreshment stand as my base, Le Dog was born (the name derived from lemonade and hot dogs, the only two items on the menu).

Michigan is neither Florida nor Hawaii. The temperature can reach

Jules Van Dyck-Dobos was born on the Danube River in Hungary and emigrated to the United States after the revolution of 1956. He owns two restaurants in Ann Arbor, Michigan, with his wife, Ika, whom he met while completing his studies in Germany. After graduating from the business school at Michigan State, he worked in many hotels and restaurants, including Louis Szathmary's The Bakery in Chicago. He is an avid skier, world traveler, and of course, cook and is grooming son Miki for the next generation of restaurateurs.

ninety degrees on some days and drop to minus ten on others. These extremes do not make it easy to push a four-hundred-pound-cart twenty blocks. On winter days it was easier to pass hot dogs to customers through an eighteen-by-twenty-four-inch take-out window and stay relatively warm. By spring I had abandoned my plan of ordering a second cart. The refreshment-stand kitchen, though small, was cozy; the overhead, manageable; the sidewalk, busy with pedestrians. But customers were rare. The menu, I realized, was all wrong. So I decided to introduce items from my prior hotel and restaurant experience. Surely Ann Arborites would go for that.

Soon, tantalizing odors wafted out from the small window to tickle the noses of passersby: roast duck, veal tarragon, cassoulet, bouillabaisse. If customers came early enough, they could order pheasant under Styrofoam, Hungarian paprikash, Cajun rice, triple-imported-chocolate shakes, or avocado soup with champagne. Reservations were necessary to order these specials, and I adhered to a strict "ten minutes late = no show" policy; those who arrived late found their lunch already sold. Even though Le Dog was open only for lunch, from 11:00 a.m. to 3:00 p.m., I worked ten- to twelve-hour days. The specials took a long time to prepare and serve to long lines of customers with limited time for lunch. So this menu was also wrong.

Even a small gourmet hot dog stand must begin with a philosophy. In order to establish your place, you have to examine the past: what works, what doesn't. And you have to figure out what you want to achieve. From there you find a niche and fill it with your passion — cooking! But do not complicate it. Follow the KISS principle: Keep It Small and Simple.

I figured out that good cooking is a good business plan. Customers will recognize it and come running. Not everyone, of course. I can't make food for everyone. At Le Dog I serve no pizza. Le Dog has no hamburgers, and the last line on the menu states emphatically, "NO Coke, NO Pepsi, NO pop or soda. EVER!!" Le Dog's fame currently rests on soups. Hundreds of soups. French, continental, Asian, seafood, vegetarian, bisques, chowders, and stews, one-pot dishes — anything I can serve in a bowl. The soups served at Le Dog are named after the main ingredient or the culture associated with the name. I don't have to explain gumbo or cream of mushroom soup in great detail, but for firedragon soup I list the ingredients. And I don't hesitate to list ingredients like rutabaga, hominy, or couscous on my fast-food menu, even though they make some customers wary.

Le Dog does not advertise. We are so low-key that I have even turned down a filming request from the Food Network (my marketing professor at Michigan State University wanted to rescind my degree when he found that out). I want my patrons, some of whom have four lunches a week at Le Dog, to spread the word by mouth. Wouldn't most restaurants be better off spending their dollars on what goes on the plate instead of on advertising? My customers include the bank teller from across the street, the president of the university, and the mayor of Ann Arbor. No one has time for a leisurely luncheon; after all, most Americans get only a half-hour break. That is why Le Dog is open now from 11:30 a.m. to 2:30 p.m., Monday through Friday. The line really moves. It's slow food, but fast!

I use local ingredients whenever I can. As a youngster in post–World War II Hungary, my contact with imported produce was very limited. Around New Year's I might see a lemon or two, oranges were even rarer, and bananas existed only in picture books. But as a first-grader, I could already name ten or twelve varieties of apples, peel and precut most vegetables, and stand in line for an hour for a loaf of bread or a liter of milk. And we had variety in our menu. Meat came from rabbits we raised; we ate fish if a friend had been lucky on the Danube River. So I understand the catchwords "locally grown" and the movement that is slowly gaining momentum in the United States. Nevertheless, I've been known to buy peppers flown in from Amsterdam and have kicked myself for my folly more than once after tasting them. But my, they looked good!

Why should a small hot dog stand have a future? Because it is simple. I know what the inventory is because I receive it, use it, and pay for it. I know the customer's name because I hand her the soup and bread myself. I know the temperature of the dishwasher because I do the dishes. I don't need a manager to tell me what labor problems are brewing. Le Dog is my baby, so it's my responsibility to watch over everything. My wife, Ika, who operates a very similar Le Dog on Main Street in the middle of town, is the only other person who shares my particular passion. In fact, she does it better than I, because she can focus on keeping it simple (some days I still want to serve roast duck or pheasant under Styrofoam).

How do I picture Le Dog in a decade? I hope I can keep it on its present course. Recently, a dear friend prompted me to research the possibility of franchising, of cloning a successful concept to reap benefits of scale and gain new vigor. Yet, much as I would like to return with my current knowledge to 1979 and cover many college campuses with Le Dogs, that is only a pipe dream. What I have today is small and specialized. It works for me, and I don't think I'll stagnate if I limit myself to two locations. New customers discover us all the time. Most important, I can follow my passion every day. I can cook!

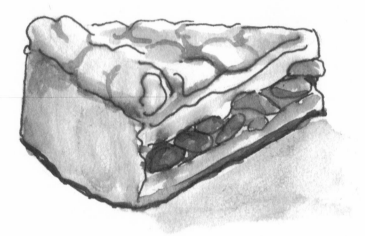

Minnesota writer Anne Dimock, who grew up in a family of pie bakers, experienced a calling to rhubarb. Remember this, says the author: Always listen when a food whispers to you. Something wonderful will happen.

The Night of the Rhubarb Kuchen

Anne Dimock

My taste in cuisines is steeped in the hearty baking traditions of Norwegian, Swedish, English, Irish, and German forebears, the ones who left their potato-blighted lands for the New World. Of course they brought rhubarb with them. It's like packing a titanium stove on a backpacking trip — essential and life-affirming — and if you forgot to pack it, well, good luck to you in finding a substitute. Had one of those immigrants forgotten to pack their pie plant, it would have meant a sorry trail of experimentation among the woodsy large-leaf stalks masquerading as rhubarb.

Of all the plants that began somewhere and then hitchhiked their way across the world, only one of them — *Rheum rhubarbarum* — has the popular moniker of "Pie Plant." For living things with limited mobility, plants are among the traveling-est species around. Why? Humans want them and need them and take them along on their transcontinental migrations as they pursue warmer climates, more game, and better real estate.

Joyously, rhubarb landed on the east coast and made its way farm by farm across the North American continent, finding its most receptive home in the Upper Midwest, Wisconsin and Minnesota in particular, where it also happily collided into the family food traditions of many Scandinavian and German families, most notably mine.

Anne Dimock is the author of *Humble Pie: Musings of What Lies beneath the Crust*, and numerous essays, features, articles, and reviews published in newspapers and magazines. She is also a poet and playwright.

What makes rhubarb a standout ingredient in classic midwestern cuisine? It is its affinity for desserts, its ability to add a pleasant sourness to what could otherwise be just too much sweetness. It thrives in midwestern soil and climate. And it was propelled into the canon of great midwestern desserts by that Scandinavian-German immigrant juggernaut of home cooks and bakers who appeared on the frozen tundra at just the right time between the Industrial Revolution and the rise of convenience foods. They were an unstoppable force and brought forth three rhubarb desserts — rhubarb pie, rhubarb kuchen (cake), and rhubarb Kram — wrought them into perfection, and gave them to the world.

I heard my call to rhubarb in 1988 when I walked the land of my new Minnesota home and discovered thirty rhubarb plants in neat three-by-ten rows. Thirty plants is an awful lot of rhubarb and I took it as a sign that I should perfect the rhubarb pie. And I did. The secret to rhubarb pie is a simple ratio that will give it enough sweetness to balance the sour and just enough thickening to slow the ooze. For a 9-inch pie pan use 5 cups of sliced rhubarb, 1¼ cups of sugar, 5 tablespoons of flour, and 2 pinches of cinnamon.

Try to refrain from adding any strawberries. You will never experience the full force and power of a rhubarb pie with strawberries to distract you.

RHUBARB KUCHEN

German and German American cooking never captured my imagination the way other cuisines did. Perhaps I echoed my grandfather's reticence to own up to German heritage — he called himself Dutch, not Deutsch, and this held for a couple of generations. He was by no means alone; memories of wars and exodus led many German expats to describe themselves in other ways. I went through three-quarters of my life thinking I was of English, Irish, and Dutch stock until I found the papers that said Grandpa Eddie was German all the way through. Then there came an occasion when I wanted to make a German statement in my baking, and I launched myself into a fact-finding mission on how to make kuchen (pronounced KOO-khehn).

There was a family nearby with whom we often got together. We shared cheesehead and Badgerland history with them, and our daughters were the same age. The other husband and I liked to cook and discuss food, and his wife and my husband liked to discuss work. He was of Wisconsin Progressive Era royalty, a scion of a prince in the movement and a prince in his own right. And he was of German heritage and did not appreciate that part of his family story. We collaborated in many food experiences — mostly French — but also Italian, Greek, and Spanish. But did we ever plan an evening to prepare and celebrate the German heritage we all had in common? Was there ever a German theme to our cooking, was there *rouladen* or spätzle or kraut? No there was not. Never. It was an unspoken agreement between us, we were not going to prepare German food when there was still more French cuisine to explore. He was deliberately eschewing his German heritage and I wasn't yet aware of mine.

Then one day I decided I would make a kuchen. I don't remember if I wanted to needle him or honor him, but the finishing flourish of an evening of potage, *daube de boeuf*, haricots verts, *beaucoup de fromage*, and Fleurie was going to be a rhubarb kuchen.

I had never made a kuchen, had hardly ever tasted one except for a memorable plum kuchen at a Sabbath dinner. It was the memory of that plum kuchen that whispered to me. Remember this — always listen when a food whispers to you — something wonderful will happen. And soon I was on a quest to find a kuchen recipe worthy of the rest of the dinner. This was in the late spring, long before there were apples or plums, so of course it would be a rhubarb kuchen.

Just as there are many things in North America that we call cakes, so too in German cuisine. The kuchen I was after was a classic fruit kuchen with a dense, almost crust-like crumb to the cake part and a custard-y addition to the fruit part. This description seems unnatural — I am a poor poet of German cuisine. It's not right to describe it only in terms of my American childhood experience of cakes, those frothy confections of airy layers slathered with frosting and dotted with cartoon characters or blue roses. A fruit kuchen is a wonderful dessert and suffers for being placed in the same category as birthday cake. A kuchen is its own wonderful thing, as we found out.

I found several recipes for *apfelkuchen* but none for rhubarb. How should I go about the substitution, the need to adjust for sourness and more moisture? There was no clear path to follow, so I blazed a new one in my dense woods of German cuisine uncertainty. A lot could go wrong. Without enough sugar to apprehend rhubarb's pucker, my kuchen would utterly fail as a dessert. Without a way to absorb the extra water trapped inside rhubarb's deceptively woody stalks, my kuchen would drown in its own juices. Without an understanding of just the right amount of spice, salt, and other unknown ingredients, I would fail in my intent to impress our family friends, enlighten us, and admit something authentically German into our faux Frenchified lives.

In the end, I created a third recipe out of parts of two that looked reliable enough. One I used for the dense cake part, one I used for the egg and cream overlay; I was on my own for the rhubarb part and the baking time. I felt like Luke Skywalker as Jedi novice who turned off his all-seeing goggles and trusted his own inner guidance system, trying to sense The Force.

But I listened to the whisper. I made a few hasty calculations on one of the recipes, then finished up my rhubarb kuchen and put it in the oven without another glance at a recipe.

Well. There is little else to say but it was likely the finest rhubarb kuchen made anywhere that year. It was perfect. It was amazing. It was the sort of revelation rhubarb is known for. And when I brought it to table, it was clear this was not a French *clafouti*; it was not an American Betty, bounce, or buckle; it was not British pudding or Spanish cream. It was a real kuchen, with just enough of all the right parts to make it unmistakably Germanic. I had no doubt my kuchen deserved its place in a long line of Minnesota and Wisconsin Lutheran church suppers and bake sales. It would be recognized and saluted there, it would be welcomed as a cousin that had dropped off the family tree and was now back.

It was only after appreciating how wonderful this dessert was, how perfectly it complemented the other foods of our dinner, how right it was in its interpretation and execution — only after all this did we admit that it was German and it was part of us and that was why it so harmoniously sang to all our senses. With this dessert, we were finally free to be as German as we wanted to be. *Ja, ja, ja!*

The next time we got together, we did not roll out the *rouladen*; we did not salt and pickle the herring or the beets or the kraut; we did not boil the bratwurst in beer or grate the *kartoffel* for pancakes. There were smaller, subtler shifts in our cooking and — dare I say it? — our regard for that part of us that descended from the millions of German immigrants who came here from the very beginning of European immigration to North America. Why did we ever think we could hold ourselves apart from this when the evidence was everywhere around us? It was in our names, our religions, in all the farms around us, and especially in those church-basement suppers and bake sales. And now that we had had our kuchen, we could walk into any one of them and belong.

Thirty rhubarb plants will teach you plenty, so I already knew that rhubarb pie was about the getting of wisdom. The rhubarb plant deserves our reverence for just this. But what I didn't know until the Night of the Rhubarb Kuchen was that rhubarb could also be a long chain and anchor that magically did not weigh us down. Instead it tethered us to our past while we sailed and sailed and sailed.

I never did again bake a rhubarb kuchen as glorious as that first one, never recalled exactly what I did in that Jedi-like moment of creation. My recipe was lost in the sands of time. But the kuchen has whispered twice, and there were others there who heard.

RHUBARB KRAM

In the Kingstad household that I married into, the recipe for Kram was possessed by Elna Bostrom Kingstad, a first-generation Swedish American who grew up in Wisconsin hearing, speaking, and eating Swedish at home. A lot of fine recipes came to me through Elna Kingstad, but because rhubarb Kram was not part of my childhood and was the most humble of immigrant and Depression-era food, it did not loom very large in my comfort food inventory. That place was occupied by apple brown Betty for my own reasons and my own family history — that's why it's comfort food. And for Jon Kingstad, whom I married, rhubarb Kram was synonymous with childlike contentment. In our household,

Kram was one of those ritual foods that could call down the Nordic gods to shield us from the arrows of an uncaring world.

Kram is a humble food, but since it is made of rhubarb, its humility comes with an extra prize for those aware enough to feel its deep, subtle power. Its only extravagance is all the sugar, which is cheap now, but sugar wasn't always cheap or plentiful, even if the rhubarb was.

For my husband, Kram was a boomerang back in time to when he was a child hearing all those Swedish elders speak around the table as they had their coffee, bread and cheese, and Kram. Flung backward in time, it gathered up the genealogy, pivoted on an invisible axis, then came right back to him with those long-gone people as if they were still alive. Saying it correctly was the difference between a Latin High Mass and a folk mass. Saying it correctly (crahm) was honoring their journey from one frigid tundra to another. Saying it correctly meant as much to him as the bowl of rhubarb Kram itself, soft olive-pink mush in a moat of milk.

Here was how Elna Bostrom Kingstad made rhubarb Kram. As in most recipes from the provenance of passed-down memory, measurements and technique are approximate, and it assumes you already know your way around a kitchen.

Rhubarb Kram

1 pound rhubarb
1 1/3 cups water
1 cup sugar
2 tablespoons potato flour or cornstarch

Clean the rhubarb and cut it into pieces.

Bring the water to a boil, add the rhubarb and the sugar; boil until tender.

Mix the potato flour or cornstarch with a small amount of water; stir into the rhubarb mixture and bring again to a boil. Cover and cool. Serve with cream.

RHUBARB JAM

A more sugared and condensed version of rhubarb Kram is simple rhubarb jam. This has been appearing in midwestern pantries and root cellars for generations, but I did not enter this slipstream until after the advent of microwave ovens. I learned how to make this and other jams without standing over the hot stove and stirring. It's the only way I make jams. I think a brighter fruit taste emerges from all that cooking and evaporation when the sugars don't caramelize as much as they do when cooked directly atop a burner.

Here is where I throw away my rule about not mixing strawberries with rhubarb. When I make my rhubarb jam, I use a four-to-one ratio of rhubarb to strawberries. It's good, and my daughter has the blue ribbons from Minnesota's Washington County Fair to prove others think so too. Our little family had to have a dozen pints of this stuff socked away to get through our seven months of winter — I had to reallocate the rhubarb stores away from the pie making in order to have it for jam. Or Kram. Or kuchen. Whichever. Because even with thirty rhubarb plants, you can still run out of rhubarb.

RHUBARB PIEKU

The knotted leaf
Unfurled to red stalk
Cleaves the earth with such happiness

Chilled air, warmed earth
Promising petioles
Pulled and yanked, bathed and cut

One part sugar, four of rhubarb
Spice, butter, wheat
An alchemy of rubies

First the crust of melting sand
Then waves of fruit and juice
Some crumbs — all done

Rhubarb Kuchen with Almond Meringue

Recipe adapted from German baker Eva Hess

2/3 cup butter, softened
1 1/4 cups sugar, separated into 1/2 cup and 3/4 cup
1 teaspoon pure vanilla extract
2 large eggs
3 large eggs, separated, at room temperature
3/4 cup flour
3/8 cup cornstarch
1 1/2 teaspoons baking powder
2 pounds rhubarb, ends cut off, strings removed, cut into 1- to
    1 1/2-inch pieces (approx. 2 2/3 cups rhubarb)
1/3 cup almonds, ground
whipped cream, optional

CAKE

Preheat the oven to 350 degrees.

To prepare the cake layer, combine the soft butter with 1/2 cup sugar and vanilla extract. Mix well.

Beat the 2 whole eggs and 3 egg yolks together with a whisk or electric beater in a medium bowl. Keep the other 3 egg whites in a bowl for later.

Add the beaten eggs to the butter mixture.

Sift the flour, cornstarch, and baking powder into a small bowl. Stir dry ingredients into the beaten eggs and sugar.

Spoon the batter into a 10-inch diameter greased springform pan. Distribute the rhubarb pieces evenly on top, lightly pushing them into the batter. Bake in the oven until the cake pulls away from the sides of the pan, about 25 minutes.

MERINGUE

While the cake is baking, whip the 3 egg whites with a pinch of salt or spritz of lemon and gradually add 3/4 cup of sugar.

Fold in the ground almonds.

Remove the cake from the oven. Smooth the meringue mix evenly over the cake. Put the pan back into the oven for another 20 minutes. Remove, and let it cool before turning it out onto a plate. If desired, add whipped cream.

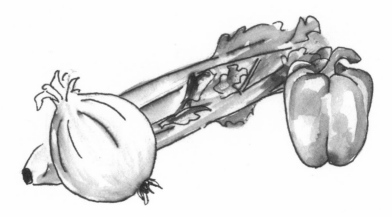

When Alabama stood behind segregation, the author's parents joined the massive migration of African Americans who made their way to uncertain futures up north. It was a hard decision for this family for it meant parting with circles of black southern culture that had touched their lives and their parents' lives—doctors, lawyers, musicians, writers, even the poet Langston Hughes and black educator Booker T. Washington.

The Black Migration

Donna Pierce

Following their June 1950 wedding, my parents, Muriel and Eliot Battle, sifted through various offers before moving from Mobile, Alabama, to the Midwest. They chose Missouri, where they were both offered jobs in that state's public school system. Their families tried to convince them to stay in Alabama's Gulf Coast following Mom's college graduation, but my dad recalls the certainty they both felt about leaving. "We made a pact to raise our children away from segregation," Dad says. "We were happy to make the social sacrifice to invest in our children's future."

So I grew up in Missouri — in an African American household migrated from Alabama's Gulf Coast. The social sacrifice my dad spoke of meant being apart from what he considered were Mobile's most exceptional families but also his and my mother's own family of physicians, lawyers, educators, musicians, and writers and their history. Dad had the photographs and keepsakes to remind us that his grandfather and Booker T. Washington were business associates and friends.

Donna Pierce is a Chicago-based contributing editor for *Upscale Magazine* and the former award-winning assistant food editor and test kitchen director for the *Chicago Tribune*. She has traveled to Africa, Europe, and the Caribbean exploring the roots of African American culinary traditions. Donna spent a decade in San Francisco and Los Angeles before a return to Missouri, where she was an adjunct assistant professor and food editor for the University of Missouri School of Journalism. She is a member of Les Dames D'Escoffier and the Southern Foodways Alliance. She is a board member of the National Association of Food Journalists. Pierce, the founder and CEO of BlackAmericaCooks.com and SkilletDiaries.com, is also the author of *Skinny Soulfood* and *Slow Cooker Soul*.

In Missouri, Mom added delicious midwestern dishes such as beef stew, chicken and dumplings, winter squash, country ham, apple cobbler, and rhubarb pie to her recipe repertoire. But she insisted on passing down culinary traditions from her Creole and southern roots. Finding her A&P produce section bereft of Creole mirliton (chayote) squash, she made the family recipe with butternut instead of the green Gulf Coast vegetable. She added a pinch of ground red pepper (cayenne) to almost every savory recipe and replaced vanilla extract in many desserts with a teaspoon of bourbon, which she described in the recipes she exchanged with our Missouri Lutheran neighbors as bourbon extract.

Dad's culinary contributions included only compliments and ready assistance. He built the fire for weekend briskets after Ollie Gates, the son of the founder of Gates Bar-B-Q, introduced my parents to sweet-sauced and tender Kansas City–style barbecue. He used a wooden spoon to beat the holiday pralines mixture, per Mom's instructions, "just until he could feel the brown sugar candy thicken and see it begin to lose its gloss." He planted a big garden behind our house where he began the season with turnip greens, then followed in the summer with green peppers, big, juicy tomatoes, and okra.

Recently, leafing through an old scrapbook with me, Dad paused when he came to the page with a photograph of the bright-eyed young couple taken a few months after they first moved to Missouri. "We brought everything north with us," he said, recalling the new Chevrolet filled with "your mother's glamorous college ball gowns, our wedding silver, china, and other formal gifts, our big dreams and hopes . . . and as much gumbo filé (a spicy herb), hot sauce, and Creole mustard as your mother could cram into little boxes tucked under the seat. Plus, everybody's handwritten recipes."

Mom, the former campus beauty queen who had grown up in a vibrant Gulf Coast city, fell in love with small midwestern towns. Here she earned the affection of the rural cooks she met by eagerly learning new traditions and unfamiliar dishes such as braised rabbit, fried funnel cakes, and quick breads made with native ingredients such as elderberries and hickory nuts.

Once at the breakfast table, when my father mentioned how much he missed beginning his day with Gulf Coast papayas and mangoes, Mom passed him the apple butter and let all of us know she would not entertain comparisons. She had five words: "Bloom where you are planted."

They moved several times, following good jobs in better schools. By the time the president of Missouri's Lincoln University hired Dad to serve as the last principal of Dalton Vocational School in the 1950s, Mom felt right at home on the 123-acre high school campus complete with horse stables, hog houses and henhouses. We lived in what is now described in history books as the Dalton "model farm house," where my mother collected eggs with my sister and me and once, to my sister's and my amazement, demonstrated the art of killing a chicken by grabbing its legs and quickly snapping its neck, under the tutelage of the school cafeteria cooks.

"I did it," she kept repeating when the job was done that cold spring day, with a triumphant glance toward her two startled daughters. "Girls, life is too short to back down from the things that scare you," she said. "We're girls with guts." I was a year away from kindergarten, but I still remember my mother's expression that day, a mix of panic, disbelief, and determination.

When the ladies left to clean the chicken, the three of us stood in the open near the henhouse breathing in the smell of fresh blood and chicken feathers.

Then my mother threw up.

As far as I know, she never killed another chicken. But that day she had proven her farm worthiness to her neighbors, and she had demonstrated the notion of what it meant to be "girls with guts" to her daughters. It's a phrase that friends and I would later print on T-shirts for a college project during the height of the women's movement.

Mom described her time spent with rural farm wives in northwestern Missouri as "rounding out her culinary skills" and introducing her to hundreds of delicious recipes she would certainly have missed on the Gulf Coast of Alabama.

She experimented with German potato salad and tart rhubarb pies. Her "Creolized" spaghetti and meatballs platter (made with celery, green peppers, and onion) always emptied quickly during every 1960s covered-dish supper I can remember.

Before she passed away in 2003, Mom still repeated a compliment she treasured from a Dalton farm wife: "You don't act like a city girl in the kitchen," the lady had once whispered to my mother, referring, my mother insisted, to both her chicken- and turkey-plucking skills, plus the wild persimmon and sweet potato bread pudding recipe she invented.

During the time my parents lived on the Dalton campus, our family's return holiday visits to Mobile included sharing our station wagon with carefully wrapped and chilled, freshly slaughtered turkeys for my grandmothers to enjoy. In the days before food was so easily transported between regions, the heritage Missouri turkeys were exotic additions to tables set with holiday gumbo.

Our grandparents returned the favor with coveted Gulf Coast specialties. When they traveled from Mobile to visit us in Missouri, we met them in St. Louis's bustling Union Station, where, in my memory, they descended the sleeping car stairs dressed as if going to the theater. All of us were filled with anticipation as the porter rolled up with a month's worth of luggage, plus a huge, heavily taped box that made my parents almost as happy to see as the arrival of our grandparents.

The oohs and ahhs over the big package began later at home, when Mom unpacked the box (cooled by wrapped packs of dry ice) to reveal at least ten pounds of fresh Gulf shrimp, Mobile Bay oysters, blue crab, and the family-favorite *chaurice*, a firm, spicy, hot, smoked sausage similar to Spanish chorizo or Portuguese *chourico*. "You brought Mobile with you," my dad always said at that moment before the valuable perishables were put away. Like Mom, he was weary of the tasteless frozen shrimp from the Missouri A&P and the kielbasa Mom used to substitute for their beloved *chaurice*. Except for ingredients needed for next-day gumbo and oyster loaf, the long-awaited seafood was frozen and saved for very special occasions.

When Dalton closed after *Brown v. Board of Education* ended the segregation policy that had created multi-county segregated campus schools, my family moved to Columbia, Missouri. There, Mom and Dad would lead the first wave of school integration as educators and administrators. My sister, Carolyn, and I became the first African American students at Grant Elementary School, where we helped Mom's midwestern culinary education advance by requesting meals introduced to us through the school lunch program.

We included chili con carne in our early requests, and Mom, having been raised almost entirely on seafood, re-created the unfamiliar ground meat menu exactly as we described — served lunchroom-style with little stacks of saltine crackers and peanut butter sandwiches on white bread.

We weren't so lucky with the hamburgers and cheeseburgers we urged her to replicate. Our mother maintained that plain pressed beef was "uncivilized" and insisted on doctoring ground beef patties with thyme, parsley, and other seasonings, plus big chunks of onion, green pepper, and celery, the vegetable seasoning widely referred to as the Creole cooking holy trinity.

Today I credit my mom's eagerness to learn the best of midwestern dishes blended with her mastery of Creole and southern cooking for stirring my curiosity about American regional recipes. Mom always said that the move north influenced our family recipe collection for the better by offering us the chance to draw the best from both regions.

Gumbo was served as a first course before the Thanksgiving turkey; hearty beef stews or shrimp Creole alternated as birthday requests for family dinners. Holiday dessert party trays were lined with Scandinavian press cookies, shortbread, Gulf Coast stuffed dates, and chocolate bourbon balls. "It's authentic to us," was always Mom's answer to someone questioning her slow-cooker gumbo or holiday turkeys filled with the Creole blend of celery ribs, onions, and green pepper halves instead of traditional dressing.

As with many families, food symbolizes much more than nourishment for our bodies. Our family recipes offer a tangible mix of love and compromise, in the form of greens with smoked turkey parts, beef roasts inserted with garlic and thyme, or beans and rice using interchanging black beans, red beans, navy beans, or the garbanzo beans my mother referred to as cici beans.

But some recipes had to remain unchanged, including gumbo, shrimp Creole, frappe punch, and oyster loaf, which called for baked, uncut bread loaves hollowed out in the center, then heavily buttered and filled with delicately fried oysters. Holiday desserts were also off limits. No changes allowed for our family fruitcakes, pralines, divinity, and Charlotte Russe (a delicate custard lined with ladyfingers). They continue to make the rounds as heirloom southern family desserts we reproduce from yellowed recipe cards passed down from our grandmothers and great-aunts.

Today, with our full Creole and southern repertoire, we claim peanut butter sandwiches and chili as family traditions. And we remember our mother's earnest reminder about not keeping recipes a secret: "The best way to keep recipes alive is to give them away."

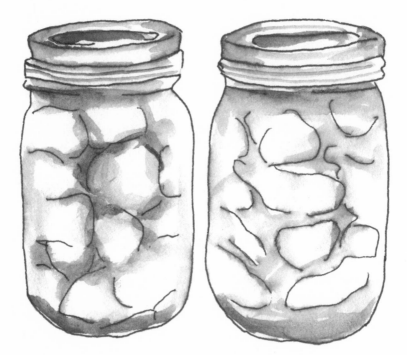

As the granddaughter of a native of the fjords, the writer saw that the no-nonsense business of feeding people wasn't always relished.

Eat Now

Phyllis Florin

My grandmother, Ingeborg Ingebrightsdatter Nornes, came to southern Minnesota from Norway in 1911. She was nineteen, didn't speak a word of English, and came over on a ticket sent by her sister Kristina who had emigrated five years earlier. Ingeborg (and don't call her Inga) left behind her mother and father, three sisters, one of whom would follow a year later, and three brothers. She couldn't have known when she sailed away on that April morning that she would never see her parents again.

While it was Kristina's intention that Ingeborg help her out with the house and children, it was also understood that the ticket was not a gift. Ingeborg was expected to pay them back. She soon got a job as a cook for the hired men who worked for the wealthy Savage family, owners of the world-famous horse Dan Patch and for whom the town of Savage was named. This always puzzled me, how someone just off the boat in a completely new culture, as young as she was, with no previous culinary experience, who couldn't speak English, could get a job as a cook. The job requirements must have been very, very simple,

Phyllis Florin was brought up never to show off or pursue anything that did not put food on the table; therefore, she did not dare to write until she was in her midforties. She is indebted to her writing group, which came out of a class taught by Anne Lamott, and to her friendship with author Elizabeth Berg, who encouraged her to transfer what's inside of her, out. Her essays have appeared in the *San Francisco Chronicle*, regional newspapers, *Iowa Woman*, and *More* magazine. She was a contributor to *Escaping into the Open: The Art of Writing True*, edited by Elizabeth Berg. She lives in Mill Valley, California, with her husband, Fabrice.

as in, can you boil potatoes and fry meat? Because even after several years of experience, my grandmother was not a good cook.

She was an abundant cook, she liked to feed people, but it was more about the feeding with her, and not so much the cooking. I don't think things like seasoning or flavor, or how she might try fixing green beans some way other than boiling them, ever crossed her mind. Gramma provided nourishment for her family in the same way she fed the calves or slopped the hogs, because it was her job. It didn't matter if the peas were mushy or if the beef was overdone and dry, which it almost always was. With nine children, a moody husband, and a household to keep up, she didn't have time to savor a sauce or experiment with ingredients. I don't think she minced a garlic clove in her life.

The cooking job ended when she met Otto, my Swedish grandfather. They were married six months later, exactly what her father had feared and predicted would happen when she got to America. Family lore goes that he sent his daughter this congratulatory note: "We'd rather have heard you were dead than married to a Swede." That must have warmed Ingeborg's lonely heart. Immediately after the wedding, the honeymooners moved up to the Red River Valley in the northwest corner of Minnesota, where they took up farming.

And that's where I grew up. My childhood geography is the prairie, one-quarter land and three-quarters sky, where the wind comes whistling down from Canada with nothing to stop it but the parliament building in Winnipeg, my dad used to say. It is a misconception that immigrants moved there because it reminded them of their homeland. Ingeborg must have blanched when she first looked out on that flat landscape, thousands of miles from the sea and not even a small hill in sight. A Norwegian can never be far from the smell of fish, it's said.

They moved there because the soil was good for farming. Being a town child, I was ignorant of what farming involved. I knew two things: they milked cows and worked in the fields. I knew they grew wheat and oats, which produced the amber waves of grain we sang about in school. But now I know they also grew, in that very short period between May and August, barley, rye, potatoes, sweet clover, and corn. I remember in the fifties, come a summer Sunday afternoon, Grampa would put on his fedora, pile as many people as could fit in the car, and we'd drive around looking at everyone's crops. He drove so slowly, we'd have to close the windows so the grasshoppers wouldn't jump in.

My mother agrees that her mother wasn't the greatest cook, but she has fond memories of her raisin pudding, an after-school treat, and her pork and brown beans, which she learned to do well despite never having had beans in Norway. Everyone agrees she made a superb apple pie. That was probably the one thing Gramma accidentally perfected over the years. She never used more than three apples per pie, partly because of her frugal nature, but also, I think, because preparing the apples was tedious work. Why peel, core, and slice six when three would do? Her pies were sunken and sad-looking, but because the ratio of crust to apples was higher, they had the density of a tart with an upper crust. And she did make an above-average crust, primarily because she used lard, but also because she didn't overwork the dough, a situation where her impatience worked in her favor. Thankfully, she understood the necessity of spices in the filling and used both cinnamon and nutmeg, which I think was as exotic as she got except for Christmas Eve dinner when allspice was dusted on the lutefisk's white sauce.

A word about lutefisk, Norwegians' gift to the world. Literally "lye fish," lutefisk is cod or other white fish that has been preserved in a lye solution. When I tell people that, the usual response is an incredulous "Lye??" Yes, lye, the same thing they use to make soap and rat poison. The prolonged soaking of the fish in lye and water solutions to preserve it is what produces its jelly-like substance. My grandparents did not preserve the fish themselves but bought it at the market, where it was well stocked at Christmas time. It was baked in a glass dish covered with tinfoil, or boiled, and served on a white platter (usually a cracked one in Gramma's case) on Christmas Eve. With the accompanying white boiled potatoes and everything smothered in a white sauce, the plate resembled a winter landscape. A side of boiled peas provided some color, and if I know my grandmother, they were an olive green. Lucky for us kids, homemade potato sausage, another tradition, and Swedish meatballs were also on the menu. But for the fish-deprived prairie immigrants, lutefisk was a Christmas treat, a special reminder of home.

Gramma was in her early to mid-sixties when I came on the scene, so even if she had had a zest for cooking, it would have been understandable if her enthusiasm had declined by then. All her nine children were grown and gone except for my uncle Harold, who never married and still lived with them. When she was eighty-five, my sister Linda recorded an interview with her. In a narrative sprinkled with Norwegian, she talked about the early days on the farm, beginning with a heavy sigh and the words "*Straben . . . straben*." Hardship. "I milked the cows and bring the milk in and separate inside . . . take the milk out to feed the calves, take the feed out, feed the pigs, carry the slop out to the pig house. . . *og* alvays tired . . ." Linda started to say something about today's conveniences, but Gramma talked over her in a loud voice, "I can't see, looking back, how I could do that." She mumbled in Norwegian, then said, "All the clothes, vashed and ironed the clothes, and cooked and baked bread every other day, cake and cookies . . . apple pies. . . . You'll never know what I had to do, and Otto, he alvays come in mad . . . he never talk."

Besides that, it must have been hard carrying around the fjords and mountains of Norway in her heart. A loneliness permeated every corner of her house. I still carry it in me. Even after seventy years in this country, she spoke with a thick accent and often fell back on Norwegian. It was frustrating for her grandchildren. We'd nod or shake our heads, hoping we had understood, but more often than not, she'd wave us away with an exasperated "You don't understand me."

She kept the pictures and postcards she received from Norway in an album. There we got a peek at her other home. Oddly dressed people with burnished cheeks and stern expressions stood in front of huts with grass growing on the roof. Turf roofs were, and still are, common in Norway, providing good insulation and sturdiness, but to a child, it was surreal. It was hard for me to comprehend that my grandmother also had a mother and family and that she had to leave them in that gray world across the ocean, so far away from the prairie. The old country. So many of the old people in our town came from an "old country," which would, of course, make sense to an eight-year-old. The first time

I heard a child speak Norwegian, it struck me as funny and incongruous, a child speaking the language of the aged.

I didn't really like staying on the farm. I was terrified of the animals, starting with the dog who barked fiercely and charged at you as soon as you stepped foot out of the car; the enormous cows that glared at you out of the sides of their eyes; even the barn cats with their sharp little teeth and claws frightened me. I dreaded going to bed in the pitch dark of the country. In late afternoon, when the sun began to sink, my homesickness began to rise. That was foolishness to my grandmother. Homesick? *Stakkars liten.* You poor thing. Now go play.

Six-o-clock supper came at that lonesome time of day and we sat down to dispiriting leftovers from the noon dinner, the main meal of the day: cold, sliced, leftover meat, usually beef or pork; warmed-up potatoes, fried or creamed; reheated home-preserved or store-bought canned vegetables; some kind of pickle, like cucumber, crabapple, or beet; homemade bread and, for my uncle Harold, white store-bought; and for dessert, sauce, which was usually the only thing I wanted.

I am surprised how many people don't know what sauce is. Fruit sauce was a staple for us. Peaches, pears, cranberries, plums, blueberries, rhubarb, apricots — almost always home preserved, but sometimes from a can. It was the easiest and most common dessert, and looking back, I realize that dessert was as important to the meal as potatoes. Maybe that's what "square meal" means: meat, potatoes, vegetable, and dessert. But sauce was not just for dessert. A dish of cranberry or rhubarb sauce swirled with cream and a side of hot buttered toast made a fine breakfast, or blueberry sauce warmed and spooned on pancakes.

In the summer of 1956, when she was sixty-five, Gramma recorded in her diary that she had put up eleven quarts of blueberries, seven quarts of pears, seven quarts of peaches, eleven quarts of apricots, two quarts of crabapples, fourteen quarts of green beans, seven pints of yellow beans, and four pints of cucumber pickles. The berries, rhubarb, and crabapples were local; the other fruit came from sunny, faraway places like Georgia and California. There was a mad rush to town as soon as folks learned of its arrival, to make sure they got it as fresh as possible.

Grampa would bring home flat wooden crates of peaches, pears, apricots, or big purple plums, each fruit wrapped in tissue paper. Almost all of it was preserved. You would never see a bowl of fresh fruit on my grandmother's table, at least I never did.

If there were no leftovers for supper, Gramma might fix *grøt*, short for *rømmegrøt*, a Norwegian cream porridge that probably dates back to the Vikings. Traditionally, it's made by boiling and reducing several cups of heavy cream, adding flour, and stirring vigorously until the butter is drawn from the cream, leaving the curd. In another pot, the flour and curd are added to scalded milk and stirred and stirred and stirred until it becomes a smooth porridge, which is served with the drawn butter, sugar, and cinnamon. One plate of *rømmegrøt* was more than enough. Because it's labor intensive, it's a safe bet it was not Gramma's favorite thing to do. My cousin Julie makes *grøt* in the microwave, which she says works great. I wonder what Gramma would think of that and how she would have felt about the microwave. My mother thinks she would have hated it, but I think she would have loved it, since she was all about the shortcut.

Cream, in all its many forms — whipped for pie, turned into *grøt*, poured into sauce or coffee, made into white sauce — was the crème de la crème of the farm. Everything was better with cream. My mother told me about the time she visited her parents in the seventies and brought along a tub of Cool Whip to go with their dessert. When she was leaving, my grandfather handed it to her and said, "You don't have to bring that again." This might also be how Gramma would feel about the microwave.

I was suspicious of Gramma's food. I liked it if it was something sweet like pie, or glorified rice with fruit cocktail and whipped cream, or any kind of cookie. We especially liked the apricot nectar she made from concentrate she got from the traveling Watkins salesman. I did not like much else, and I especially did not like the glass of raw blue milk, often warm from the cow. She insisted we have this with every meal. Gramma got mad if you didn't eat, it made no sense to her. Eating was for nourishment, it didn't matter if you "liked" it or if it was "good." I've often wondered how I made it through those meals with Gramma insisting I eat because I was too "tin," and me, homesick and queasy, not being able to. I think I learned to eat and swallow quickly before I could taste the food, an unfortunate habit I still have.

We ate in the kitchen, next to the entry room where the work clothes hung, so mixed in with supper was the faint smell of the barn. I see us sitting there at the gray linoleum-topped table that jutted out from the wall, a little farm supper tableau: Grampa and Uncle Harold on one side, Gramma at the head, and on the other side my sister Margie and me, two little tow-headed girls, swinging our skinny legs under the table. *I Jesu navn går vil til bords, å spise, drikke på ditt ord. Deg Gud til ære oss till gavn, så får vi mat I Jesu navn. Amen.* We are bathed in the pale lavender fluorescence of the ceiling light if it is winter, or in the natural low light of summer. The only sounds are the scrape of silverware on a plate, a slurp of coffee, and the occasional "yah." Outside, the lonesome call of the mourning dove and darkness approaching.

I think of Gramma when I'm at some fancy restaurant eating, say, sand dabs over carrots and grilled spring onions in a garlicky salsa verde, or when my friends and I discuss the quality of tomatoes or our inability to eat something because it's not done quite to our liking; it's not fresh enough, or it's too sweet or too salty, or the steak is not rare enough. I see her then wearily limping to the stove to poach yet another egg or fry up another piece of meat or peel her millionth potato. The way she matter-of-factly put the bowls and platters of food on the table. How she'd walk around the table making sure everyone had enough, ladling another spoonful of mashed potatoes or over-cooked string beans on plates that still had plenty. This was her job as woman, wife, and mother: to put food on the table, to feed her family, to make sure they had enough, to keep them from sickness, to make them strong. It was not a request, it was an imperative: eat now.

In Wisconsin, where modest cottages meet the shores of the lake, style is pleasantly stuck somewhere back in the seventies; people still sit on front porches after dinner watching the mating antics of fireflies. Waterfront, beach, kayak, hammock. That just about sums it up. Except for the fish boil, the reason the author is here.

The Door County Fish Boil

Peggy Wolff

There is a meal I have hungered for ever since visiting Door County, Wisconsin, on a fall bike trip in 1985, the trip where I met my husband. Called the fish boil, it is equal parts dinner and entertainment where a very big chef with a weathered expression stages a fiery spectacle of cooking freshly caught Lake Michigan whitefish, probably from a boat that went out around five that morning with a name like *So'Wester* or *Leif* or *Norska*.

I let those names slowly roll off my tongue because they add a faraway dreaminess to the beauty of this Wisconsin peninsula where Scandinavians settled 150 years ago. Four thousand miles from home, they found their culinary heaven afloat: Lake Michigan to the east, Sturgeon Bay to the south, Green Bay to the west, and Death's Door, with its smattering of islands, to the north. Although I have lived on the Illinois side of Lake Michigan most of my life, it came as something of a surprise to

---

Peggy Wolff's stories on what, where, and how people eat have appeared in the *Chicago Tribune*. She has also written articles on ultra sports and photography for *Chicago Magazine*, *ArtNews*, and more. She received a BFA in cinema from California Institute of the Arts, where she completed two films, one on t'ai chi, which went on to win awards, the other an animated film set to a Henry Mancini tune, which aired on his musical-variety network show. Immediately afterward, digital animation came about along with her grave realization that the two-minute film that took months of inking and painting could have been done in fifteen minutes on a computer. She wrote, produced, and directed short films and did story research for 20th Century Fox TV and a large documentary film studio. Wolff divides her time between Chicago and Park City, Utah, where she has happily discovered mountain trout.

discover that I lived a mere few hours from a place where there were strong Scandinavian influences, including deep-seated culinary traditions like meatballs, herring salads, and rye breads.

Needing a little late afternoon snack before the evening's fish boil meal, I disappear into Al Johnson's Swedish restaurant, which is about as emblematic of this region as the fish boil. To most people, Al Johnson's is not identified by the fruit soup, lingonberries, pancake breakfasts, or Swedish meatballs but by the goats grazing on the roof. That's right, a turf roof. Grass was planted up there to follow a Scandinavian custom that began when farmers in the old country built their homes into the sides of hills, so goats and other animals could meander onto the roof from the mountainsides and feed on the lawn.

It'd be unfair to write a piece about Door County without mentioning that Swedish cooks are particularly skillful with fish. Inside Al Johnson's I find a box of crackers, pickled herring, and smoked whitefish paté, a food that carries no frilly adjectives like it might on the east or west coast, such as wild caught or cold smoked. At Al Johnson's, it is just smoked whitefish paté.

The fish boil is very far from its humble origins of feeding large groups of people who settled in Wisconsin over a century ago. Though the boil still feeds large groups of people, now there's an admission charge to watch the dexterity of the chef.

It's a fast mover, pure heaven on any restaurant's books. Tables turn over every seventy-five minutes, and travelers to the peninsula feel they must indulge in a fish boil or they haven't really been to Door, as this strip of land is known to practically everybody here.

The whitefish are caught along the shoreline thumb of Wisconsin that sticks out into the acres and acres of smooth blue water that shines like chrome. Maybe this fact is important only to the Swedes and Norwegians who were drawn to the familiarity of bountiful fishing and logging opportunities, but Door lies at forty-five degrees latitude, exactly halfway between the equator and the North Pole.

Earlier this morning at the Norwegian-owned Hickey Brothers fish market in Bailey's Harbor, sixteen hundred pounds of whitefish arrived, having been scooped in on live entrapment nets, kept on ice, then trucked off the boat. One by one they were fed into a scaling machine and shot out into a bucket, cleaned of all scales. The three- to four-pounders, which are big enough for fillets, rolled through a machine that removed the backbone and rib bone. The beautiful fillet came off the belt and splashed into a final tub of water, quickly turning it pink. If the fish was smaller, say a two-pounder, it was slit down the underbelly, emptied of its guts, and hand cut into two- to three-inch chunks. Perfect for a fish boil.

They catch, they clean, they chunk, they deliver.

After watching five fish boils and dining at two, I can say with some authority that the fish boil meal is the same all over the peninsula: small, boiled red potatoes, slaw, and sour cherry pie. Some restaurants add onions to the boiling water, but it seems that true sons of Door view this as foolish. They claim it overpowers the flavor of freshly caught fish.

No self-respecting restaurant here that serves the fish boil, whether lunch counter, humble hole in the wall, or historic inn, can make do without a proper outdoor gravel pit.

That's because the cooking method specifies that the fish is boiled outdoors in a huge pot of water over flames, while steaming oils and water gush up and spill over the sides and onto the ground. There are no kitchen burners roaring, no fryers superheated, no flattop grills cooking up a crisp, edible skin. Just a cauldron of boiling water suspended over shooting flames.

A fashion editor at *Women's Wear Daily* once told me that style lies in the ability to walk across a room without having anyone notice you. What speaks for fashion, I think, also holds true for food.

Take a lake perch fillet, gently, lovingly dredged through a pan of room-temperature beer batter made sweet with buttermilk and a craft beer, then jacketed with flour and slipped into a hot fryer, the batter tightening around the fish as the oil bubbles away and you salivating as it turns into perfectly fried fish, golden brown and puffy, crisp around the edges. That's the plunging neckline of fish dinners. Whereas the more subtle and mild tasting day catch of whitefish, embellished with melted butter, lemon juice, or tartar sauce holds the true, slightly sweet flavor of a perfectly cooked fish. That fillet has real style, especially when plated alongside creamy coleslaw with the toothy crunch of life.

At the White Gull Inn in Fish Creek, we give the hostess our name. She looks at the reservation I made earlier that day for three fish dinners and one chicken dinner for our son.

"Three adults and one chicken," she repeats the reservation out loud, looking straight at Jordan, our twenty-one-year-old son, as if the Wisconsin culinary cops will be after him for having a food hangup. Jordan was not as heavily invested as we were in the menu — in fact he vetoed the fish — but he didn't take kindly to being called a chicken either.

In a place where obtaining calories is very nearly effortless, we join the happy hour guests on the patio who have also come for the $18.95 boil but are warming up with drinks. Nothing remarkable stands out; they could be locals or just other tourists like us, part of the anonymous population of summer travelers that thickens our world, wearing the clothing and accessories synonymous with informality. Khaki and denim, madly printed purses, a few madly printed slacks, sailor-striped T-shirts, black camera bags, long lenses.

The crowd looks like the prime demographic for the fish boil — kids, parents, and grandparents, a reunion destination. To listen to them, there's a pleasant air of expectation, as if we are in a happy crowd gathering for a free summer concert. With Marlboro Lights.

Team Whitefish emerges from the restaurant kitchen carrying a huge mesh basket of half-pound fish fillets. The two men look like they could've done some rough sea time with the Merchant Marines, with tanned arms and faces flat as a flounder.

There is a full basket of small red potatoes with the ends sliced off so that the salt in the boiling water penetrates. Salt is the only spice used but it's not to make the fish salty. In addition to giving the potatoes some flavor, it raises the specific gravity of the water, making everything float. It also helps firm up the fish.

They lower the potato basket into a black kettle of heavily salted water. Five pounds of salt, the chef says, as I feel my customary shock at how much. Potatoes need thirty minutes to cook. Plenty of time for another beer, and since austerity is not the rule, I take out those white Cheddar cheese curds I snagged earlier at a convenience store. This is Wisconsin, the dairy state par excellence, cheesemania wherever you drive. Curds have a mild flavor due to their youth but what they don't have in flavor they make up in texture — firm and springy — which causes them to squeak in your mouth when you bite into them.

Master boiler Tom Christiansen is our emcee for the night, a gray-bearded man with a Swedish, German, and Norwegian ancestry mix. He wears gym shoes, dark pants, and a Depression-era newsboy cap with a snap brim and a short visor. By now he's a virtuoso and cooks up this fish with guesswork, heart's leap, memory. He introduces us to the infamous boil with an introduction he has probably given a thousand times.

"It was invented as a fast way of serving laborers in lumber camps." Stay in Wisconsin long enough and you'll learn that the identity of the inventor is the subject of some dispute. Local historian Beverly Hudson says that Scandinavian fishermen coming in from their day on the boat were so hungry that they couldn't wait to get to dock. The easiest thing to do was to boil their day catch of fish in pots of water over the stove onboard. When they caught lake trout, there was a lot of oil in the fish, and it did boil over.

You can believe either legend, but the practice of boiling fish became an economical way of feeding fishermen and lumberjacks. Later on, church and civic groups picked up the fish boil theme as a fundraiser, much like chili suppers in other parts of the Midwest.

Christiansen will host two more seatings this night, an hour and fifteen minutes apart. I did the math: about 120 pounds of fish each night for 240 diners makes five to six tons of fish a year — and this is just one restaurant — an indication of the inroads this tradition has made.

After a mere fifteen minutes Christiansen tests the doneness of the potatoes by sticking a long-handled fork in. From his doubtful expression, they're not ready.

The black kettle of water is foaming, bubbling, steaming; he lowers the fish fillets into the same water with the red potatoes, throws in a five-pound bag of salt, then deadpans, "Another pinch of salt." The inebriated crowd howls with laughter. The fish need ten to twelve minutes to cook. Although whitefish are not as oily as trout, they do have some fat to survive the icy northern lake, which, in the gloomy, cool water at depths of up to two hundred feet, is about thirty-four degrees Fahrenheit.

Soon, fish oil rises and pools on top, forming a filmy layer. When water bubbles rise, Christiansen yells and waves his arm at people to move back. Last night a woman's hair was singed.

It is one minute to the boil over. There's an eccentric movement of people scurrying around before cameras come out to grab the moment when Christiansen amps up the fire with kerosene and screams "Boil over" at the crowd. The blaze flares up; my head jerks back like a Pez dispenser to follow this inferno twenty feet high. Half the water in the pot and all the grayish filmy oil spill over the sides and into the gravel pit, quenching the fire. His prowess and popularity are uncontested; the crowd applauds for a seamless job.

"It looks like a special effect, like a mushroom," says our computer graphics–conscious nineteen-year-old daughter Zoe, who has videotaped it and will put it on YouTube this night.

The blaze is a grand send-off for people to leave the patio and head indoors for the one-pass-only buffet line. Believing that this fish needs a little enlivening with seasoning, but not quite the ladle of butter the guy in front of me craved, I ask for a modest amount of melted butter, with a spoonful of tartar sauce. We fill our china plates, knowing that the waitress will bring seconds for the people who love red potatoes (our daughter), for people who can't manage without several baskets of house-made tea breads (our son), and for the ones who want more coleslaw (my husband).

I am admiring the glossiness of the entrée and how much its whiteness resembles cod, another fish with an opaque and flaky flesh, when I overhear a guest who cannot avoid Whining Diner Syndrome. "Bones, bones, and more bones," she mumbles, mashing the fish with her fork.

The staff immediately bring her another fillet because when she's done mashing, she sure isn't going to eat it.

Carla, our waitress, comes around for tableside lessons in deboning. She says that if she doesn't give folks her mini-tutorial, people are likely to pick it apart in pieces.

Find the center part of the backbone, she instructs. Slide a knife underneath and lift. She pauses to let that sink in. When a fish is cooked, the backbone with the pin bones — the ones that come out sideways — will just lift out. I follow her directions and — Bingo! I will not be going through any epic to get rid of bones.

"If they complain," Carla goes on, "I tell them they won't find any bones in the pie . . . maybe a cherry pit. If there were no bones, it'd be mush, and then we'd be serving it with a number-ten scoop. Y'know, like an ice cream scoop." Carla sees me writing notes. "Now I'm gonna get fired."

Carla won't get fired. In fact, the White Gull Inn could add her to the breakfast shift to handle the tables after they won *Good Morning America*'s "Best Breakfast Challenge" in 2010 for their cherry-stuffed French toast, made with the local Montmorency cherries. Nice award for small-town America. I could snack on that all the way back to Chicago, the way some people pop Tic Tacs.

Until now, I had never tasted a fresher catch of fish. I grew up eating the tailpiece of Lake Michigan whitefish and always prized it for its mild flavor, for the whiteness of its flesh, and for the thick flakes that come apart, nearly shining on the plate. The biggest surprise tonight is that freshly caught fish, even boiled outdoors in a cauldron, has some sweetness. And that makes all the difference, or as R. W. Apple said as succinctly as anyone ever put it in his essay "A Prime Kettle of Fish": "Where it's caught and how it's caught and when it's caught matter at least as much as how it's cooked in determining how it will taste."

Smell, that loyal sentry, warns me of the incredible sour-smelling sweetness of the finale, the Door County cherry pie. Regardless of the tonic for the body the boiled fish just provided, my instincts for sugar are firing off, a longing that's a cornerstone of my diet. The craving arrives with the force of a cattle prod and when I'm in the early stages, I just turn myself in. Every slice carried past us makes my eyes grow round in anticipation. We order our pie à la mode, with vanilla ice cream. I ask for another Diet Coke — an exercise in futility if I ever saw one — so Carla returns to the kitchen.

As many see it, the mention of Wisconsin to a visitor, particularly an American tourist, instantly conjures up images of north woods, canoes, beer, moose, and anything German because in the 1860s, Milwaukee was the largest German settlement in the nation. The list goes on, but it usually does not include the fire-engine-red cherry, packed with sour power, an image that appears on billboards and T-shirts all over Door.

I was already an intravenous user of cherry pie. Growing up in between Michigan and Wisconsin, two tart-cherry-producing states, I devoured them in cobblers and crisps or popped them in my mouth dried.

Like so much in life that is desirable, sour cherries are perishable, very hard to keep, but worth going after. I have eaten my way through acres of trees dripping with the delicate, mouth-puckering fruit, first with children who couldn't reach the heavily laden branches unless we helped them up a ladder with a bucket slung around their necks. And more recently when these toddlers became college kids, tall enough to reach those ruby-red cherries high up on the tree, the ones that took in the most sun.

The season is all too brief, and if you pick cherries, even leaving them in a basket in the sunlight for an hour will cause their ruby-red color to fade. This is why the vast majority of the crop — also called the old-fashioned pie cherry — ends up not in the grocery store produce aisle but in cans or jars as pie filling. Call me a food snob, but I have never been able to rise above a deep and irrational prejudice against the gooey canned pie filling stuff. It is a gazillion miles away from the excellent version we are about to enjoy.

Here it is, the real deal, the culinary destiny of the local Montmorency cherry, baked in a show-stopping, irresistible, flaky double crust. This is a party worth going after, saving for, putting all your eggs in one basket for. The top is as smooth as a confectioner's toffee candy, the edges are perfectly pinched.

If I were blessed with a quick metabolism, I'd ask for seconds right now because the White Gull Inn's kitchen makes their crusts with lard. A full cup of lard.

Even without a patisserie degree, I can see that the crust will be stiff enough to hang together from the cherry juices drooling out when I take a bite. With full knowledge there could be pits, my big first bite still flashes through my mind. A brash, full frontal sweet-tart flavor. And it lasts, even as my summer appetite picks up momentum.

Oh, when did sweet and sour find each other, opposites that, thrown together, highlight the essence of each? The pie is Door County's American statement and the most durable impression of the meal.

That the fish boil was simple and not genuinely new doesn't mean that it was without value. It's been added to my personal list of Wisconsin's culinary charms that are impossible to find anywhere else, like the Sheboygan brat (the name rhymes with cot, not cat), a stubby sausage boiled in beer before it's grilled; a Milwaukee Friday night fish fry; and the big, oval, butter-layered Danish kringle pastry from Racine, a city on Lake Michigan once known as the most Danish in America.

We travel back to Chicago, our Styrofoam cooler packed with five-year Cheddar (loaded with cholesterol), Swedish limpa bread (packed with calories), sour cherry jams (packed with sugar), and as many fish fillets as we can put on ice. We'll never duplicate the boil over, but we surely talked about slathering our fish in local craft beer and frying them up in a pan. Then slicing up another Door County cherry pie.

White Gull Inn Door County Cherry Pie

Makes 8 servings

CRUST

2 ½ cups flour
1 tablespoon sugar
1 cup lard
4 to 5 tablespoons ice water

FILLING

4 cups pitted, fresh or frozen tart Montmorency cherries
¼ teaspoon almond extract
1 ¼ cups sugar
1 ½ tablespoons cornstarch

Preheat oven to 425 degrees.

Combine flour and sugar in a large bowl. Cut in lard with a pastry blender until dough begins to stick together. Add ice water, a tablespoon at a time, and toss with a fork until all flour is moistened and pastry forms a slightly sticky ball. Divide dough in half and pat into two rounds. On a lightly floured surface, roll each round of dough to 2 inches larger than an inverted 9-inch pie plate. Place one round in bottom of pie plate.

To make filling, combine cherries and almond extract in a medium bowl. In a separate bowl, stir together sugar and cornstarch. Gently toss sugar mixture into cherries to combine. Pour filling over prepared crust and cover with top crust. Pinch edges and seal; trim excess dough. Cut several slits in top crust to allow steam to escape.

Bake 35 to 45 minutes, or until crust is golden brown and filling is bubbly.

Note: If using frozen cherries, drain for two hours and reserve ¼ cup juice. Combine cherries and reserved juice.

White Gull Inn Fish Boil Recipe for Home Cooks

Makes 4 generous servings

This recipe is for cooking at home on your kitchen stove. You will need a large pot (5 gallons is ideal), preferably with a removable basket or net, for draining. For smaller quantities, one basket or net is sufficient for both the potatoes and fish. If your pot does not have a removable basket for draining, you can make one cheesecloth bag to hold the potatoes and one to hold the fish. Or, using a colander, drain the fish and potatoes in the sink.

Try to make the weight of the fish chunks, and thus the portions, as similar as possible.

The amount of salt used in the fish boil is based on the amount of water. To expand this recipe, add 1 cup salt for each additional gallon of water.

12 small red potatoes

8 quarts water

2 cups salt

**12 whitefish steaks, cut 2 inches thick, approximately 2 1/2 to
    4 1/2 ounces each**

Melted butter

Lemon wedges

EQUIPMENT

5-gallon pot

**Removable basket for pot, or 2 24-inch by 24-inch pieces
    of cheesecloth, or colander**

Wash potatoes and cut a small slice from each end, for flavor penetration. Bring the water to a boil in the pot; keep it boiling as much as possible throughout the cooking procedure.

Add the potatoes and half the salt; cook 20 minutes. Check doneness of potatoes with a fork; they should be almost done.

When potatoes are almost done, add whitefish with the remaining salt. Cook approximately 8 to 10 minutes, until fish are still firm but begin to pull away from the bone when lifted with a fork. At the inn, when cooking outside, we toss a small amount of kerosene on the fire when the fish is done, causing the fish oils, which have risen to the surface of the water, to boil over the sides. Do not attempt this at home; simply skim the oils off the surface with a spoon while the fish is cooking.

Lift cooked potatoes and fish from the water; drain. Serve immediately with melted butter and lemon.

Traditional fish boil accompaniments are coleslaw, homemade limpa bread, lemon, orange date nut bread and pumpkin bread, and Door County cherry pie for dessert.

Holidays, Fairs, and Events

Grill man Markus, who says he knows more about barbecu-
ing than any Jew ought to, finds the deep-fried food at his
county fair equally tasty.

Thrill Food

John Markus

I came of age in the rural Midwest, and my most vivid memories of pubescence place me at the Madison County Fair. This is no soft-focus reminiscence of goofy sexual innocence. No, as a clarinet player in the marching band — the bottom rung of the pecking order of initiation — I had to settle for walks down the county fair's midway, where, pained, I could only gaze at halter-topped objects of desire, strolling arm in arm with jersey-wearing football players. And, driving home the point of my unworthiness, each girl had her free arm around a near-life-sized stuffed animal, proof that her selected mate could club the wooly mammoth and bring home its bacon. Girl, guy, and trophy all seemed to utter contemptuously to me, "You can't have."

Fortunately for the beta male, there was fair food. Available just once a year and off the charts in saturated fat, these deeply satisfying eats

---

John Markus, comedy television writer, producer, and co-creator of many long-running episodic sitcoms, such as NBC's *A Different World* and *Lateline* with Al Franken, was the head writer of *The Cosby Show*. During his tenure on the acclaimed series, he wrote or co-wrote sixty-seven episodes, earning an Emmy, a Peabody, and two Humanitas Prizes. After apprenticing under world-champion pitmasters and competing on the New England circuit with his own Central Pork West team, he is now a baron of barbecue, winning awards in the categories of chicken, ribs, and brisket. In 2010 Markus, accompanied by a film crew and five of America's top BBQ Pitmasters from his series for TLC, traveled to Kuwait to feed our troops. Markus divides his time between a Manhattan apartment and a gentleman's farm in upstate New York, which, as he says, "allows him to experience elevated blood pressure in only one location."

were essential to boys in the woodwind section hoping to sublimate the emotional and physical pain of early unrequited lust. Elephant ears: deep-fried flaps of dough. Funnel cakes: also fried dough. And corn dogs: batter-dipped frankfurters, also fried. But please don't think of these as comfort food. Born of hot flames and angry, hissing oil and feasted on in the electrically charged atmosphere of the midway, this stuff goes beyond comfort. This is the *fugu* of comfort. This is Thrill Food.

It is now October 2002, and I am on the midway of the American Royal, the esteemed Kansas City barbecue festival and championship. Days earlier, a doctor told me my blood pressure and "bad" cholesterol were elevated, giving new, middle-aged meaning to the concept of Thrill Food. (Let's face it: once the Lipitor kicks in, the Thrill is gone.)

A small cardboard square is duct-taped to the concession stand's metal awning, hand-printed, like an afterthought to the menu: "Deep-Fried Twinkie — $1.95." Whoa, I almost missed it! My blood pressure shoots up, and I can't allow my bad cholesterol to be left behind, so I approach the counter. But when the aproned, grandmotherly proprietor hears my order, her response is curious. She simply looks at me, cocks her head, and narrows one eye, as if to admonish, "Are you sure?" I will not be deterred. Thrill Food seekers must never heed warnings, even from pushers.

The Twinkie is peeled from its cellophane jacket and a Popsicle stick inserted into the south end. Next, my new grandma — I quickly bond with anyone preparing my Thrill Food — dunks the snack cake in apple fritter batter and drops it in hot peanut oil. Using tongs, she gently logrolls it to a golden brown — a minute and a half — shakes off the excess oil (at thirty-four grams of fat you might say what's the point), and dusts it with powdered sugar.

A moment before my first bite, I pause to look up. I am the only person in sight holding a deep-fried Twinkie on a stick, and yet a small crowd has gathered. I feel like a Wright brother at Kitty Hawk.

It is extraordinarily tasty. The intense heat has melted both cake and cream filling, fusing the combo into a single sensation tucked inside a crisped pancakey wrap. Sweet, warm oil lingers in my throat.

And with each bite, the thing gets better and better. I wash it down with nothing. Then, as I work the final morsel off the stick, a dusting of sugar on my moustache, I catch the stare of one of the onlookers, a young halter-topped woman. Sure, she's standing next to a burly guy, but I swear, she gives me the nicest smile. Closure. I go back for another.

An expatriate from Hoosier land is gripped by the nostalgia of the foods served up during May, when the Indy 500 racers and spectators fill the town. If you can't get up close and personal with drivers like Paul Newman at the track, you definitely can in diners like Charlie Brown's Pancake and Steak House.

Under the Checkered Flag

Melanie Benjamin

I was twenty-seven years old before I realized that Memorial Day is not known throughout the land as "the day after the Indy 500."

That was my age when I moved away from Indiana — specifically, Indianapolis, Indiana, home of the Indianapolis Motor Speedway. That was my age when I discovered that other — non-Hoosier — people did not look forward to May all year long, as much as they looked forward to Christmas; that they did not plan their entire May wardrobes to reflect some kind of combination of black and white; that not every drugstore sold checkered flag party favors, nor did every bakery feature cakes in the shape of racecars. Indeed, it was the first time I realized that other — non-Hoosier — people didn't even understand the need for cakes in the shape of racecars.

It was a rude awakening, to be honest. That first race day not spent in Indianapolis, my husband and I stood in front of our TV with our hands placed over our hearts, tears streaming down our faces as first Florence Henderson performed the national anthem, and then — Shivers! Chills! — Jim Nabors launched into "Back Home Again in Indiana."

As he sang, a million colored balloons were released from their nets, rising and then dotting the sky above the grandstand, and I recalled waiting breathlessly for that moment when I was a little girl. Listening

---

Born and raised in the shadow of the Indianapolis Motor Speedway, **Melanie Benjamin** now lives with her family in Chicago, where she writes historical fiction. She is the nationally bestselling author of *The Autobiography of Mrs. Tom Thumb* and *Alice I Have Been*; you can visit her at her website, www.melaniebenjamin.com.

to our little transistor radio for the burst of applause following that last, grand, "How I long for my Indiana ho-o-me," I'd stare at the sky, my gaze sure and watchful, in case any of the balloons caught the wind and flew a few miles west, over my house. Many times, they did. Oh, the joy when my brother and I spied them! Oh, the ecstasy if one or two got caught in a tree, colorful souvenirs of the race taking place even as we jumped up and down and begged our father to climb a ladder and get them down for us. He never did, of course. A day later, they would be sad and deflated, and they'd remain there all summer until all of us were tired of the heat and humidity, our joy over the bright promise of May long gone.

That memorable, miserable race day, my husband and I huddled in front of the T v, missing it all so. Not the race itself, exactly, but all that it symbolized — every glorious day in May leading up to it, a series of parties and picnics and weekday afternoons spent playing hooky at the track, hoping for a glimpse of a favorite driver. May was joy; it was happiness; it was the end of school and the beginning of summer and it all was wrapped up in a black-and-white checkered flag, as familiar to us as the Stars and Stripes and just as apt to stir up warm feelings of home and patriotism and the urge to defend man's God-given right to drive five hundred miles making left turns only, at very high speeds.

That was what we missed.

Well, that — and all the food. *Hoosier* food: comforting and uncomplicated, just like childhood itself. For a moment, I could almost hear the cast-iron skillet being pulled out from a cabinet as my mother prepared to fry the first green tomatoes of the summer — soaked in salt water, coated in flour and salt and pepper.

When I was a child growing up in the late sixties and seventies, my father's appliance store was only about a quarter of a mile from the track. (That's what we call the Motor Speedway in Indiana — it's simply "the track." As the 500 is simply "the race" — back then, anyway, there was no other.) Dad painted the outside of the store in black-and-white checks to honor its proximity, and he always closed on race day because the traffic was just too terrible — and because, of course, all his customers would be glued to the radio, listening.

I absorbed the Indianapolis 500 in a way that's hard to explain to someone who didn't grow up playing with the children of racecar drivers, seeing people like Paul Newman in local diners, or setting their clocks by what time the Goodyear Blimp flew overhead on its daily trips to the track. In fact, we set our *calendars* by the Goodyear Blimp; the day it arrived, the first time we saw its strange, silvery, vaguely mammary shape flying overhead, we knew that May had officially begun.

Pit Stop: Milk is the traditional celebratory beverage for the winner of the Indianapolis 500. This tradition started in 1933 when Louis Meyer won his second race and requested a glass of buttermilk. After winning his third title in 1936, he requested a bottle of buttermilk and was photographed drinking it. Since then, with the exception of the years 1947–55, every winner is offered his choice of 2 percent, skim, or whole milk. (Buttermilk has apparently gone out of style.) In 1993 Emerson Fittipaldi notoriously drank orange juice instead; there are many fans who have yet to forgive him.

Now that I'm an adult, I may not be able to remember all the state capitols, but I can recite the name of every winner of the race in chronological order, which has sometimes come in handy as a party trick. People who did not grow up in Speedway — the city within a city that houses the actual track — are astounded by this feat. But honestly, it would be more astounding if I didn't possess this information. Street signs are painted with the name, number, and year of every winner. And the wall of the mcl Cafeteria in Speedway — one of my parents' favorite restaurants — is lined with every winner's photo, as well; as there is always a long line, you have ample opportunity to memorize names and years.

Hoosiers love a good cafeteria, and I'm not sure why; I've not encountered this in other states. And I'm not talking about an all-you-can-eat buffet. No, a good cafeteria requires hair-net-clad workers standing behind steaming trays of fresh, home-cooked food that tempts you into a fit because you have to *choose*; you can't have it all because every single item has a price, and there's some iron-clad rule about not going back to the end of the line for more once you've paid the first time. Only the most gluttonous would do this, and woe to the child who, in a panic, invariably chose the chocolate pie instead of the pecan pie, only to discover, too late, that the chocolate had meringue on it, which was yucky. Too bad. I was not allowed, under the inviolate rule of the cafeteria, to go back and stand at the end of the line just to buy a piece of pecan pie when I had already paid for the chocolate. No, I had to suffer the penance of watching everyone else enjoy their desserts and try to remember not to make the same mistake again. But honestly, I thought the meringue looked like whipped cream!

> Pit Stop: If you ever find yourself driving between Indianapolis and Bloomington, you must stop at a beloved Hoosier institution known as Gray Brothers' Cafeteria, in Mooresville. The line winds itself outdoors even in bad weather but the wait is worth it; mounds of golden fried chicken, tiny dishes of deviled eggs, vegetables slathered in cheese, ethereal, flaky biscuits, and homemade pies with meringue swirled as high as Dolly Parton's hair. Which apparently, if you like meringue, is a good thing.

So when I say that, as a child, I absorbed the race, had it coming out of my pores, you understand why. There was just no getting around it. To this day, if I hear someone shout out a year — "1963," for example — I'll reply, "Parnelli Jones!" I just can't help it.

But oh, it's the food that I remember the most, because that was the one thing that never changed from year to year. Drivers came and went; changes were made to the cars and to the track. One thing you could always be sure of, though, was that somewhere around May first, picnic baskets would be dusted off and packed full of deviled eggs and sandwiches, a thermos of iced tea, a can or two of Bud for the men. Then Hoosiers by the hundreds would descend upon the track to soak up the sun and catch a glimpse of A. J. Foyt or Mario Andretti flexing their muscles, stretching out their cars, trying to get a sense of who might have the best chance to win this year's pole.

What outsiders don't understand is that the race itself, at least back then, was just an afterthought. Those of us growing up around the track didn't actually attend — we couldn't afford the price of the ticket and only the very brave (or young and stupid) dared to wade into the

"Snake Pit," the general admission in the center of the field where, it was rumored, people went in but never came out. *Bad* people were there. People who smoked funny-smelling cigarettes and danced topless and indulged in all sorts of un-midwestern practices. It was rumored they trucked all these uninhibited, long-haired people in from California and trucked them all back out again after the race.

No, true Hoosiers only went to the track during the week to watch practice, or if you were really lucky, during time trials. The rest of the time we celebrated in time-honored Hoosier fashion: by eating.

If you couldn't get up close and personal with the drivers and owners at the track, you definitely could in the restaurants surrounding it. The drivers liked to frequent a little diner called Charlie Brown's Pancake and Steak House. I once saw a silver-haired Paul Newman sitting at a wobbly little Formica table, crowded around on all sides by other wobbly little Formica tables, eating eggs and the thinnest, crispiest home fries ever. The amazing thing about Charlie Brown's was the speed, perhaps a reflection of its location and clientele; the waitresses zipped about like demons, and no sooner had you placed your order and unfolded your napkin than your food was in front of you. Nothing fancy; just eggs and potatoes, ketchup on every table (Hoosiers pour ketchup on everything, including — or maybe especially — scrambled eggs). Charlie Brown's is still open, although it's moved a few blocks; whenever we go back to visit, we try to have breakfast there. It still has Hoosier staples such as biscuits and gravy and chicken-fried steak. And of course, the thinnest, crispiest home fries ever.

If breakfast wasn't your thing, you could buy your favorite driver a beer at Union Jack's Pub (also still around); that's where everyone went after the track closed at night. Or, if you were really well-off, you could spot Roger Penske at St. Elmo's Steakhouse downtown, one of the very best restaurants on earth, then and now. Known for its steaks and shrimp cocktails, it's really the cocktail sauce you remember. So much horseradish, just a whiff of it can clear out the sinuses with a force that would make even the most stoic Midwestern farmer weep.

But back when I was a child, there weren't a lot of celebrities around (with the exception of Paul Newman, who was a true racer, not just a dabbler). Drivers didn't necessarily have corporate sponsorships; there were a lot of owner-drivers, and these men were just overgrown kids, really. They lived simply, most of them born and raised in Indiana, and they raced dirt bikes and karts the rest of the year. Oh, the tragedy of discovering that the winner of the 1973 and 1982 races, Gordon Johncock, lived in an apartment complex near my high school! And it wasn't a very nice apartment complex at that. While I knew that a lot of drivers lived modestly — I grew up with some of their children — I'd assumed that those anointed gods of speed who had their name engraved on the Borg Warner Trophy lived in palaces. Palaces with private racetracks in the backyard and swimming pools in the shape of carburetors. To discover that even these deities lived in crummy apartment complexes was a disappointment from which I've yet to recover.

Pit Stop: One year a skinny, quiet girl who worked at my father's store asked if she could have the month of May off. It turned out she had been chosen 500 festival queen, a glorious title made up of angel wings, tiaras, and STP stickers. For the entire month, we watched in awe as she — transported into this beautiful, ethereal creature wearing gowns and long gloves — waved from floats, presided over balls, and finally gave the winner of the race the ceremonial kiss. Then, May over, she returned to work, just another skinny, quiet girl once more — Cinderella after the ball. She lived in a crummy apartment complex, too.

Of course, everything was simpler, then.

May marked not only the beginning of the race festivities, but the end of the school year. Back then we didn't have computers and flat-screen TVs in every classroom. No, when the heat crept in those half-opened casement windows — no air conditioning, of course, only a desperate old fan — and the teacher decided we needed to know nothing more under her watch, she simply carted in a projector, popped in a film, and took a quick nap in the back of the room. And that film was, more often than not, a highlight reel of a previous year's Indy 500, which we all watched with open-mouthed, drooling absorption. Because as soon as it was over, we would eat.

The picnic! The school or church picnic was *always* held in May. On tables clad in black-and-white checked cloths, our mothers would pile up Hoosier picnic food. Fried chicken, of course; ham sandwiches on white hamburger buns with mayonnaise, naturally. Potato salad, nothing fancy — just potatoes and mayonnaise and yellow mustard and some sweet pickle relish, none of that Grey Poupon stuff, no chives or shallots or other vegetables that I never encountered until I moved away. Now, some people would argue about the relish; should it be sweet, or tangy? Whole baby gherkins cut up instead, maybe, with a couple of teaspoons of pickle juice tossed in?

But you would never find anyone arguing about the mustard. Yellow mustard only. *Finis.* And the potatoes? Please do not insult a Hoosier by talking about red potatoes or new potatoes or fingerling potatoes. Russet potatoes boiled and cut up in big, uneven chunks. Now, THAT's how you make potato salad.

Of course, there were tiny toothpick checkered flags planted in everything; in brownies, cookies, sandwiches, olives. A few ambitious mothers might try to make a black-and-white checkered cake. But the most common race-themed dessert involved Circus Peanuts.

Now, the Circus Peanut is a little-understood confection. I wasn't even aware it was called a Circus Peanut until I was an adult; I always referred to them as "those marshmallow things that look like racecars." Because they do; they do look like racecars. Especially after you stick a toothpick through each end and attach a gumdrop to all four ends of the protruding toothpicks. Suddenly this odd little candy looks like a four-wheeled racecar. Plates and plates of thirty-three Circus Peanut racecars, eleven rows of three, exactly like the cars in the race. Most of them were left untouched, because even small children think that Circus Peanuts are just nasty. But they sure did look festive, and the picnic simply wouldn't have been the same without them.

Pit Stop: The Circus Peanut, while shaped like a peanut, actually tastes like a banana. No one knows why. The Circus Peanut is also responsible for Lucky Charms breakfast cereal; in 1963 a General Mills vice president discovered that Circus Peanut shavings added that extra something in his breakfast cereal that apparently he had been looking for all his life.

However, the race food of all race food, the one item for which I would willingly strap myself into a racecar and be dragged along at speeds over two hundred miles per hour just so I could taste it one more time, is a Hoosier tradition called fried biscuits and apple butter. If you were lucky; if your company or church or neighbor decided to cater the ubiquitous May party — or if you were fortunate enough to be invited to a corporate tent at the track itself — chances were the caterer was an establishment called Jug's Catering. Fortunately, Jug's is still around. And even more fortunately, they're still famous for their fried biscuits and apple butter.

Now, you can find these delectable treats elsewhere in Indiana — notably, the Nashville House in Nashville, which also fries a mean chicken. But the fried biscuits from Jug's are the fried biscuits of my childhood, my memory, and sometimes, I must admit — my dreams.

First you have the biscuit. It's small — bite-sized, almost. It's a bit doughy on the inside, but not too doughy; it still retains a lightness. It's not dense. And on the outside — oh, the outside! It's ethereal and crunchy all at the same time; it melts inside your mouth with a satisfying sweetness, delicately flavored with just a little oil.

But before you bite into it for that first, airy taste, you slather it with apple butter.

Apple butter. Again, somewhat of a misnomer. There is no dairy involved; it's simply a gooey form of applesauce, rich with caramelized sugar so that it has a sticky, brown, spreadable consistency. You place a dollop of this on your warm fried biscuit, watch it melt just a little, then bite into it; apple and dough and sugar and grease explode in your mouth, and there's nothing better on this earth. Especially on a warm day in May, with black-and-white checkered flags everywhere, fried chicken and your mother's potato salad on the plate in front of you, cold milk in your hand, and the Goodyear Blimp hovering noisily overhead.

It's summer, and school's almost out, and you might just go knock on Gordon Johncock's door, even though you heard of one kid who did and got yelled at by him, and when you go visit your father at his store tomorrow, you'll probably hear the whine of racecars not a quarter of a mile away, whipping around the track at speeds you can't imagine. The cars are just blurs, but the people inside them are real. As real as you are, only better, somehow.

But nothing's better than this moment, when you're a child and you live in Indianapolis, Indiana, home of the Indianapolis Motor Speedway; it's practically in your backyard and you know that's special, although you won't know how special until you grow up and move away from it.

The race is different now. Not so magical; not able to transform skinny girls into princesses and grumpy men living in bachelor apartments into gods. The names of the drivers are foreign; there aren't a lot of overgrown Hoosier dirt-car drivers able to catch a ride these days. Big corporations are behind everything; the track itself now is home to other races — Formula 1, NASCAR.

May is different, I hear from family and friends who still live there. The whole month isn't a grand holiday; everything's wedged into about two weeks of jam-packed activity. There's a red carpet, and celebrities are everywhere; instead of Florence Henderson, pop stars take turns singing the national anthem. But Jim Nabors still sings "Back Home Again in Indiana" while they release a million balloons, which then fly over Speedway, coming to rest in some other little girl's yard.

And my husband and I, watching from our home in Chicago, still stand with our hands over our hearts and tears in our eyes — and fried biscuits and apple butter in our dreams.

Before he embarks on a mission to Ethiopia, a teenage boy feels a surge of patriotism at his small-town Kansas Fourth of July. There are flags in the wind, a sun lowering over the horizon, trumpets scattered on the lawn, and a spread of pies, cakes, and cobblers that he fears he may never see again.

Bicentennial Pie

Timothy Bascom

In the summer of 1976 I spent a lot of time at our town pool next to the brown-baked fields of the 4-H Club, where I kept cool by dunking or getting dunked. I was a fifteen-year-old Kansas boy with a fifteen-year-old's perspective on the world, much of it filtered through the pool's PA system. Radio DJs were still interrupting songs, two years after the Watergate scandal, to insinuate that President Ford had made a secret deal with Nixon: a full pardon in exchange for keys to the White House. They were also joking about the Statue of Liberty needing a face-lift before the Bicentennial celebrations.

I hoisted myself out of the water and pattered down the hot concrete in my dripping swimsuit, glad to hear Bachman-Turner Overdrive come over the PA, shouting over the poolside screams, "You Ain't Seen Nothing Yet." I did my own mock rendition as I ran. Then I gave twenty-five cents to the pretty seventeen-year-old at the concession window and asked for a Suicide, watching in a happy, interested way as she twisted in her yellow bikini to mix a cup of Coke and Dr. Pepper and root beer, sun-bleached hair bouncing to the music.

Timothy Bascom, whose memoir *Chameleon Days* won the Bakeless Literary Prize in nonfiction, has written often about his unique bicultural childhood, half in Kansas and half in Ethiopia. Though he no longer has access to the peach cobbler he ate in Troy, Kansas, on July 4, 1976, he stops often at roadside cafes, looking for a local equivalent. His essays have won editor's prizes at the *Missouri Review* and *Florida Review*, being selected for the anthologies *Best American Travel Writing* and *Best Creative Nonfiction*. Currently he lives in Des Moines, Iowa, where his wife bakes a mean cherry pie. He teaches creative writing at Drake University and the University of Missouri.

The singer on the radio stuttered out his signature "B-b-b-baby," and I was struck suddenly that this girl was so wondrously tan she might as well be from the family of Bertie Hamilton, one of the four black residents in Troy, Kansas. Eighty-year-old Bertie, whose skin was closer to the color of caramel, attended our church, and she was one of my favorite old people — in part because of her famous peach cobbler. In fact, just a few days later I would see her down at our church — Troy Baptist — for a Sunday evening potluck, where she appeared in her standard pink dress and white go-go boots.

Bertie was, perhaps, the most energetic "old person" I knew. At the time, she was trying to get her college degree, despite having to drive to Atchison twice a week. She was also taking violin lessons. And when she made peach cobbler, often from fruit grown in her own yard, she tended to make two or three pans at a time, delivering them to neighbors or mysteriously selected church members.

Her cobbler was the one thing I absolutely knew I had to eat, so I didn't wait for dessert time, instead scooping a square onto my plate next to some chicken casserole and green beans. I opted for Bertie's cobbler over all the brownies and Bundt cake and pineapple turnover, and as soon as I had done the required damage to my main dishes, I forked into that luscious stuff, savoring its balance of dumpling-like crust and succulent fruit. All the acid of the peaches was buttered and sugared away, which meant that I felt lifted into culinary heaven, raised to a rapturous bliss even though seated on a metal folding chair in a paneled basement. It's amazing how, even while eating underground, in a dark hall of a room with polyester suit jackets all around, those soft-baked peaches could taste like sunlight and honey. They sang on my tongue like the music down at the pool, full of let-go-of-all-your-worries exultation.

Of course, everyone at our table had something worrisome to say about the moral decline of the nation. This was a Baptist gathering, after all. They feared that, if our founding fathers could see the state of things, they would roll in their graves this Fourth of July, two hundred years after independence. What would George Washington think of Nixon and his stooges, not to mention the Doobie Brothers or Cheryl Tiegs wearing virtually nothing on the cover of *Sports Illustrated*?

I noticed, though, that Bertie didn't jump into this running commentary. She just smiled an enigmatic seen-it-all smile and said, "What goes around comes around."

I happened to know, through my parents, that Bertie had once had a baby who died and that her husband had left her long ago. Also that she had worked for decades as a housemaid, cooking and washing other people's clothes. She had a proven graciousness that gave her an almost regal poise, so I found it paradoxical to think that she had practically leapt right out of slavery, a fact she shared with my parents earlier that year while we were helping her move a broken clothes dryer. "You know," she said to them as I kneeled with her two collies, ruffling their ears, "my mama was actually born a slave! She didn't get free until after the war, when her parents moved out this way."

Of course, with 1976 being the year of the Bicentennial, our teachers at Troy High School had made a big deal about history all the previous school year. In one class I had been required to write a ten-page report about local historic events, which led to borrowing a rare book from a neighbor who was a member of the state legislature. After I brought home *Gray's Doniphan County History*, published in 1905, I became unexpectedly intrigued as I flipped through the yellowing pages. I couldn't believe there had been knife fights right here on the streets of Troy, sparked by arguments over slavery. Or that the Squatters' Sovereign Association had taken an abolitionist minister down to the Missouri River and tied him to a log, then thrown him in, to drift indefinitely or to roll under, pecked by carp.

While I read further, I began to see that the United States, as a whole, had not only survived its original war of independence but had gone through a second, even more brutal revolution back in that era when Bertie's mother was still a slave — back when the very word *slavery* was so heated that it split Kansas into warring factions, causing the state to get dubbed "Bloody Kansas." Gray reported in his book that Abraham Lincoln had visited our highly contested county on a frigid day in December 1859, dropping in on a Troy resident who owned a house with a secret cellar, a hideout for escaping slaves. Gray also wrote that

Lincoln had not crossed back into Missouri when news arrived of the abolitionist John Brown being executed for trying to start a full-scale slave rebellion, which meant Lincoln had to make an official statement. Apparently, he had declared that even though he admired the courage and commitment of this native Kansan, such courage could not "excuse violence, bloodshed, and treason."

For a moment, as I pondered that comment from a hundred years earlier, I could almost picture John Brown the way I had seen him depicted on a mural at our state capitol: a wrathful Moses of a man, wild-bearded, arms outstretched, holding a rifle instead of a staff. I wasn't sure whether or not I should trust him, but I felt his power as I imagined him standing, prophet-like, between two waves of advancing soldiers. This, now, was part of my personal sense of history. I could value it more fully because of Bertie Hamilton, whose mother had actually lived as a slave before being freed. I could prize it because I had eaten a peach cobbler that was probably baked in the same fashion that Bertie had learned from that older, more-experienced mother, who had outlived such horrible injustice.

Of course, all this right-or-wrong, life-or-death conflict had the magical charm that is the special property of adolescent males. It tasted of adventure, something that made me hungry to get closer. The only problem with being so near to history — almost able to touch it — is that it will remain lodged in the past, back in some era that seems more exciting than one's own. That is probably why I smirked when July Fourth arrived and the town fathers made a big to-do about burying a stainless steel time capsule under a flagpole in front of our courthouse. That capsule seemed trivial next to all the large events of the past. It included, among other oddities, what seemed to be an overly sincere description of a Doniphan County home economics club known as the Pollyanna Club, renowned for prize-winning pies. Sure, I loved pie, but did that seemingly insignificant news clipping qualify to be memorialized and dug up two hundred years later as a representation of the life we had once lived?

I was too self-important in my own fifteen-year-old way to see the irony of my own enthusiasm a few minutes later, when it was time to make a personal contribution to this small-town celebration — that is, by playing trumpet on the courthouse lawn alongside Dad and my older brother and the other members of the Troy Summer Band. When our time came, we carried folding chairs onto the grass then sat down and played very intently, wet at the armpits. We played "Yankee Doodle Dandy" and "Stars and Stripes Forever." We played "America, the Beautiful." Then we stood and bowed to a hearty round of applause.

Concert over, I walked around the edge of the milling crowd in a please-notice-me way, finally joining a long line so that I could reach a table where members of the still-functioning Pollyanna Club were setting out slices of pie. By the time I got to the front, the other band members had been served and almost everyone was drifting away, so one of the ladies behind the makeshift counter winked, whispering that I could have more than one kind of pie, plus a scoop of ice cream — that is, if I wanted.

I certainly did. I had spotted Bertie close by, in a blue-and-red dress with white patent-leather sandals, which meant I could get not only a piece of cherry pie but some cobbler. I waited longer, facing the late-afternoon sun and salivating as the women passed the plate to Bertie. I waited, too, as the plate went to one of the men in the background, who were palming ice and salt off the lids of hand-cranked buckets, then lifting out the metal paddles to scoop spoonfuls of cold vanilla onto plates.

My friends from the brass section had perched on the upper steps of the courthouse, but I waited awhile by myself and started into the cherry pie, chewing on a tart forkful with a dollop of frozen cream. All quiet there, I savored the sheer Americanness of the moment: flags in the wind, sun lowering over the horizon, trumpets scattered on the lawn. I felt suddenly proud to just be part of the large community called America — one member of a nation that had lasted two hundred years, surviving its own revolution and civil war, not to mention the troubles Nixon had brought upon us.

I had the faith of a young man, which is a powerful but short-lived thing, and I think I could already sense the never-again nature of this moment. My excitement was magnified because I was now carrying a life-changing secret — something that no one else knew except my parents and brothers. Just a few days earlier, Dad had called us into the living room for a family conference, and he had announced that a mission organization in Africa was requesting him to serve as a doctor in Ethiopia, a country currently going through a full-scale Marxist revolution.

My parents were people who had always responded to need. During their early marriage they had let homeless drifters stay on their living room couch, sometimes for weeks. Dad had chosen to do his residency in a state hospital across the river — in St. Joseph, Missouri — one of the few places where poor people could afford treatment. Here, now, was another stated need. Dad said that, due to the revolution, the mission had lost most of its staff. Doctors and nurses had left. The only mission doctor in Addis was taking a furlough, so a replacement was critical.

"Are you saying it's decided?" I asked.

"No. It might not even be possible, since the Ethiopian government is denying most visas . . ."

"Do you want to go?" asked my older brother, who looked queasy.

"We just know that everyone may have to leave the country, so this could be a last window to go in and do what's possible."

I could hear the eagerness under my father's noncommittal response. The way he said "go in" sounded like a beach landing on D-Day or a paratrooper strike. There was a kind of dramatic urgency to it: "Your mission, should you choose to accept it, . . . " And frankly I thrilled at the thought. To live with courage and conviction, taking on a worthwhile cause that sounded tantalizing to me as a fifteen-year-old American boy full of the desire to do something large.

As Mom and Dad went on to explain more about the situation in Ethiopia, I became sobered. After the overthrow of the emperor Haile Selassie, a new socialist state had been declared, run by a group of hard-line Marxists called the Derg, or "Committee of Equals." This shadowy junta had been dominated by its most brutal member, Colonel Mengistu, who arranged the execution of several other members. Mengistu had also instituted a neighborhood police force called the *kebele*, and these cadres of loyal followers gave him eyes and ears everywhere. Business owners and landlords were being stripped of property. Student protesters were being dragged off in the dark.

"We don't have to go at all," Mom said, trying to be very clear. "It's only if you're willing."

The odd thing is that I *was* willing. Even though the Cold War had begun to thaw due to the American exit from Vietnam, the Iron Curtain was still an ominous fixture in Europe, and I tended to imagine a dark, dark shadow that hovered up there in the northeast quadrant of the map, threatening to ooze out onto places like Ethiopia or maybe even as far as Kansas. To go right into that darkness, hoping to push it back a bit, was frightening. Yet it made me feel as if I might enter into history at last, getting involved in something that mattered as much as the abolition movement that freed Bertie's mother.

I was too young, of course, to know that shades of gray will exist where light meets dark or to realize the costs of entering into such ill-defined territory. However, as I stood on the courthouse lawn, relishing bites of that soft-baked cherry pie with its flaky crust, I began to feel for the first time what would be lost by leaving Troy, Kansas.

I bit into Bertie's cobbler — shifting to its softer, warmer taste, so rich with butter and brown sugar — and I felt genuine grief. Even without having left, I missed this town that had been my one true home. I missed Bertie and the graceful way she went about life. Missed the ladies in the Pollyanna Club, with their inherited Kansas recipes. Missed the church members grumbling about the decline of the nation. And the pretty girl at the pool, humming along with Bachman-Turner Overdrive. I suddenly missed all twelve hundred of the people who called Troy home, living out their lives inside a big embrace of the looping Missouri River. In a few months I would be looking back at Troy from the other side of the globe, exiled to a place where everything tasted of red pepper and cumin, and for the first time I realized that pie could never taste the same.

COME TO THE FAIR

When you think of a beautiful August day at a state fair in the Midwest, is there a dish that more readily comes to mind than the infamous belly-bomber of a sausage, the corn dog?

So You'll Diet Tomorrow

Lorna Landvik

In general, Minnesotans are a prudent people who regularly place high in overall health rankings, but for twelve days in late summer, we forget about tracking calories, ignore cholesterol and glycemic levels, unbutton the top button of our shorts (or better yet, find the ones with the elasticized waistband) and make a pledge to *indulge*. The Great Minnesota Get-Together is the official nickname of our state fair, the largest in the Midwest according to daily attendance. The unofficial nickname, used by natives in the know, is the Great Minnesota Pig Out.

Our covenant has been made: pounds will be gained. Gas will be expelled. Guilt will try to shadow pleasure, but as we bite into a key lime ice cream bar or sample a Korean taco, we understand it's all worth it.

Lorna Landvik is the best-selling author of *Patty Jane's House of Curl*, *Your Oasis on Flame Lake*, *The Tall Pine Polka*, *Welcome to the Great Mysterious*, *Angry Housewives Eating Bon Bons*, *Oh My Stars*, *The View from Mount Joy*, and *'Tis the Season*. She is also an actor and most recently has been performing her all-improvised one-woman show *Party in the Rec Room*. That she makes margaritas on stage ensures sell-out runs. After high school she went to Europe with her best friend and, when funds ran low, found work as a chambermaid in a hotel in Bavaria. There she became skilled at fluffing eiderdown duvets and yodeling. She attended the University of Minnesota before moving to California, where she performed in comedy clubs and theaters in San Francisco and Los Angeles. While in LA, she worked many temp jobs, including a clerical job at the Playboy Mansion. She was not required to wear any bunny ears or cottontails. Married to the guy she met when he crashed her high school dance, she lives in Minneapolis and is the mother of two daughters and the owner of the most handsome dog ever.

Especially if we've planned ahead and tucked a roll of Tums into our back pockets.

There are many specialty fragrances to be found in the fairgrounds: farmers appreciate the smells of hay and milk and dung emanating from the cow or sheep barns, those mechanically inclined are drawn to Machinery Hill's smells of fuel and metal, but everyone is intoxicated by the most pervasive fair perfume, the smell of food, heady with top notes of grease and spun sugar, the musk of grilling meats.

The fair has hundreds of cultural, entertainment, and educational enticements, but on this trip we're going to bypass the Clydesdale horse show, the 4-H fashion revue, the belly dancing invitational and the Terror-Bungee-Ride. As we enter the gates, let us remember our visit today is all about eating, so people, start your metabolisms.

Passing the Creative Arts building, where homemade quilts, wood carvings, crocheted baptismal dresses, and rhubarb preserves vie for blue ribbons, we see a booth and face our first dilemma: the corn dog or the pronto pup? Both? I like your style. Each begins with a hot dog, but the corn dog's batter is, as its name infers, made of cornmeal whereas a pronto pup's is flour-based. They're both dipped in a boiling bath of oil and equally well-paired with a splurt of mustard. They are also, like over sixty other food items here, served on a stick.

Thanks to this most utilitarian utensil, it is entirely possible to eat all day at the fair without lifting a spoon or fork to your lips. Cotton candy may have been one of the first foods (if cotton candy can indeed be considered a food) to incorporate the stick as cutlery, but now you can eat everything from hot dish (Minnesotan for *casserole*) to a giant dill pickle to camel (tastes like desert bison) on a long pressed-paper or wood cylinder.

The following foods, believe it or not, are also served on a stick: Bacon Cheddar mashed potatoes. Reuben sandwiches. Cheesecake. Walleye. Spaghetti and meatballs. Candy bars. Shrimp toast. Chocolate-covered bananas. Spam. Teriyaki ostrich. Cheese pizza. Caramel apples. Egg rolls. Alligator (tastes like swampy chicken). Macaroni and cheese. Scallops. Mushrooms and cauliflower. Salmon. Bologna. Fudge puppies (Belgian waffles dipped in chocolate).

With some foods—the fruit and vegetable kabobs—it makes sense to *spear* them, but how do you wrangle hot dish on a stick? Or mashed potatoes? The secret is in the deep fryer. Anything that can be molded will keep its shaped when dipped in batter and deep-fried. But can be doesn't necessarily mean should be. Take deep-fried candy bars. As a lifelong fan of Misters Mars and Hershey, I often have their products in my purse or desk drawer, but deep-frying a Snickers or Reese's Peanut Butter Cup is too much, forcing one's tastebuds into overload, to wave a flag of surrender.

Then again, la cuisine de la State Fair is, of course, overkill.

What a perfect introduction to a food on many people's must-eat list: the cheese curd. A food homely in execution (golden, lumpy knobs and puffy blobs), the deep-fried cheese curd offers a molten lava cheesy center surrounded by hot, fried batter. There is a definite ahhh factor to be found in that first bite, but careful you don't singe the roof of your mouth. See that guy over there in the Grateful Dead T-shirt fanning his mouth as he eats a cheese curd? Is he tearing up from pain or from pleasure? Probably a combination of both.

What *is* the great allure of these foods served from kiosks and booths and stands? Certainly the holiday element is at play—the fair's open for less than two weeks and you'd better celebrate while you can—but it is my belief that we love these foods because so many of them can't be re-created at home. Even if you could make them—even if you had the deep fryer, the industrial-size cans of oil, and the ingredients, local and far-flung—how could you recapture the calliope music, the baiting shouts of carneys asking you to "try your luck!," the screams of roller-coaster riders as they plunge forward in a vertical drop? Parades don't march by as you're adding syrup to your Sno-Cone machine, the heavy staccato of clog dancers won't accompany you while you stretch out ribbons of saltwater taffy, and you can't tour the horse barn as you pop up a bushel of kettle corn. Dang it, you just can't bring a carnival into your own kitchen.

As you finish the last bite of our catfish on a stick, and I dip this corn fritter in ranch dressing, let us now pause to consider the romance of fair food. Sharing is the most practical way to enjoy all there is to be ingested here, as it allows for a wider sampling. And to share is, in a small way, to love.

Mini-donuts, tossed in a cinnamon-sugar coating as soon as they emerge hot from the fryer, are served in a little waxed-paper bag, perfect for passing back and forth. It is not unusual to see couples sharing a kiss after sharing mini-donuts — is it to taste that last residual tinge of grease and sugar on each other's lips, or is it an acknowledgement that sharing contributed to the experience's sweetness?

There's no written law, but everyone abides by the unwritten one: Sweet Martha's chocolate chip cookies must be shared. How many marriage proposals have been tendered when there is only one cookie remaining in the cardboard bucket and the generous offer "You take it, honey," is made? How many teenagers, after co-licking the chocolate and vanilla swirls of a frozen yogurt cone, are awakened to the romantic possibilities of someone who just yesterday was considered a dweeb, a dork, or totally *not* chill?

Oops, watch out for that poor guy carrying around that six-foot chartreuse plush dinosaur he just won at the midway. I don't think he can tell where he's going. His girlfriend doesn't look too happy either — she's probably thinking, "Where am I supposed to put that ugly thing?" They definitely could use some mini-donuts.

Platonic friendships, too, are solidified by sharing. When I, like Friar Tuck in days of yore, pass you a gigantic turkey leg, don't you feel mine is a merry band worth joining? And don't we cement our new-found camaraderie by raising a glass or two in the beer garden? When we push the pile of garlic French fries back and forth, are we not participating in some small minuet of grace?

Oh boy, the hotter the sun, the more purple the prose — how about we duck inside this diner for an iced-tea? These eateries, often church-sponsored and staffed by their congregants, offer sanctuary from the fair's razzle-dazzle, as well as more traditional fare — ham and egg breakfasts, meatloaf sandwich lunches, and blueberry pie for dessert. I appreciate their earnestness and bottomless cups of coffee, but why fill up on stuff you can get anywhere or anytime?

In the Agriculture Horticulture Building there's a room that displays fruits and vegetables — red apples so polished you can see your reflection in them, orange carrots with their green plumage of leaves still attached, elegant fingers of asparagus. Corralled behind a fence are the freakish "biggest" winners: pumpkins the size of Volkswagens, squash you could hit a home run with. Here we're invited to examine barrels of different seeds and grains, inspect the silk trailing from an ear of corn, and read about wheat's journey from farm field to mill to grocery store bread aisle. It's a nice grounding place, reminding us, as we dip a fried green tomato in ranch dressing or spoon up caramel drizzled over an apple sundae, of how food begins: its naked self, pre–dolled up, processed, and cooked.

Oh, and there's a wine bar right around the corner! Are we cosmopolitan or what?

The answer, when we visit the International Bazaar is *oui, yawhol, sí, yah, hai*, and *yes*es spoken in dozens of other languages. Here you can sample Greek olives and baklava, Caribbean jerk chicken, tamales, West Indian sweet potato pie, Middle Eastern gyros and falafel, hibiscus lemonade and roasted almonds, and any number of Chinese/Cuban/Mexican combination plates. You can also buy African shirts, Ecuadorean hats, or Indian jewelry, if you're inclined to bring home a souvenir other than a stomachache. (This might be a good time to be proactive and take a Tums.)

If you got a hankering for Scandinavian food — and being that you're in Minnesota, you should — let's try some *lefsa*. Made from riced potatoes, *lefsa* is like a Norwegian tortilla and is usually buttered and sprinkled with brown or white sugar and rolled up into delicious tubular goodness. Let's ask for extra lingonberries, a red berry as tasty as a blueberry, but without the publicity.

If you're still feeling Euro, we might try some German bratwurst or Wiener schnitzel, French crêpes or Polish pierogies. Or maybe some fish and chips, English style. In the mood for Irish soda bread? Umm, try this Scotch egg (hard-boiled and rolled in sausage and breadcrumbs, deep-fried, and, wonder of wonders, served on a stick).

For the carnivores in the crowd, gnaw on this: you will not find meat prepared in as many creative (and occasionally bizarre) ways as you will at our state fair. Pig Lickers are strips of bacon dipped in chocolate and you feel both sinful and giddy eating them. There's also bacon fried and caramelized in maple syrup. Bull Bites are blackened tenderloin with horseradish. There are sausages — from traditional Italian to nontraditional Asian to sausages encased in spirals of bread and served — hey, whaddya know — on a stick. The state fair is a meat-eater's delight, but vegetarians can easily reach Nirvana, or at least see its outlying suburbs.

Spiral chips are potatoes cut in a spiral and deep-fat-fried. (Do I need to tell you what they're served on?) A blooming onion, cut open to look like a flower, is battered, deep-fried, and served with a dipping sauce, just in case you're worried about not getting enough fat. The roasted corn, served in its husk and dripping with butter, is about as good as corn gets. Napkins are at a premium in front of this particular booth.

Yes, you're right: there are a lot of teenagers working the many booths. It's a premium summer job — who wouldn't want to work in the midst of a fair? — and it's easy to work long hours when it's only for twelve days. I did, however, know a high schooler who made malts for ten hours a day and, while she says she definitely gained some bicep definition, she lost her taste for ice cream. That may be one hazard of working a booth; your enthusiasm for its product wanes after the two-thousand-seven-hundredth serving of it.

Look, the sun's setting. How're you doing? You look a little peaked. Maybe I shouldn't have insisted we share that London broil sandwich. Whoo. How many calories do you suppose we've ingested? Maybe the same as a sumo wrestler eats on the day before his big match, or at least close to that of the winner of a pie-eating contest. I can't really read your expression: is it one of disbelief or horror? Fortunately, my pants have an elasticized waistband. And don't worry, we did walk a lot. I'll bet we burned off at least five hundred calories. And really, wasn't it all worth it?

Look, an empty bench! That's prized real estate around here. Now we can relax and take a load off. And it's close enough to the grandstand that we can hear tonight's headliner. Hope you're a heavy metal fan.

Pretty soon the fire works'll start, but until they do, let's just settle back and watch our fellow fairgoers. Look at the guy over there rubbing the marinara sauce off the bib of his overalls while his wife finishes the pizza kabob. Or that woman in the Golden Gopher T-shirt, a cloud of powdered-sugar rising as she bites into a grilled marshmallow cream, chocolate, and banana sandwich. And look at that kid in a stroller wrangling that elephant ear pastry. Have you ever seen such bliss?

Seems I've gotten a second wind — how's about if I run over to the Dippin' Dots booth and get us a cup of those delicious frozen ice cream pellets, or maybe you'd like to try a deep-fried Twinkie? I'll get some cappuccino chasers too — decaf if you like.

Excuse me! That burp has been a long time coming.

Thanks for joining me at the fair. I'm sure you'll be able to fit into your regular clothes in a week or two. And next year, if you come back, we can try all the food we missed this time — plus they always have new stuff. I must admit, this particular food tour's inspired me; I'm even thinking of applying for a license and opening up my own booth. I haven't exactly figured out my main ingredient, but I know it'll be deep-fried-flash-frozen-battered-frittered-hand-tossed-machine-rolled-toasted-roasted-chocolate-covered-caramel-coated and dipped in sprinkles, twinkles, crushed peanuts, or whole cashews. At the Minnesota State Fair, it can't miss.

Shanley shares her extended family's sacred ritual of Thanksgiving in the farmhouse where her mother grew up. The meal centers on turkey and trimmings — ingredients measured by a multitude of cooks. But the soul here is a story that weaves through generations of stability and change. Life as it was. Life as it is.

Thanksgiving Dinner

Mary Kay Shanley

Diabetes finally triumphed in 1952, mere days before the doctor was scheduled to amputate Grandpa Henry's second leg. When Aunt Frances called Webster City, Iowa, to tell us, I wondered who would take his place at the head of the dining room table come Thanksgiving. At nine, I understood innately that was Grandpa's chair. No one else's.

Henry — Hank to others — farmed the rich black soil that is Kossuth County in north-central Iowa. A big man, cattle farmer, smart and German-stern. Farms were islands then, each with its own cacophony — hogs snorting, chickens cackling, Skippy barking as he rounded up cattle wandering too far into the grove. The endless wind, weaving its way eastward through the pines along the gravel road, delivered respite. Not so, though, when it blew out of the north, passing through the cattle barn and the hog pens, on into the house. The cousins would

---

Mary Kay Shanley is a born-and-bred midwesterner who can't figure out why everyone doesn't crave to live here but is glad they don't. She loves the welcoming openness of the region's people, the greens-blues-browns-blacks of its landscape, the energy of its cities and rhythm of its small towns and rural areas. And she loves its food. She's the author of ten books, including *Our State Fair — Iowa's Blue Ribbon Story*, a coffee-table book about the fair's first 150 years that's actually fun to read. A best seller, *She Taught Me to Eat Artichokes*, was one of two of her books considered for the *Oprah Winfrey Show*. (Being considered and being on the show are not the same.) Mary Kay is an instructor with the University of Iowa Summer Writing Festival and co-sponsors Writing from the Soul retreats with Sr. Joyce Rupp, an international retreat and conference speaker. She also teaches at the Iowa Correctional Institution for Women in Mitchellville.

chide me for plugging my nose and holding my breath. "Mary Kay," they'd say, "that's the smell of money."

Okay, I didn't like the well water, either. It smelled like rotten eggs. It tasted musty. I wasn't allowed to drink it with my nose plugged — which would have been flat-out rude. So I learned to drink an entire glass without taking a breath by the age of five.

The farm was Grandpa Henry. Even after he'd turned day-to-day operations over to his son-in-law and moved sixteen miles away to the county seat of Algona, he remained in charge of the land he'd purchased a half-century earlier.

Even after diabetes took half of his first leg in 1950, he went everywhere crutches would take him. That didn't include his corn and bean fields, and the cattle yard was verboten. My mother and Aunt Frances acquiesced to his walking through the hog house if the cement floor was clean. Well, farmer clean.

Two years after that surgery, the diabetes broke into a gallop, sending him to bed back on his beloved farm. Aunt Frances the daughter became Aunt Frances the nurse, and her sewing room off the parlor, his hospital room. Until he died, he called the shots from there.

I think I loved my grandpa, but I know I respectfully feared him. And I wondered for months after his funeral how we could have Thanksgiving dinner on the farm without him. Even at my young age, I feared tampering with our sacred ritual of sameness.

After Thanksgiving Mass in St. Joe — which was too small to even be called a village — Grandpa would drive out to the big, square, white farmhouse with its exciting wraparound porch. The pumpkin pies — half a cup of butter and half a cup of lard per every two crusts and handle the dough as little as possible — had been baked the day before. Cholesterol be damned, I still use that recipe. On Wednesday evening, Aunt Frances would extend the dining room table to accommodate sixteen, then cover it with her fine linen tablecloth. "Someday when you have a house of your own," my mother always said, "I'll give you my Irish linen tablecloth. It's like Frances's so whenever you wash it, you'll have to sprinkle it, roll it up, and keep it inside a plastic bag for a day. And it'll take more than an hour to iron."

I wasn't sure she should be telling me this.

Thanksgiving morning, my cousin — 4-H trained — set the table properly with fine china and good silverware — salad and dinner forks, knife, and both spoons placed exactly one inch from the edge of the table. Around eleven, relatives began pulling into the yard. The farmers, and the generation of older boys who would one day replace them in the fields, settled in the parlor to talk — okay, to argue — shorthorns and weather and what a bushel of corn should bring. Just before noon, one of the girls slipped out of the kitchen to announce the turkey had been carved and the gravy whisked. Final tasks. Trumpets heralding the meal.

Grandpa took his place at the head of the table, followed by the men — none in bibs this day. Then the older boys — none in blue jeans this day. When the last seat at the table was claimed, the younger boys stepped back. They'd have to wait for the second round, eating with the women and girls, who were quietly filing into the dining room for the prayer before the meal.

Recited in unison:

Bless-us-oh-Lord-and-these-thy-gifts-which-we-are-about-to-receive-from-thy-bounty-through-Christ-our-Lord-Amen.

You did not pause between the words. Then began the passing of platters and bowls until each plate disappeared under piping-hot mounds of hand-mashed potatoes, green beans and corn, cranberries, turkey, stuffing, and gravy. Salad plates held pickled beets, sweet pickles, olives (special occasion treats), and Jell-O. Strawberry Jell-O with shredded carrots or lime Jell-O with crushed pineapple. Oh, and white bread with yellow oleomargarine, which tasted way better than butter because it was new. (In the beginning margarine was almost, but not quite, white. For a long while, manufacturers were not allowed to add yellow coloring agents, the dairy industry's hope being that a bland-looking margarine spread would send consumers scurrying back to bright-yellow butter.)

The potatoes, green beans, corn, beets, and pickles grew in the women's gardens. By October, chest freezers were full-up with beans, corn, and butchered chickens, cut up and packed tidily in milk cartons. Cellar shelves were stocked with canned Bing cherries, pickled beets, a multitude of pickled cucumbers, tomatoes, pears, peaches, and apricots. The brick walls and cement floor in our closet-sized cellar under the front porch cooled you off on long summer afternoons when the threat of polio kept you away from the pool. Aunt Frances's cellar was dank, with one bare lightbulb and an outside entrance. That place was flat-out scary.

Thanksgiving's main event — tom turkey — didn't come from the farm, however. Grandpa raised corn-fed purebred shorthorns, keeping the heifers for breeding stock, selling some of the bull calves, castrating others and feeding them out as steers to butcher for the family. And he raised Poland China hogs — big and fat. Fat was good.

While Aunt Frances raised chickens, she never gave a thought to keeping black-feathered turkeys, which, incidentally, grew up without hormones and steroids. So like most farm families in the area, they bought a frozen turkey from the locker in town until grocery stores began installing their own freezer cases.

The son-in-law, Uncle Frank, succeeded Grandpa at the head of the Thanksgiving table. And with his and subsequent generations came changes, large and small. Field horses of Frank's youth gave way to tractors; running water and electricity became commonplace. Uncle Frank bought yearlings weighing six to seven hundred pounds and ran them up to about twelve hundred pounds before selling them to packing plants in Fort Dodge and Estherville. And his hogs were crossbreeds. Grandpa had raised field corn, oats, hay, and pasture. With Frank, it was corn, beans, hay, and to a lesser extent, pasture. As new generations marched across the land, oats disappeared; combines meant no more picking corn by hand. Equipment was bigger, fancier, more expensive — amazing machines that did it all. And then technology showed up. Everywhere.

Small in stature compared with Henry, Frank finished eighth grade. After that, no need for schooling what with corn and beans to plant, cultivate, and harvest; animals to raise to slaughter; machinery to repair; silage to put up; and the commodities market to play. I thought my uncle *always* sold high until a cousin pointed out that he simply didn't talk about it when he sold low. Same with the ponies at Ak-Sar-Ben. You always knew when Frank had a winning ticket.

Different from Henry, yes, but Frank was just as German, with an accent so thick you needed a butcher knife to cut it. Interesting, since neither man had ever been in Germany.

Thanksgiving still started with morning Mass in St. Joe. The table still spanned the length of the dining room. It was still set properly, and the tablecloth still took an hour to iron. Around eleven, relatives — including young ones who never knew Grandpa Henry — began pulling into the yard. The men settled in the parlor to argue about shorthorns and the weather and what a bushel of corn was bringing. Most of the older boys joined them, but not all of them. Not the ones who already knew they wouldn't be farming. Just before noon, one of the girls would slip out of the kitchen to say the turkey had been carved and the gravy whisked.

Over the years, slowly, and surely without a game plan, the kitchen women tampered with the menu. Replacing canned green beans from the garden with cans of French-style green beans from Del Monte. They'd mix the fancy beans with milk, mushroom soup, and soy sauce (so oriental). The beans tasted better than plain old garden green beans because of those French-fried onions. Instead of canning the garden sweet corn, they were freezing it — sometimes in whipping cream. Whoa! Warm dinner rolls replaced passé white loaves of Colonial bread, although the jam still started out as strawberries from my mother's patch. And they added iceberg lettuce with French dressing. How'd we miss the fact that there were zero nutrients in a head of iceberg lettuce?

Being midwestern, we still passed the staples: strawberry Jell-O with shredded carrots, lime Jell-O with crushed pineapple, and occasionally, orange Jell-O with miniature marshmallows. Then one year my mother's bowl of Jell-O deviated from the family norms. Majorly. Cherry Jell-O with little white balls suspended throughout. The bowl joined the endless procession, following the potatoes and gravy and corn around the table. The procession stopped abruptly when somebody handed the bowl to Jerry, who looked into the shimmering maroon to wonder at those little white balls. "What the hell is in this Jell-O?" he asked.

"Jerry, hush!" his wife said.

"No, really, what's in this Jell-O? Who made Jell-O with white balls?"

"Jerry, hush!"

"I did," my mother leaned forward. "From a recipe in *Better Homes and Gardens*. You soften some cream cheese and make little balls out of it with a melon-ball scoop. I had to go clear back to Hy-Vee just to get one of those scoops."

"Your magazine said to put cream cheese in the Jell-O? You are kidding, Irene."

"Jerry! Hush!"

"Yes," my mother replied. "I think you'll like it. My bridge club did."

And so did Jerry because, by this time, my mother had become the matriarch of our extended family. That's probably why she and the other women her age were finally eating with the men.

Once you sit the women with the men, there's no stopping parameter-shifting. Changes didn't follow in a predictable manner, nor with uniformly acceptable outcomes. I attributed most of that to postsecondary education, with young adults heading off in droves beginning in the sixties. They listened to professors urging, "Think outside the box," and the next logical step was personalized dance cards filled with crisp, new thoughts and mighty challenges, with righteous dissent and proclamations that teetered on the edge. Still, every Thanksgiving Day during college and beyond, the drive from Webster City to the farm was a journey back into a cocoon quilted with the silken threads of family and familiarity.

The men in the parlor, arguing about chisel plowing and farm subsidies and crop sharing until someone — still a female — announced the turkey was carved and the gravy whisked. Last tasks. Trumpets announcing the meal.

These days, little kids were served first in the kitchen. Then followed the procession of platters and bowls until each plate disappeared under piping-hot mounds of food, mostly homemade, sometimes homegrown. One year a cousin brought sweet potatoes smothered in marshmallows. The consensus? Marshmallows belong in Jell-O and s'mores. Another time an aunt brought coleslaw with fruit in it. The consensus? Fruit should be next to coleslaw, not in it.

What was turning our Thanksgivings spicy were the discussions, not the food. When Aunt Frances asked if anybody had read *The Godfather*, I said I'd not only read it but had seen the movie and wasn't Mario Puzo one powerful author. All conversation at our end of the table skidded to a stop. "Mary Kay," Aunt Frances said finally, and quite slowly, "I cannot believe you read that book. It was absolutely filthy. Just trash."

"Oh, Aunt Frances. Um, did you read it or just hear about it?"

"I read the first twenty pages; then I went out behind the chicken coop and burned it in the trash barrel."

I wondered if it had been hardcover or paperback.

Assassinations, integration (or not), hippies and Woodstock, a war on the other side of the world in a millenniums-old country most of us had only recently heard of — great table topics if you like to get all riled up. Some of us liked to and most of us did. Until the farm crisis of the 1980s, the sizzler was the post–Vatican II changes slowly manifesting their presence inside the quaintly small, visually joyful churches of rural north-central Iowa.

First it was, "Did you know, in St. Joe, dey are turning dat altar around so Fr. Schumacher has to face the people? What was wrong with looking at his back? Dat's how it's always been done. Dat church is damn near a hundred years old and now we got to turn around an altar."

Then it was, "Did you know dat last Sunday dey had a woman reading the Epistle? A woman!"

Finally, it was, "Dis can't be. I heard women are going to serve communion."

A thunderous silence sliced through the dining room. "I said dey are going to let women give out communion. Dat's not right. Goddamn it."

Silence.

"Dat is wrong. Dat is flat-out wrong." A fist pounds the table, the German gesture for inherent egregiousness. "I tell you, if dey let women serve communion, I ain't going back to church. I don't give a fu—

"I don't give a goddamnn."

More pounding, dangerously close to the china.

When I was twenty-four years old, I brought a young man with me to the Thanksgiving table. He wasn't Catholic and although he'd heard the prayer before meals at my parents' house, he didn't recognize the cousins' version. The extended family had, long before, received a heads-up that this guy was a Protestant. Actually, a member of the Disciples of Christ church, although Protestant sufficed. A year later, when we announced we were to marry, they were happy. If you're a quarter of a century old and unmarried, a Protestant is better than nothing at all.

My favorite picture in our wedding album remains Aunt Frances pouring punch.

By the time she died ten years later, young marrieds were splitting Thanksgiving dinners between his family one year, hers the next. (Not everybody lived within shouting distance anymore.) Next-generation cousins moved the holiday out of the big, square white farmhouse — now on a paved road — to their farms. More acres, more cattle in the yards, more hogs in the lot, but no more chickens to butcher. "Butchering chickens," by the way, is pabulum talk for slapping the bird's neck down on a flat-topped tree stump by the grove and whacking its head off with an ax. Nobody tells you that, afterward, the bird chases you around the yard. Ichabod Crane's Headless Horseman nemesis. Far worse than Freddy Krueger, that villain from *A Nightmare on Elm Street*.

Come Thanksgiving, those nearby still gather. No matter whose house, the menu remains constant, although store-bought stuff now slips into some of those bowls wending their way around the table. But one unspoken kitchen missive remains: no store-bought pies. One year, with my mother in her eighties and Aunt Frances gone, I decided I'd make a cherry pie. How hard could it be? Pie filling in a can couldn't count as store-bought if you made the crust.

The night before I gingerly mixed the lard, butter, and flour together with my fingers, being Aunt-Frances careful not to over-handle it. Good advice, but when it's your first piecrust, when is too much too much? Not knowing, at some point I just stopped handling it, added the lemon juice, beaten egg, and water, rolled out pastry for the bottom crust, and placed it gingerly in the pie pan. It looked pretty rough, but once I dumped in the filling, who'd know?

More carefully now, I rolled out the remaining pastry. Three times. The minute a semblance of circle appeared, I placed the pastry even more gingerly atop the filling. It pretty much covered everything. Still, realizing you can't pinch top and bottom pastries together unless they touch, I took some leftover dough away from the kids and cobbled a top together.

The fluting didn't work so well, either.

That Thanksgiving morning, I quietly slipped the pie in amongst the others on the sideboard. When one of the boys walked past for a look-see, he turned to his cousin and said, "Wow, looks like somebody dropped that pie."

So, at one point, I had brought home that Protestant. A generation later, our older daughter brought home a California boy who doesn't own a single drop of Caucasian blood. His Japanese-Mexican-Filipino heritage gifts him with shining black eyes, thick hair the color of midnight, and a hue that causes strangers to ask what tribe he's from. Navajo? Cherokee? As far as I'm concerned, such traits upgrade the family bloodline.

A couple of years after their wedding on a cliff by the ocean, we joined our new extended family at our daughter and son-in-law's home in Los Angeles for Thanksgiving. The adults gathered around the rich cherrywood table that had been my mother's. She'd needlepointed the deep-burgundy, purple, and rose chair cushions. She'd purchased the bone china on a family trip to Canada with the cousins half a century earlier. Once again, the platters and bowls offered up (real) mashed potatoes, green beans still topped with French-fried onions, corn casseroles, cranberries boiled in pomegranate juice, turkey, cornbread stuffing with sausage and apples straight from www.thepioneerwoman. com and not-too-lumpy gravy.

And tiny Filipino *lumpia* stuffed with ground pork, deep-fat-fried, and passed with sweet chili sauce.

And rice from the steamer, zested up with soy sauce. "You eat it like mashed potatoes," our daughter said, "so put gravy on your potatoes and your rice."

And tamales made from corn masa, filled with chilies and cheese, then wrapped in cornhusks and steamed.

Our daughter gets up before dawn on Thanksgiving, forgoing the Macy's parade for serious pie making. "It's an all-butter crust, Mom. I don't know where you find lard in the grocery store."

Plus the dough emerges from a food processor. What would Aunt Frances say!?

The chocolate pecan and Dutch apple pies are made from scratch. Pumpkin still comes from a can, but there's whiskey in the whipped-cream topping. "I never ask anyone to bring pie because I know they'd go to Marie Callender's," she says. "Right there, that would ruin Thanksgiving."

Thanksgiving Stuffing with Cast-Iron Skillet Corn Bread

Makes 10 servings

This is a two-part recipe, adapted from the Pioneer Woman website. It makes one 9 by 13-inch pan of stuffing. Start the day before. Make the corn bread first, and while it is baking, cut the French bread (from the second recipe) into cubes. Both breads should dry out overnight.

CAST-IRON SKILLET CORN BREAD

1 ¼ cups coarsely ground yellow cornmeal
¾ cup all-purpose flour
2 tablespoons sugar
1 teaspoon kosher salt
1 tablespoon baking powder
½ teaspoon baking soda
1 cup buttermilk
⅓ cup whole milk
2 eggs, lightly beaten
1 stick unsalted butter, melted

Preheat the oven to 450 degrees and place a 9-inch cast-iron skillet inside to heat while you prepare the batter.

In a large bowl, mix together the cornmeal, flour, sugar, salt, baking powder, and baking soda. Whisk in the buttermilk, milk, and beaten eggs.

Whisk in almost all of the melted butter, reserving 1 tablespoon for greasing the skillet later.

Remove the hot skillet from the oven and lower the temperature to 375 degrees. Coat the bottom and sides of the skillet with the reserved tablespoon of butter.

Pour the batter into the skillet and bake in the center of the oven for 20 to 25 minutes. Test with a toothpick inserted into the center, making sure it is firm and the edges are crispy.

Cool completely. Cut into 1-inch cubes, spread them out on a baking sheet, and let them dry out overnight.

STUFFING

1 stick butter
1 medium onion, diced
2 cups celery, chopped
1/2 teaspoon dried basil
1/2 teaspoon ground thyme
2 teaspoons fresh rosemary, chopped
1/3 cup parsley, chopped
4 cups low-sodium chicken broth
1 loaf crusty French bread, about 10 ounces, cut into 1-inch cubes
    and left out on a baking sheet overnight
1 recipe skillet corn bread (above), cut into 1-inch cubes and dried
    out overnight
Scant teaspoon kosher salt

Warm up a large skillet over medium heat and melt the stick of butter. Sauté the onion and celery for a few minutes until onions are almost translucent.

Add basil, thyme, rosemary and parsley. Add chicken broth and bring to a boil. Stir until combined.

Place all of the dried bread cubes into a bowl and mix them up a bit. Gradually ladle the broth mixture onto the bread, tossing lightly as you go. Gradually add more of the broth mixture, adding salt as you go and tasting. You don't want to over salt your stuffing. If the mixture is not moist enough, add a bit more chicken broth and stir.

Place in a 9 by 13-inch baking dish and bake at 350 degrees until golden brown on top, about 35 to 40 minutes.

A Full Belly

Nearly all of us have memories of some tavern we visited. Curved leather booths drew you in. Cocktails, steaks, fried shrimp, and delicious fried walleye dinners made you stay all night. Flick learned that nothing shows the stuff of a small city more quickly than the five-thirty tavern. Much of what people do and believe and share is evident there.

The Tam-O-Shanter, Lincoln, Nebraska

Sherrie Flick

When I moved to Lincoln, Nebraska, in the summer of 1994, it's safe to say I had no idea what I was doing. I had been living in the Lower Haight district of San Francisco for five years and hadn't really traveled from the Bay Area much in the last two. It's not that I assumed everyone could buy organic tofu and fresh beet-carrot-ginger juice at the corner market — but.

In Nebraska, I reasoned, I would meet cowboys and eat grilled cheese sandwiches. I would score amazing thrift store deals. I moved there not knowing a soul. I had forgotten, it seems, about the conservative nature of the middle. About the overarching, passed-over reality of the plains. This was before Facebook! Before e-mail! (I wouldn't have my first dial-up connection until 1996.) Before cell phones and Google. I sent postcards to my friends on the coasts, and it took a long time to get one in return. I faced how alone the middle could feel. I felt empathy for the pioneers.

Relocating to Lincoln was, as one West Coast friend suggested at

Sherrie Flick is author of the novel *Reconsidering Happiness* (University of Nebraska Press Flyover Fiction series), which was a semifinalist for the VCU Cabell First Novelist Award, and the flash fiction chapbook *I Call This Flirting* (Flume). Her work appears in many literary journals and anthologies, including the Norton anthologies *Flash Fiction Forward* and *New Sudden Fiction* and *The Rose Metal Press Field Guide to Writing Flash Fiction*. She has been granted fellowships from the Sewanee Writers' Conference, Ucross Foundation, Atlantic Center for the Arts, and Pennsylvania Council on the Arts. She teaches in Chatham University's MFA and food studies programs. Her blog *Sentences and Food* chronicles the food she makes and the artists who eat at her house.

the time, "like deciding to move to Mars." Back in San Francisco, at Sally's Bakery where I worked, some of my fellow bakers consistently confused Alaska and Nebraska — saying things like, "Maybe you'll get to see a polar bear!"

I would patiently reply, "No, Nebraska. Nebraska, the one in the middle? It's landlocked and kind of rectangular with a little knob on the left-hand side that pats Colorado on the head?"

And they'd say, "Tell me again why you're going there?"

There were other alienating details. My previous jobs had always been connected to food — baked goods in particular — first in New Hampshire and then California. This relocation signaled the first time I had to define myself solely as a fiction writer. The first time I couldn't cling to flour and yeast for easy definition. I had to step forward with words, and I found this identity difficult to slip on.

Two things happened to make the Midwest mine. I met Billy, who took me to the Tam-O-Shanter Restaurant and Pub. Billy was an artist and photographer who worked as a chef in Lincoln, outside of academia, although not outside of intellectual conversation. His was conversation mixed with food — something I was used to.

Fancy food and bar food, our life together was centered on eating. Billy cooked for me, and I cooked for him. We became friends in that way that two single people in their late twenties who are sick of relationships become friends. Fast friends who make phone calls in the middle of the night, who meet for breakfast with mussed hair; friends who drive to the farmers' market at 6:00 a.m. to buy sunflower sprouts or, alternately, drink until 6:00 a.m. talking about messed-up shit. Good friends.

The first time I went to the Tam-O-Shanter — a nondescript hunch of a building on the far end of O Street with a curved red roof and newspaper boxes to the left of the front door — it was in the middle of the afternoon. A blazing Nebraskan summer day, when the sun scorches through your eyeballs to touch the tips of your toes. Take-your-breath-away-you-think-you-understand-hot-after-working-as-a-baker heat. It was boiling, and Billy had called and left instructions on my answering machine to meet him there for lunch.

When you stepped inside the Tam-O-Shanter, it was dim. 1970s dim. And because of that, cool in a variety of ways. The walls had a fine sheen of red shag carpet, and the curved leather booths by the bar snuggled people in and made regular old conversations seem important and mysterious. The imitation crystal chandeliers glittering in the corners gave off a subtle, ineffective shine while cushy black Naugahyde bar stools lined up with slender wooden legs in front of the main bar. A "Warm Nuts" machine rested on its counter — salted cashews, almonds, and peanuts gathered in tidy trays, warmed by an overhead bulb. There was a slippery quality to the air — dark and moist. Entering the Tam-O-Shanter felt like traveling underground. The overlarge door handles at the entrance made it seem part medieval castle, part Mafia den. The pebbled-pressed concrete exterior did not give away the interior's secrets. You couldn't possibly know the Tam-O-Shanter unless you'd been inside, stepped through the red door with the tiny sign that read: entrance. They served crisp, perfectly fried foods and offered a tiny steak dinner that everyone loved, called the Tammy. The no-nonsense bartenders there made stiff drinks, served in a wide array of appropriately sized glasses. The entire mystique of the place made you want to simultaneously eat French fries, drink a martini, and confess your innermost secrets to your friend. The Tam-O-Shanter showed me something that I couldn't yet articulate that afternoon. It showed me a way through to a simple savoring of the undiscovered.

This is the story of finding my place in the Midwest through a dimly lit bar.

The first day I met Billy at the Tam-O-Shanter was the first and last time I sat in the dining area off to the right of the hostess station. I pushed through the heavy front door, through the vestibule door, and then blinked and squinted my way to him, already seated by the shuttered windows. Billy with his dark, wavy, Latino hair and black-framed glasses. Billy with his wrinkled white button-down shirt, sleeves rolled to his elbows, with his pursed lips, quick to smile as I told a story. Workers surrounded us, people who did things — measurable things like pounding nails, like driving trucks. A small TV blinked the day's news in the corner.

The world of the mind was — and still is — intimidating to me. I'd spent my childhood in a small, industrial turning postindustrial, steel town. People worked shifts, and they worked — labored — hard each day with their bodies. They did this until they were laid off, and then they turned to drinking and complaining with the same physical intensity at corner bars and local diners.

My father wasn't a millworker. He was — is — a life insurance salesman. We lived in a nice house, in a nice neighborhood — located on a hill above the tiny, gritty city. I descended with my pals to eat D&G pizza and drink coffee at Eat'n Park restaurant, the Rust Belt work ethic seeping into my bones.

Our high school teachers encouraged us to become engineers or to pursue degrees in business. It was maniacal, this push. And so I came to believe work was associated with labor — with numbers and formulas and the body pushing things around. Touching things, not pondering, led to success. And perhaps this is why baking appealed to me, why I applied for a counter position in a French bakery once I started college. Soon thereafter I took a job as one of two bread bakers at another bakery in the small New England town I'd escaped to. Waking up at midnight to begin a shift, rolling out loaves of oatmeal molasses and anadama bread. It seemed like the right way to work my way through an English literature degree.

And yet, there I was, five years after receiving my BA, applying to graduate school and then suddenly in graduate school with my department paying my way for a master's degree in English literature with a thesis in fiction. I felt like a sham, a pretend intellectual. I baked baguettes for my fiction workshop. Cooked elaborate dinners for myself. Taught the women writers in my department how to properly bank a pool ball. Wrote an explosion of short stories trying to capture the space and sounds of this new place.

The place of Nebraska — its expanse — caused a slow hysteria to build in me. The sky never ended, and it seemed that one day it would just up and swallow me if I wasn't careful. The mournful sound of trains hooting their horns, reaching out over hundreds of miles, broke my heart. The constant wind followed after me, as I walked cautiously in my (ironically purchased) cowboy boots. I nestled my black-framed glasses securely on the bridge of my nose. I hesitated. I hesitated. I peeked at this flat world, could it really do me in?

One of the keys to Tam-O-Shanter's siren pull was that it didn't judge anyone. It just stood steady in itself while patrons, who did not gawk or pose, came to eat there. They slid into the curved booths wearing their unironic western snap shirts. They walked past the shag-carpeted walls on their way to the bathrooms with pink neon signs above each door announcing "ladies" and "men." I rarely heard anyone say, "This is so cool." But it was.

Billy and I sat that day in the dining room, hunched over our food, talking about movies, books, art, the failed catastrophe of a date from the previous weekend who *would not stop calling*. I remember the outside world cut off entirely behind thick shutters that kept the long rectangle of a room from both sunlight and heat — and in this way kept out any reality too. This instant timelessness — like a cloak of invisibility — descended like a gentle mist of the Prozac everyone in the English Department seemed to be taking at the time. I remember thinking, "A person could get lost in here." Billy there across from me, smiling his warm, curious smile, digging into a steak, chewing through our discussion, stabbing his knife at the air to make a point. Saying, "You are ridiculous." And, "There is no way you said that to him." And we were alone there in that crowded room. Alone with ourselves, and this moment let me take a breath.

The servers and bartenders wore black pants and white button-up shirts. This prim contrast to its bland concrete exterior added to the Tam-O-Shanter's otherworldly nature. Years later when I asked my husband to describe the Tam, he said, "It's a bar with blue-collar food and country club service." And it's true. We disagreed, however, about where we traditionally sat. I said in the booth across from the bar, where we could be by ourselves but still talk with the bartenders. He said at the bar itself, on the corner stools under the brass overhang of the glass rack, where we sat and talked to the bartenders. And the truth is, we're both probably right. We spent a lot of nights hiding out there. When I first met my future husband, Rick, not only did Billy (who didn't approve of anyone) approve of him, Rick also already knew of the Tam-O-Shanter. Not in an oh-that's-so-retro-and-hip kind of way, but more like — yes, let's drink some whiskey. I want to get a drink with you and talk.

There was an authentic-ness to Rick that the hipster guys I had dated for years lacked. Rick didn't have a gigantic record collection back at his apartment, and he didn't sport ironic sideburns. His first present to me was a newly bought bread knife, because he noticed I needed one. It was a practical present — and sweetly thought out, since he knew I still liked to bake bread.

Rick is, like the Tam-O-Shanter, a born-and-bred Nebraskan. He grew up in that flat world that was bothering me so much. His slow, one-fingered nod of a hello while driving showed that. He had an earnest, unforced curiosity and said "sack" instead of "bag" at the grocery store. Perhaps in some way, finding this bar led me to him. I'll never know, but it definitely had a part in our courtship, such a big part that we sent a wedding announcement to the Tam when we decided to tie the knot. It hung on the speckled backbar mirror for some time, to the left of the hulking metal cash register.

I had spent my formative years floating in the wake of Reaganomics, embracing an alternative, Gen X worldview where "selling out" was the biggest mistake one could make. Bands sold out when they signed with a major label. A person could sell out by taking a job with a 401K or by turning from thrift store scores to buying new at J. Crew. I was of this generation that had, instead of dealing with mainstream culture and an administration's priorities we couldn't understand, gone underground for our music and our zines and our humor and our jobs. I dropped out, got into my car, and drove from one coast to another — took time off to explore the crazy mix of small-town and big-city worlds that made up America. Like my peers, I carefully honed my cool-restaurant- and motel-finding skills; I had a practiced competitive eye for sifting through a rack to find excellent vintage dresses and sweaters. Those cowboy boots that I mentioned earlier that I rarely took off in those days were not dug up from the dusty bins of Lincoln but found in a vintage shop in the Castro. The coasts were, for lack of a better term, competitive in their living skills. Coming to live in Nebraska let the air out of something I once held dear. In Lincoln, I would clutch a trio of vintage Le Creuset ware to my chest and scurry to the register like a football player breaking tackles. But no one was really fighting me for the pans. My score was personal. I wanted the pans, yes, but buying them gained me no clout. Nebraska taught me that I could slow down, take my time.

The Tam-O-Shanter was the kind of bar, if someone had discovered it on a side street in San Francisco, they would try to swear friends to secrecy in order to keep its luscious, privileged purity to themselves. Located at Twenty-Fifth and O Street, it squared itself off in the corner of a crowded parking lot near the less appealing section of town, away from the college bars and the crazy university drinking scene. It was also not near the places where most of my fellow graduate students and professors gossiped and talked shop. It was, as we liked to say then in our theory classes, "other."

I settled myself in my seat that afternoon, the air shushing out of its black cushion as I fingered the paper placemat, the cloth napkin. Billy had ordered a Tammy. I ordered a grilled cheese and steak fries. When my sandwich came, the stiff planks of white bread were buttered and golden, a thin line of orange cheese melting out the sides. Later, this order would turn to onion rings with a side of ranch dressing or the walleye or fried shrimp dinner with a baked potato, served with a roll and thin pats of butter, each pressed onto its own white paper square, topped with a translucent covering. We each had a beer, probably a crisp, clear Miller High Life, and when we shoved open the glass door to re-enter the world, it was startling to me that daylight still existed.

Tam O' Shanter — with a tiny pom-pommed hat poised atop the cursive *T*, with a single right-facing quotation mark following the *O*. A subtitle read in cursive, "Restaurant and Pub," two generic golf clubs crossed in the empty space to the right. No golf course in sight. Who knows how the place got its name — but it stood there, not calling out for anyone to join in or sell out, just to stop by when you had a chance to escape and wanted a strong drink or perfectly deep-fried nuggets of bar food. No pretensions. No looking over your shoulder to see who else was in the bar, to see what you could and could not say. No whispering. No theory. No judgment.

Here I drank my first Rusty Nail. Drambuie and scotch in a tiny rocks glass, sitting on a cushioned stool at the bar with Rick. Even still, when I order that drink I think of flat, cold lands. I think of fields and their ocean-like rustling, calling me out on myself, letting me let myself back in.

The author reveals a connection and intimacy to the agrarian life that only a farm kid could know. From watching the dual labors of field work and kitchen chores, he asserts that the constant job of bringing a meal together is the hardest.

What Was Served

Douglas Bauer

Our farmhouse sat atop a slight rise in the middle of the acreage. The land, as lawn, sloped away from the foundation and flattened out in all directions until it reached the surrounding corn and soybean fields, then continued extremely into the four distances. A wide, pillared porch wrapped around the north and east sides of the house. As a boy, during the summer months, I sometimes sat for a time on the east porch railing and, if my father and grandfather Bauer happened to be working in the field that was my view, I looked out to watch the two of them on their tractors moving the day's tending implements along the Iowa horizon.

And if the hour were any time from midmorning till noon, I could also look, from that same perch on the porch, just to my right and through the screen door into our kitchen. There my mother was moving about

---

Douglas Bauer was raised on a small family farm in central Iowa. He has written many articles and essays and two books about that place and that life. His novels are *Dexterity*, *The Very Air*, and *The Book of Famous Iowans*. He's also written two nonfiction books, *Prairie City, Iowa* and *The Stuff of Fiction*, and has edited two anthologies, *Prime Times: Writers on Their Favorite Television Shows* and *Death by Pad Thai and Other Unforgettable Meals*. His stories, essays, and reviews have appeared in *Esquire*, the *New York Times Magazine*, the *New York Times Book Review*, *Atlantic*, *Harper's*, *Sports Illustrated*, *Tin House*, *Agni*, and many other magazines. He's received grants in both fiction and creative nonfiction from the National Endowment for the Arts. He divides his time between rural Vermont, where he's a professor of literature at Bennington College, and Boston, where he's thinking of growing cherry tomatoes in pots on his terrace this summer.

the big floral-patterned-wallpapered room, frequently glancing herself out the windows that gave to that same east field to see where the men were. There was a clock mounted on the wall above the refrigerator, but their location was the way she told the time.

Thinking back, I concoct a daily synchrony: my father and grandfather, out there at their work; my mother just inside, busy at hers. The tractors inching along at an almost imperceptible pace, their sounds made soundless by their distance from the house, and my mother close by in the kitchen, all bustle and noise. The sharp metallic clang of a spoon against a pot, stovetop burners rattling, oven door opening and thudding shut. And woven through it all, the voices from the radio that sat atop the refrigerator. The absentminded mumbles of Arthur Godfrey. "The real-life drama of Helen Trent, who . . . fights bravely, successfully, to prove what so many women long to prove, that because a woman is thirty-five or more, romance in life need not be over." In truth I don't recall if Helen Trent's romantic travails happened in the morning or the afternoon, and I've no idea if my mother, a woman living through her thirties at the time of which I write, brought irony or escape or some sort of identification to her interest as she listened. But she listened.

Surely my memory exaggerates the nature of the dual labors I've described, both the agrarian stateliness of machinery silently progressing and the short-order-cook urgency audible through the screen. Still, this *is* how I remember them and what lingers within it is the impression that of the two, my mother's work was the harder and more manual.

The full, hot midday meal she prepared every day but Sunday from the first field work in spring to the end of autumn harvest was called *dinner* (which, obviously enough, made the only slightly less ambitious evening meal *supper*). And what was typically for dinner? Maybe a roast of pork or beef with mashed potatoes and brown gravy. Maybe a baked ham with her signature potato salad — its secret, she claimed, substituting Miracle Whip for mayonnaise; go figure. Maybe beef and homemade egg noodles, or beef stew with carrots and potatoes and onions, the noodle or stew beef simmering in the pressure cooker through the morning.

But for my purposes here I can order anything I want from that summer dinner menu, so I choose my favorite childhood dish — creamed chicken and biscuits. The chicken (until quite recently squawking clue-lessly in the henhouse a hundred yards from the kitchen door) was cut into pieces, which were skinned, poached in broth, and removed to cool, then their meat pulled from the bone into loosely shredded strips. Next, cream was slowly stirred into the broth, making a kind of ambrosial prairie velouté. Finally the strips of chicken were returned to the pot, salt and pepper were added to season, and it was brought to the table to be ladled over baking-powder biscuits and mounds of mashed potatoes.

Can you fathom the gustatory insult of calling such meals — and oh, yes, most every day a baked dessert, often a fruit pie — *lunch*? Neither can I.

I said I sensed my mother's work to be one of mounting manual effort and this impression had a lot to do with her usual mood as she brought the meal together. I can best describe it as a preoccupied brooding of varying strength, sometimes seeming nothing more than her need to hurry, to have everything ready (to make the men wait to eat was to cost them precious field time); often something palpably more layered than that; and always suggesting she was deep in her own world and not all that pleased to be there. I'm confident I can say that she often felt besieged by the terms of her farmwife life and that this feeling steadily intensified, like something heating on the stove, as she cooked through the morning.

I don't believe she felt uniquely put upon. She knew her domestic chores were entirely typical of the place and the times. In fact, she knew that they were fewer than those of many women married to farmers, women who frequently shared the field work with their husbands. And she very much liked being known as a good cook, especially for the things she made especially well. Oatmeal cookies, for one, crisp flat ovals that might better be called the Joy of Butter. And that potato salad for another. No matter where you stand on Miracle Whip, my mother's potato salad was incredibly good, owing, *I* think, as I taste it in my mind, to the indulgent quantity of chopped eggs and the exactly right measurement of chopped onions — just letting you know they're there — blended in.

Instead, I suspect that sense of burden as she moved about the kitchen was brought on in great part by her knowing that the considerable meal she was in the act of making would be followed, after a brief pause, by the need to begin making another one — supper. I suspect much else that frustrated her was neatly symbolized in that.

This sense she had of her days as a farm kitchen version of the *Woman in the Dunes* never really left her, even decades after my father had sold the farm and spent his time puttering and tinkering in the garage and, as often as not, came into the house around noon to make himself a sandwich: *lunch*. I remember her predictably complaining about her three young grandsons, my brother's sons, devouring those addictive oatmeal cookies, which she'd baked for their visit. Peering into the big cookie jar, shaking her head, and making her patented "Tsk!" sound with her tongue against her teeth, she would say, not happily, "I just made these this morning and they're already gone." What she saw in the almost instantly empty jar was not the pleasure her food gave her grandsons but rather that she must now make more of it.

It was noon, maybe fifteen minutes past, when my father and grandfather brought their tractors to a stop. They got down from their seats to unhook the plows or discs or whatever they were pulling, then climbed back up and turned in the direction of the house. It was as if the kitchen's summoning smells had escaped through the open windows into the thick summer heat and moved on like a kind of aromatic weather front until they reached my father and grandfather.

At that age — nine, ten, even eleven — I was beguiled by the world of early television cowboys. (I once asked my fifth-grade teacher to call me by the surname Crockett, after Davy, and she gave me, with her, "No," an appropriately impatient frown.) Watching from our porch, I was a cavalry scout alert for any suspicious movement appearing suddenly out there on the far rim of the world and my father and grandfather were a pair of nasty Apaches on horseback pulling hijacked covered wagons.

Seeing them turning and heading in, I alerted the kitchen. "They're coming."

To which my mother replied, "Come set the table," thus ending the fantasy. Cavalry scouts did not set the table.

Inside, I soon began to hear the tractors approaching, their sounds starting faint as rumors and growing as they got closer to the house until they made the loud, raw announcement of their arrival in the barnyard. A minute, two minutes, later, my father, in his blue chambray shirt and darker blue loose-fitting jeans, and my grandfather, in his shirt and pants of matching tan khaki, appeared at the back door, removed their caps, and hung them on hooks. Their protected foreheads looked artificially white, so great was the contrast with the rest of their sun-browned faces. Farmers' tans.

Entering the kitchen, father and son and a life of shared husbandry, they seemed intimately *teamed*. My father was, in his midthirties, a very handsome man. His thick, dark pompadour, of which he was quite proud, was matted down now from his cap and the morning's sweat. He greeted my mother and me and hurried into the small room next to the kitchen to wash up and my grandfather sat down, waiting to go next. His shyness gave him a sweet courtliness, his manner that of a grateful guest. He managed to look fresh no matter how much field dirt powdered his face. It was as if he'd learned from half a century of this work the trick of how to spend hours in the eye of heat and dust without appearing to get any of it on him.

He remarked to my mother that whatever was for dinner smelled awfully good, which was both a compliment and the truth. He was thin, hard-muscled, and walked with a pronounced limp, one hip permanently cocked, from a childhood accident that had made his left leg stiff. It says something about him and how much I loved him that his gait in my memory was a fluidly graceful thing.

Dinner was often the only time I got to see him during the day. He drove in the morning, the sun starting up the sky, from the little house he and my grandmother had built at the edge of the town. I called it "little" — though my child's perspective didn't see it as particularly small — but in fact it was even littler than that; it was as tiny as a cottage in a clearing in a fable. It sat on a large corner lot, so the size of the spot was not the reason for the house's miniature size. Or, as I think about it, probably it was. I suspect the farmer in my grandfather wanted, as much as absolutely possible, to keep the land as land.

The men's hands and faces scrubbed clean and the dishes on the table, we all took our usual chairs, my grandfather on my right, my mother on my left, my father directly across from me. The farm's two worlds of work coming together; my mother's food and the men's, mostly, field talk.

While I ate the portions of a Cather hired hand and listened closely to the work conversation, I was part of neither world. I had my place at the table but no place in the life. I certainly had no thought of learning how to cook and helping my mother prepare the meal. Any wish to participate in the kitchen began and ended with the happy acceptance of a spoon to scrape the smears of batter or frosting from a bowl.

But I wanted keenly to be with the men. Some of my classmates who were farmer's sons, fluent in the language of gearboxes and plow size and yields per acre, had, at what seems to me now a very early age, begun their field lives. Like them, I wanted to be integral, to have a daily assignment.

My problem was twofold. My childhood asthma rendered me seriously allergic to any kind of crop dust. This ruled out helping with the harvest. Also, and all too apparent early on, I brought a stunning lack of talent to every facet of the work — how to read a tilled field, for instance, something as simple as distinguishing where the harrow had passed and where it hadn't; or how to smoothly operate a tractor together with the implement it was pulling. Which ruled out pretty much everything else. Now and then I got to drive a tractor somewhere, to take a wagon from one field to another. That was about the extent of what I could do and be trusted to do.

The closest, then, that I could come to being a farmer was to eat like one.

More creamed chicken would be great.

And another sliver of pie.

And while you adults drink your coffee, a last biscuit with butter and jam. (A kind of farm kitchen petit four.)

Obviously, I don't mean that I ate to pretend I was a farmer, at least not in any conscious way. I mean that I loved the rhythm and the ritual. To sit across from my father and next to my grandfather and listen to them review the morning and plot the afternoon. How cleanly the soil was turning; where were the spots still too wet from recent rains; how the combine was behaving after its repair. I loved dinner, yes, because my mother's food was damned good. But I loved it more for its culinary power to draw my father and grandfather's privately entwined life in from where they lived it.

Eating these hot, heavy meals, and with no opportunity to work off the calories through an afternoon of sweat and whatever effort might be required, and with *supper* still to come, I was a fat boy. Not till adolescence did I begin to lose the weight. Photos of me from my portly days show a lad smiling bravely into the camera. The fourth-grade class photo particularly haunts my memory. I'm sitting cross-legged on the floor in the first row, dressed in an ill-advised plaid shirt and my husky-section jeans, hunched slightly forward, elbows resting on my thighs, and thus posed, the degree to which my shape is perfectly round is quite remarkable.

Finished, we sat digesting all that food while my father and grandfather listened to the radio market report. This went on for what seemed hours, the reader's voice that recognizably midwestern flat, adenoidal twang, droning on and on, quoting the current and futures prices. March soybeans . . . November hogs . . . August wheat. First from the Chicago Mercantile Exchange, then, when you'd thought he was done, from Omaha's, while the farmers at the table listened, sipping coffee, with the silent, rooting concentration I brought to getting the nightly baseball scores. "Um," my father might say. "Huh," my grandfather might add. For all I know there was a scheme proposed and responded to in that.

I understood generally why this market news was vital, which made it no less tedious to listen to. And I think I disliked it not just because it was so deadly boring. I could sense my father and grandfather beginning as they listened to move away from the flavors of the table back into their life.

When at last it was finished, my father looked up at the wall clock. "Well, Dad, what do you say?" And they pushed back their chairs. My grandfather once again thanked my mother and she said, "You're welcome, Dad." I hear her voice in this exchange as undefended and warm and each day freshly pleased, as his thanks was to her. She would tell me years later — when she told me much about the difficult complexities of those years — that she loved him, too, her father-in-law; that she thought he was a kind and lovely man.

I walked with the two of them down the sidewalk, through the gate, and over to their tractors. I helped fill the tanks with gasoline. I placed the crank that started my grandfather's ancient Case in the proper position, below the radiator at the nose of the tractor. Then I stepped away as he stepped in, for I wasn't strong enough to turn it with the necessary force. He assured me the issue wasn't so much strength as getting a feel for the precise leverage. He seemed to take a conjuring moment, then with what I saw as an effortless wrist flick he turned the crank and the tractor woke and belched as if from a huge meal into life.

I watched them mount. My grandfather as always rode sidesaddle, his rod-stiff leg making it impossible for him to sit conventionally. Then the tractors eased away with the rhythmic sashay of horses from the hitching rail. I could imagine them as cowboys and in that way be with them, while the evidence of what they were and I was not was everywhere around me and there was nothing my imagination could do about that.

I waved to them as they headed back out. Picturing it now, I give myself a grand, semaphorical gesture. It's as mawkish a moment in memory's eye as the boy standing in the dusty street waving good-bye to Shane.

Half a century would pass, my father recently having died, when my mother talked to me about those years.

"Your grandfather was the love of your dad's life," she said to me that day she told me, with much else, that she had loved my grandfather, too. "Nobody else, and sure not me, had a chance to get your dad's attention. After Grandpa Bauer died, he retreated more and more into himself. I don't think he ever thought there could be something else to love like he loved his dad. I don't think he ever figured he might want to."

And so, she felt in a vastly different way as much an exile, as excluded from my father and grandfather's world, as I did. My father would have had *his* story, *his* version, of course. But this was hers and it was clear from her tone how completely she believed it. She blamed my grandfather for none of it. Savvy as he was about the work and about the commerce of land, buying and selling a few acres here and there in a lifelong game of farm monopoly, he was as guileless as anyone I've known.

Still, guileless or not, he did, my mother said, strongly urge my father to join him in the life. Yes, I'm sure he loved farming with his son. But that's in part because, unlike his son, he loved farming.

Knowing how she felt, it's little wonder my mother's unhappiness built as the hours of morning passed; as she cooked those marvelous meals; as she brought such generosity to the table sometimes so begrudgingly. In a very real sense, she was feeding her competition in a game she couldn't win. But as a boy, I knew nothing, suspected nothing, of whatever else was being wordlessly passed around the table, what portions and flavors were being shared.

Leaving the barnyard and starting back toward the house, the men and their tractors no longer in view, I assign myself the chore of standing at the sink beside her — a short, pretty woman in her early thirties, wearing what was called a house dress of printed cotton and summer sandals — helping her wash the dishes. It seems only right, given everything she served me, and everything she labored not to.

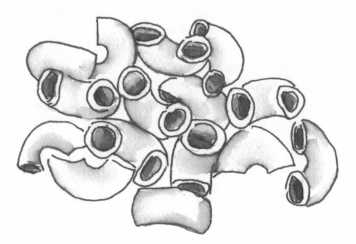

Is there some key linking Chicago's long-established food giant Kraft to the imaginative cuisine being served in places like Grant Achatz's Michelin three-star restaurant Alinea? Did both embrace technology as a means to cook more creatively?

Tomorrowland

Peter Meehan

When I was growing up in River Forest, a Chicago suburb, I ate hot dogs, hamburgers, and (if I was cooking) Kraft Macaroni & Cheese with unrelenting regularity. So it was somewhat of a surprise, even to me, that part of my coming-of-age rebellion involved rejecting my mainly supermarket-supplied culinary upbringing. After I followed my girlfriend, Hannah Clark, to New York, we fed ourselves from our local farmers' market and spent weekends tackling the often complicated and always rewarding kinds of recipes they don't print on box tops. That Hannah's father, Dr. J. Peter Clark, was a food engineer who spent his days designing beef patties for McDonald's and race car–shaped corn chips for Frito-Lay only enhanced our sense of revolt.

But while I was distancing myself from the processed foods of my youth, a style of cooking inspired as much by Kraft as by craft was finding its way into some of the world's best restaurants. Following the lead of forward-thinking chefs like Ferran Adrià (in Spain) and Heston Blumenthal (in England), cooks around the world — those who might have at one time considered science to be a threat to honest-to-goodness food — were embracing technology as a tool to help them cook more creatively. And over the past few years, Chicago has become known

---

Peter Meehan wrote the *New York Times* column $25 and Under. As well, he has four books, all with shared bylines: *Brunch: 100 Recipes from Five Points Restaurant*, with Marc Meyer, *How I Learned to Cook*, with Kimberly Witherspoon, *Momofuku* with David Chang, and *The Frankies Spuntino Kitchen Companion and Cooking Manual*, with Frank Castronovo and Frank Falcinelli.

to many as the North American capital of that movement, thanks in large part to chefs like Homaru Cantu of Moto and Grant Achatz of Alinea.

The fact that my hometown was earning a reputation as a center for avant-garde cooking struck me as more than a coincidence. The city has long been a hub for people, like Hannah's father, who work in the trenches of food technology. Many of the world's largest food manufacturing and food service companies — including Quaker, Sara Lee, McDonald's, and Kraft — are based here, as are the Institute of Food Technologists and the nation's largest regional chapter of the Research Chefs Association, whose members work for both restaurants and food companies. The quiet suburbs that surround the city are home to many high-tech research and development kitchens. I learned from Hannah's father that many of these businesses could trace their presence in Chicago to the vast stockyards that once dominated the city's commercial life and to the readily accessible bounty from nearby farms.

I knew that many respected chefs around the country, and in Chicago, had worked with accredited food scientists — not to produce shelf-stable versions of their namesake salad dressings to sell in supermarkets but to learn how to manipulate food in new ways — and that many of those scientists also consulted for Kraft and other local companies. And I knew that many chefs who cook in this modernist style have used processed foods in their restaurant dishes. I wondered whether there was a causal connection that linked Chicago's long-established industrial food culture to the imaginative cuisine being served in places like Alinea. Did some kind of crossover esprit de corps exist between chefs in pioneering restaurants and those in the processed-food business?

Arguably, the granddaddy of Chicago's food giants is Kraft. The company was started in this city in 1903 by a farm boy named J. L. Kraft, who went on to devise a series of techniques for making processed cheese. Today, Kraft Foods, based in Northfield, Illinois, is one of the world's largest food conglomerates, with $34 billion in annual sales and factories and branch offices in 155 countries. Its products include everything from Kraft Macaroni & Cheese to Oreo cookies. And its research kitchens, in Glenview, a northern suburb, seemed as good a place as any to start my inquiry.

My guide was Harry Crane, an affable sixty-year-old chef who manages Kraft's kitchens. As we walked through his work space, which looks like a series of Corian-countered residential kitchens strung together, Crane told me that he had met some of Chicago's most progressive restaurant chefs through his affiliation with the Research Chefs Association (he's on its executive board). As he described the nature of his work at Kraft, however, it didn't sound very scientific: he and his six-person team test, retest, and refine the simple step-by-step recipes that appear on their products' boxes, bags, bottles, and jars. Their job is to ensure that the instructions are foolproof and yield consistent results. Crane's crew also suggest adjustments to the foods (which are developed at another facility) for improving their taste and texture.

"Say they're reformulating a barbecue sauce, and it's pretty close to being perfect," Crane told me. "They have two or three or four varieties; then we would maybe get involved, taste it, see if it performs the way we want it to." While most of Crane's staff come from a culinary background, they are comfortable with and clearly guided by the methodology of science: one woman, for instance, spends day after day baking frozen pizzas over and over again in ovens of different strengths, determining how many minutes each should be exposed to heat, in which part of the oven it should be cooked, and on what part of the sheet pan it should be placed. Still, there was little science of the test tube variety on display, even in the slightly flashier Kitchen of the Future, a showpiece facility down the block. There I spotted standard induction ranges but none of the high-tech devices that chefs are starting to bring into restaurant kitchens, like immersion circulators (used for sous-vide cooking, a slow-poaching, low-temperature technique) and food extruders (devices that force ingredient mixes into various shapes, like noodles).

When I prodded Crane for evidence of cutting-edge cooking, he told me that most of the hard-core scientific work went on in labs that are off-limits to outsiders for proprietary reasons. And when I asked him for examples in which his background as a trained cook with a knowledge of food science might benefit the products coming out of

Kraft's kitchens, his answer had more to do with taste than with technology. He related a story about precooked bacon. Kraft's scientists had designed a way to package it at the ideal stage of crispness so that customers would only have to heat it in the microwave oven for sixty seconds before eating it: an impressive feat, indeed. "But tons and tons of people were calling and wondering how to cook it in the oven or skillet," he said. "So we tested it, figured out how to do both, and now those directions are on the package." It was an interesting illustration, I thought, of how customers often reject technology when it shatters traditional notions of food and cooking. But is that always the case?

Chef Grant Achatz's restaurant, Alinea, where I'd booked a table that night, occupies a brick building on a busy downtown block of Halsted Street, opposite the Steppenwolf Theater. You enter the dining room through a dark, narrow hallway that conjures images of Willy Wonka's chocolate factory — the Tim Burton version of it, anyway. Achatz, who is thirty-three years old, has spent his life in kitchens: his parents were restaurateurs, and by his early twenties he was a sous-chef to Thomas Keller at the French Laundry in Yountville, California. Everything I'd heard about his food pointed to the inquisitive mind of a cook who has spent years exploring the whys and what-ifs of cooking.

Here I expected to encounter some of the mad-scientist food chemistry — or at least edible evidence of it — I'd been unable to find at the Kraft kitchens, spilling over into the dining room. After all, on his website Achatz refers to PolyScience, a Chicago-area company that manufactures equipment used in large-scale food processing, as a "collaborator." I'd read that he worked with the company to invent what's known as the Anti-Griddle, which freezes food on contact instead of searing it. Indeed, most of the attention Alinea has received has been focused less on the food itself than on Achatz's embrace of novel technology and cooking techniques.

In this regard, Alinea did not disappoint: during my twenty-seven-course meal, I ate single-bite dishes that had the texture of meringue, made without the use of eggs (a trick enabled by methylcellulose, a chemical compound used by food companies to alter textures);

lavender-scented air created with a vaporizer called a Volcano that contributed to the flavor of duck confit; a sliver of dehydrated tuna jerky; foods that went from piping hot to refreshingly cold between bites; and all manner of gelatinous elements achieved by methods natural and scientifically engineered.

In every instance, however, the most memorable aspect of each dish was, simply, that it was delicious. Dipping into a plate of monkfish — a silky scoop of the fish's liver, a crisp piece of fried flesh, and a meltingly tender filet — I realized that I had never understood the full potential of that fish, let alone that it paired well with bananas (present in pudding form). When I asked my waiter how one course was made — the black truffle "explosion," which tasted like the most incredible black truffle and parmesan pasta stuck inside a futuristic ravioli — he coyly replied, "Magic."

The answer — quite likely given because a tableside explanation of the chemistry behind the dish might disturb the mood — said a lot about how food science will probably always operate beyond most customers' grasp. Chicago's avant-garde cuisine and its industrial counterparts may have cross-pollinated, but a fundamental distinction separated the two worlds: that is, at places like Alinea, the science is celebrated if not entirely exposed; it is part of the overarching pleasure of the dining experience — the joy of revelation and shared discovery. Having eaten plenty of instant mac and cheese in my lifetime, I won't deny that the people at Kraft also successfully use science to make food taste good. But as my meal at Alinea wound down, it occurred to me that when I visited Kraft's kitchens, I hadn't been offered so much as a bite of anything.

SPLENDID ICE CREAMS

During her quest to define American cuisine, the author returns to her hometown and finds it is no longer the epicenter of average. The food revolution in America has gone mainstream, and its center of gravity is shifting from the coasts to the middle of the country, in places just like Columbus, Ohio.

I'll Eat Columbus

Molly O'Neill

I grew up in Columbus, Ohio, in the middle of a conversation between two Americas. My mother's America had horses, higher education, and good silver. My father's had a dairy farm, a dustbowl, and base-ball. Their tireless effort to reconcile these two Americas took place primarily at the dinner table. As if campaigning for public office, my mother sat at one end of the kitchen table arguing for personal sacri-fice in the name of the greater good. At the other end of the table, my father defended the individual's right to life, liberty, and the pursuit of happiness. Seated on either side of the long table between them, my five younger brothers and I were their New Hampshire. We were the constituents they wanted, the votes they needed. Night after night, we scrambled to support the America that we wanted when we grew up.

The meals may have groomed us to maintain our hometown's habit of voting for winning presidents. The dinner debates also aligned us with the tastes of the nation and prepared us to do our part in sustaining the

Molly O'Neill is the author of four cookbooks, including *One Big Table: A Portrait of American Cooking*, the editor of the Library of America's anthology *American Food Writing*, and the host of the PBS series *Great Food*. O'Neill won the prestigious Julia Child/IACP Award for cookbooks and has been awarded three James Beard citations for books, journalism, and television and, during her ten-year tenure at the *New York Times*, the society's Lifetime Achievement Award. Born in Columbus, Ohio, O'Neill graduated from Denison University and attended La Varenne in Paris. *Mostly True*, her memoir of growing up in a Major League Baseball family, was described in the *New York Times Book Review* as "a magical tale of growing up in the middle of the American dream."

city's legendary ability to anoint the next McDonald's–Kentucky Fried Chicken–Domino's Pizza–Doritos. From the first White Castle in 1922 to the introduction of the Wendy's and Subway chains in the 1970s, rare was the successful packaged-food product or chain-restaurant concept that was not test-marketed in my hometown. During the 1960s, when we were growing up there, Columbus was still the nation's premier test-market capital for new food products. The taste preferences of the local citizenry were uncannily and consistently average.

Our parents did not intend to cultivate average Americans, particularly not ones with a taste for cheesy Manwich sandwiches and ranch-flavored dips. They may have disagreed on civil rights, Vietnam, long hair, "women's lib," the gas crisis, Reaganomics, and the color of the sky, but my parents were in complete accord on dietary policy. They did not believe in junk food.

My mother thought that food wrapped in plastic was for *other* people. My father thought it was a Communist plot.

They were freaks. Everybody else got to eat Oreos and Fig Newtons straight from the bag. Our mother *baked* cookies and forced us to make our selection from the waxed-paper layers she painstakingly arranged in an antique tin. Other people's fathers applauded progress. Our father shook his head when acres of the cornfields surrounding the city were razed to create shopping malls. He'd grown up on a farm. "You lose more than corn when you lose your cornfields, kiddos." When a set of Golden Arches sprouted across the street from the Red Pig, a greasy spoon that he favored, he grew red in the face.

"Next it'll be a price war and the Red Pig will be gone," he railed. "That nice family, working all those years. Mark my words, kiddos. You lose more than pulled pork when you lose a place like the ole Red Pig."

They were hopeless. It was humiliating. Who would choose a chipped plate heaped with sloppy, greasy shredded hog if they could have a nice, tidy Happy Meal? My brothers and I were the youth whom marketers credited, along with a stable, well-balanced economy and a lack of ethnic distinction, with making Columbus the epicenter of average. And when we were young, that is exactly what we wanted to be.

We wanted TV dinners and macaroni and cheese from a box. We

wanted to drink Coca-Cola and to eat at McDonald's. Average was the compromise that evaded our parents, the neutrality we pined for, the blessed condition of being just like everybody else.

My adolescence was dedicated to the pursuit of the average. Babysitting money in hand, I made secret forays to the grocery store. I took my first cooking lesson there. The lady who passed out free samples taught me how to turn half a hamburger bun into a small pizza. What magic. Suddenly the arty impulses that had hampered my quest to be average could be directed toward an average, everyday achievement. What bliss.

I am not sure when average began to feel less like a happy medium and more like a failure to achieve excellence. There was no single moment of reversal, just a growing sense of what Woody Allen would call ennui and my father would have called "boooor-or-or-RING." The shift was connected to cooking, which had, by the time I was fourteen, lead to making art and writing poems. It was connected to Kent State and *The Feminine Mystique*. My growing intolerance for the average also had elements of amnesia. By the time my madeleines were earning me accolades at the high school bake sale, I'd lost all memory of waxed-paper layers and antique cookie tins. When terms such as *real food* and *authentic cuisine* entered my lexicon, I was thinking along the lines of croissants and chicken Marrakesh, not the Red Pig.

By the time I was eighteen, I was sure that life was elsewhere. I couldn't get out of Columbus fast enough.

I returned with a set of real knives from cooking school in Paris, and then with bottles of real olive oil from Tuscany, and then with a suitcase full of oysters from Cape Cod. "You see," I told my brothers, "they come in shells, not cans."

Through twenty years of culinary globetrotting, I never failed to go back to Columbus bearing epicurean mementos. I carried jars of mole back from Oaxaca, fish sauce from Vietnam, *sambal* from Bali. Once, returning from my home in New York City, I carried approximately half the inventory from Zabars in order that the family I'd left behind might taste the real thing. Poor things.

I was a restaurant critic for a newspaper in New York City by then, an author of cookbooks, a recognized authority. Even my own family acknowledged my sophisticated taste and superior location, at least for a while.

Sometime between Pasta Nation and the onset of molecular cuisine in Manhattan, however, things began to shift. My hulking, athletic, alpha-male brothers (my father's athletic gene, if not his worldview, had prevailed) called from central Ohio to share recipes. Long in charge of family holiday menus, I was increasingly advised not to worry about cooking.

"We got that," said one brother, "you just get here." They called with restaurant recommendations gleaned from the Internet, passed along cellar-building tips they'd picked up at their wine clubs, offered cooking advice.

"There's more to cooking than backyard barbecue," one informed me. "You ought to get into some Food T v."

The food revolution — *my revolution!* — had gone mainstream. The brother I'd taught to make a traditional, Genovese-style pesto was now making his own tagliatelle that he served with his own, superb lamb ragout.

"There's a guy a couple miles from my house raising lamb," he said. "You should meet him. He's the president of the national grass-fed lamb society. Unlike most big American cities, Columbus didn't lose all its farmland."

"Move over Alice Waters," said my mother, who never had a taste for lamb. "This is delicious," she told my brother, pressing the well-pressed Frette napkin he'd supplied to her lips, "just like Felidia in New York."

In 2001, twenty-five years after I moved to Manhattan, I began venturing west of the Hudson River on a regular basis. The pull was powerful, though unconscious, as atavistic as that of the salmon I'd watched hurdling themselves upstream toward home in the Alaskan Yukon. I began writing a book about American cuisine and traveling almost constantly.

First I zigzagged around the country giving potlucks and collecting recipes, then I followed the perimeters and waterways, then I followed weather patterns and agricultural shifts. Defining the nation's discrete growing regions was the first major hurdle. Tracking the historic and contemporary immigration patterns was the next. By 2008 I'd gone to farmers' markets, church suppers, Little League cookouts, big-rig barbecues, and chefs' private retreats. I'd ridden food trucks, fishing boats, and Mardi Gras floats, cast and cooked in private trout clubs, run with the sheep in Idaho, dug truffles in Tennessee, and become an honorary member of most major ethnic and cultural clubs in the country. I'd completed a draft of the book. It perfectly mirrored the demographic picture I'd found, and it was perfectly boring. There is more to American cuisine than recipes and over three hundred thousand miles. I hadn't found it.

During that time, food in America had changed more than in any other period I'd observed. The food revolution was, after all, televised. Fast Food Nation had been exposed as the multinational agri-industry my father had predicted. The United States of (eat local) Arugula had been born. But there was something else going on, something that felt like tectonic plates shifting beneath the wheels of my car as I drove north to south, east to west.

The addresses for "the best Mexican *barbacoa* and rodeo," the best bowl of Vietnamese *pho*, and the best Iranian kebobs were no longer in the outer boroughs of New York City or in mini-malls on the fringes of Los Angeles, Miami, Houston, or Minneapolis. Instead, they were tucked in midcentury suburbs in Charlotte, South Carolina; Indianapolis, Indiana; Missoula, Montana; Ann Arbor, Michigan; Portland, Oregon; and, yes, Columbus, Ohio.

At the end of the nineteenth century the nation's first great wave of immigrants arrived in its major ports and remained. Even as successive generations "moved on up," they selected suburbs near the cities of their forefathers. But in the mid-twentieth century, when the nation's immigration policy was expanded to include nonwhite, non-European people, the more affordable suburbs in the middle of the country beckoned. Instead of funneling immigrants through a central clearing spot such as the Great Hall at Ellis Island, churches in the middle of the country began to sponsor refugees — from Vietnam and Cambodia, Pakistan, Bosnia, Jamaica, Trinidad, Puerto Rico, Pueblo, Rwanda.

The nation's restaurants had long offered work to recent immigrants. By the late twentieth century *authentic* was a buzzword and more and more immigrants worked in restaurants only long enough to fund a food truck, a pop-up, or a storefront of their own.

"Remember that mall where the s&h Green Stamp store was? Well, that is a Vietnamese superstore now and you just have to get the recipe for their *pho*," my mother said. "It is stupendous. Saigon-style, so fresh and vibrant. I like it better than the one we had at Vong in New York."

In my quest to define American cuisine, the only place I hadn't studied was Columbus. My father had died and my visits, though frequent, consisted only of the drive from the airport to my mother's house. I'd heard rumors about the city's vibrant food-truck scene. I'd heard that someone was even giving ethnic food tours of the city. These reports were difficult to reconcile with the city I'd known, the city I'd fled. I didn't rush out to investigate.

There was, as well, a growing body of evidence that the same gentle rents and cost of living that attracted recent immigrants were also attracting young food entrepreneurs.

"I'm *addicted* to the lavender ice cream at Jeni's Splendid," one brother confided. "This woman can make some cream. She has her own cows, I swear, only uses Ohio ingredients. Well, of course, Ohio has a long ice cream history. Did you know that banana splits were invented in Columbus?"

Another brother sang the praises of Oyo spirits. "It's the first distillery opened in a retail location since Prohibition," he said. "These guys can make some whiskey, I'm telling you. Heirloom corn whisky and rye. They have this copper still in an old taxi garage downtown."

Yet another brother waxed rhapsodic about the macaroons that a brother-and-sister team was selling in the patisserie they'd opened in the German Village section of town.

"It's like Brooklyn down there," he said, "all these little joints. And these macaroons! Better than anything I've had in Paris *or* New York."

Pausing, he said softly, "If you'd just stuck around we coulda done something like that."

My mother picked me up at the airport. She is eighty-five years old and she drives a pearly white Cadillac that, like her designer clothing and stylish coiffure, is impeccably maintained. She was excited about our plan.

"Just imagine! *Me* taking *you* on the foodie tour of Columbus!" she said. "Get in the car! Hurry up, we're meeting the food-truck tour lady, she is absolutely darling, by the way. She's taking us out to some parking lot for the *taco al pastor* and it's a good thing, it's quite a scene. *Everybody* goes on Friday night now and Bethia Woolf is going to move us right to the head of the line. You know about *pastor* right? Its pork cooked gyro-style with pineapple and all these exotic spices! Apparently the Mexicans learned it from Arab traders in the fourteenth century. Well, it's absolutely delicious, Molly. I just can't wait to hear what you think."

Over the next several weeks, we would eat at food trucks and shopping malls and tiny storefront restaurants. I would cook with a Vietnamese woman, several people from Africa, and a Mexican family. I would swoon for Jeni and her splendid ice cream. Standing in Columbus nibbling a macaroon, I would remember being in Paris, wide-eyed, on fire, nineteen years old. I would feel that burst of belief that occurs when you witness a work of art. Anything seemed possible at that moment. Especially moving back to Ohio.

But that first day, as we sped toward dusk in my mother's Cadillac, I was, for a few minutes, three years old and I was standing between my parents in the front seat of a 1955 Plymouth. They were driving to the North Market downtown. It was still a farmers' depot back then and my parents were talking about what to have for dinner. They didn't have a plan. They didn't have recipes. They each had their own Americas, but they both had Ohio, where the capacity for wonder, a big appetite, and the willingness to be surprised were considered normal. Even average.

"Well, you just never know what they'll have today," said my mother.

"We'll just wait and see," said my father, "and then we'll roll with it, won't we, kiddo?"

Can eating locally work? As far north as Michigan? Mather learned to recalibrate her life to a more natural rhythm in tune with the seasons in the western part of the state.

On Cider, Cornmeal, and Comfort

Robin Mather

A lthough you'd more frequently find me studying the constellations at 2:00 a.m. than greeting the rising sun at dawn, in early fall I become a natural morning person. Something in the crisp daybreak wakes me effortlessly. When night's cool air collided with the lake's warm waters, the resultant morning mists, quavering visibly, were often dense enough that I couldn't see my own dock. It was ineffably beautiful, and I typically took my coffee standing on the deck, to better appreciate the view, relaxing into the scene's glory.

Hunters' pickup trucks stood in all the pullouts that dot the dirt roads winding through the Barry State Game Area. Some were bowmen, taking advantage of the early deer season, but most were gunners, scouting the best spot for their tree stands and blinds. Many, if not most, of the hunters are responsible sportsmen who want only to bag a little meat for the family's freezer, and I'm lucky to know several. While I have no quarrel with hunters or their sport, it's hard to miss the empty whiskey

Robin Mather is a Michigan native and third-generation journalist who has written about food for more than thirty years. She has written for newspapers, including the *Detroit News* and the *Chicago Tribune*, and magazines, including *Cooking Light* and *Relish*. Now a senior associate editor at *Mother Earth News*, she lives in Topeka, Kansas, with the young brown standard poodle Callebaut, who succeeded the late Boon of the memoir from which this excerpt was taken; Pippin, her voluble African Grey parrot; and Guffy, her irascible cat. Mather continues to eat locally and on a budget; she cans, freezes, and dehydrates the food from her garden and buys at farmers' markets or directly from growers. She is at work on a novel and is considering a third nonfiction book.

bottles and boxes of beer cans scattered about many of the campsites where they've pitched their tents or parked their campers. It takes just one jittery, still-drunk or hungover hunter with a gun and buck fever to wreak havoc: in 2008 a man standing in his own yard not two miles from my house was killed by a stray bullet fired from a drunken hunter's gun a quarter-mile away. So I stuck to the road on my walks, even with the fluorescent-yellow vest I wore to signal that I am not a deer. It seemed prudent as well to leave Boon at home, and I missed his lolling-tongued, happy company. I tried to squelch my resentment that the hunters take over the woods from early October to January — a time when a walk in the woods seems especially appealing — but I frequently failed.

The peppery, dusty, sharp scents of summer had given way to the earthier odors of leaf mold and goldenrod. Where goldenrod grows, though, so does ragweed, which meant my fall allergies roared in. I sometimes punctuated the day with a dozen or more mind-fogging sneezes in a row.

Still, despite the hunters and the allergies and the cooling nights, autumn is perhaps my favorite season. I adore its golden streaming light, so different from the high summer's harsh brilliance, and the way that light sets the coloring leaves afire. The trees' beauty is redoubled by their reflection in the glassy lake. I love, too, the braises and long-simmered dishes for which fall's chilly temperatures create an appetite.

Of all the glories that autumn has to offer, however, the biggest and foremost in my mind is apples. I'm in love with apples, in love especially with names of the older varieties: Sheepnose, Wolf River, Macoun, Seek-No-Further, Cox's Orange Pippin — poetical names that whisper of older times and simpler values. Hundreds of apple varieties still grow all over the country — apples meant for sauce, or pies, or eating out of hand; apples meant for long-keeping or for making into cider; apples meant for drying or for pairing with cheeses. But commercial apple growers seem to concentrate on only a few. It seems pitiful to me that even a well-stocked supermarket carries just a handful of varieties, and those the same no matter where you live: the trusty Empire, the insipid Red and Golden Delicious, the bright-tart Granny Smith, and, these days, the ubiquitous, sugary Galas, Honey Crisps, and Fujis.

Farmers' markets and farm stands often offer a wider variety — especially the Northern Spies and Romes that I like for pies, occasionally Baldwins and russeted Pippins with their rough skin — but every year, more orchards fall to developers who build subdivisions where the humble rows of apple trees once rooted.

If you buy apples at any season other than the late summer and fall when they ripen, you're buying apples from cold storage, a process in which growers store their harvests in controlled-atmosphere closed bins, where piped-in nitrogen replaces the oxygen that apples need to ripen and rot. It is a system that has made it possible for apple growers to spread their income over the year, which is a good thing, I reckon; yet, even under the best of circumstances, I find those controlled-atmosphere apples are often mealy and dissatisfying.

A better solution, perhaps, than buying out-of-season apples might be what people used to do, back when I was young. Nearly every mudroom and glassed-in sunporch in the houses I visited boasted a couple of bushels of apples, and we ravenous kids coming in from school were encouraged to help ourselves. The apples would be gone just about the time everyone tired of eating them, sometime after the New Year, and then we would go without until the following fall. Because I live alone, I don't need bushel after bushel, but I will buy a half bushel each of a couple varieties — both for cooking and for eating out-of-hand — to set in my cool, dark basement. They will store there comfortably, along with the rest of my home-canned pantry items.

Michigan has always been among the premier apple-growing states, of course; the moderating effect of the Great Lakes creates a climate that suits apples to a T, with enough deep snow to protect the trees from dry, cold winter winds and enough dormancy days to encourage the trees to set a good crop. Washington State grows more apples, but Michigan grows more varieties of apples, something of which I am unjustly proud. I felt that pride even as a kid. I remember dressing as Johnny Appleseed for Halloween when I was about ten, going out to trick-or-treat with one of my mom's Revere copper-clad saucepans on my head and wearing a burlap feed sack tied with rope at my waist. So perhaps my apple love is but another part of my sense of place.

The apple harvest naturally means cider, too, another glory of the season. So when Jim told me that Bowens Mills, a privately owned historic gristmill in nearby Yankee Springs, had a cider festival coming up and wondered if I'd like to go with him, I said yes with alacrity.

Cider might be the most truly American of all drinks. The colonists started their day with mugs of cider, probably the lightly alcoholic "hard," or fermented, type, drawing on their traditions in England and elsewhere. It may have been a good choice, given that safe, potable water was sometimes scarce and that fermented beverages may destroy intestinal bugs. English ciders remain my favorite, although I also love the peculiar French ciders, which often have a whiff of the barnyard about them. I even like domestic hard ciders, such as Woodchuck and Hornsby, although they have been dumbed down for mass consumption by upping the sugar to make them sticky-sweet.

It's sweet cider we think of, though, when we think of cider and doughnuts and pumpkin patches. Nowadays, thanks to our panicky attitudes about food, sweet cider must be pasteurized before sale in many states after an E. coli outbreak in raw cider a few years ago — remember that? A cider maker used apples contaminated by cow manure in his cider and it sickened some people. So many states rushed to require that cider be pasteurized.

The United States Department of Agriculture oversees food labeling and has created thousands of "standards of identity" for the foods we eat. The standards of identity are meant to ensure that the ice cream we buy actually has cream in it or that the Velveeta on sale last week is labeled "cheese food product," because it isn't really cheese. So if you have ever wondered what the difference is between apple juice and cider, well, this is it: nothing. The standard of identity for apple juice says it must be pasteurized. In the loopy world of government regulation, today, cider must also be pasteurized. Therefore, apple juice and cider — both often sold with sodium benzoate added to further reduce the chances of bacterial contamination — are the same thing. The cider we all look forward to drinking each fall is now nothing much different from the Tree Top or Welch's frozen concentrate in cans you can pick up year-round. Unless, perhaps, we informally agree that cider is usually fresh-pressed, generally within a couple days of its sale, and typically unfiltered. The government sees no such distinction.

I hadn't visited Bowens Mills before and was pleased to see a parking lot full of cars when we arrived. At one side of the lot, men unloaded horses from their trailers — draft types, butternut-brown Belgians with flaxen manes and tails, dappled gray Percherons, and chestnut and bay Clydesdales with their flashing white stockings and hooves as big as dinner plates — to ready for the pulling contest. Children scampered hither and yon like the bees drawn to the cider press, and parents pushing strollers clogged the paths. I could hear the fiddles and banjos of a bluegrass band off in the distance. I could see that vendors had set up tables, and one of the concessionaires offered what smelled like very good barbecue.

Jim and I wandered around a bit, and then, seeing that he was going to spend some time looking at the muzzle-loading rifles offered at one booth, I excused myself to step over to the horse pull. I couldn't care less about a tractor pull or anything else that involves machines and motors and engines, but if an animal is involved, especially one that wants to work, I will stop dead in my tracks to observe. I could have watched those extraordinary horses pull for hours — their dancing anticipation as they backed to the loaded sled, their straining muscles as they dug for purchase before leaning into the collar to pull, their pride and dignity and grace as they were unhitched — and sat happily in the sun, completely contented and at peace, until Jim found me, a new rifle in his hand.

We set off to watch the cider press, powered by the musical stream rushing over moss-covered rocks, crush and juice the mountains of apples stacked in wooden crates nearby. I asked the cider maker what type of apples he was using and, recognizing all the varieties he named as dessert apples, knew his cider would be sweet and good. Not terribly complex — the best ciders mix sweet, sharp, bitter, and tart varieties, whereas he was using just sweet varieties — but it would be cool and delectable, and taste of fall.

"Think I'm going to buy a couple gallons of that cider, Jim, and make hard cider," I said. At this, Jim's ears perked up.

"Teach me how?" he said.

"Sure. It won't be the finest hard cider in the world, but it'll taste good. We'll both like it, I think."

The cider maker told us that gallon jugs of his cider were available in the mill's gift shop, so we headed that way.

A temporary cooler housed gallons of cider, so it was easy to snag a few. Tucked on a shelf to the right of the cooler were two-pound bags of coarse cornmeal, each dressed in a little faux burlap sack. Although the bags were labeled "Bowens Mills," I wasn't sure if they were simply souvenirs or products of the mill.

I turned to the woman staffing the cash register. "Do you grind this cornmeal? Here?"

"Yes," she said. "We grind it every week or so." She handed me a brochure that detailed the mill's history — built in 1836 as a sawmill, with the addition of a gristmill around 1864, Bowens Mills started making cider in 1902 — and I saw that the brochure mentioned that the old French stone millstones had been renovated and redressed to make them operable.

I don't use a great deal of cornmeal, probably less than ten pounds a year. But I do like to keep some on hand for cornbread and muffins, for polenta and its kinfolk, and to use to add a little gritty body to waffles, pancakes, and breads. When I lived in the Deep South, I never cultivated a passion for grits at breakfast — no self-respecting Michigan girl would choose grits over hash browns! But a little study showed me that grits is coarse cornmeal is polenta. They're all essentially the same thing, although I think technically some have the germ of the corn sifted out, some don't. (Note that there are two kinds of grits: hominy grits and regular grits, and I am referring to regular grits.) The stone-ground stuff that Bowens Mills had on offer was whole grain, with germ and everything. All the better, to my mind. After confirming that the gift store was open all year and that it always had cornmeal in stock, I picked up two, two-pound bags to add to my purchase.

With cornmeal stashed in the pantry, I literally have a world of dishes at hand. Naturally, you and I both think of cornbread first, because it is the most familiar. Cornbread is so easy to make that I can't figure the appeal of mixes; stir together one cup each cornmeal and self-rising flour, two beaten eggs, three tablespoons vegetable oil or melted butter, two tablespoons of sugar if you're not a breast-pounding southerner, and enough buttermilk or milk to make a stiff batter; bake at 350 degrees Fahrenheit until golden, preferably in a well-greased ten-inch cast-iron skillet. When I bake a batch of cornbread, I usually plan to use the leftovers for cornbread dressing to go with pork chops or chicken within a couple of days.

Good coarse cornmeal can also lead to polenta, which is plain old midwestern cornmeal mush or southern grits in a dressier, slightly more exotic guise — and which is treated as a much-loved peasant food in its native Italy. Although I sometimes make polenta to serve with spaghetti sauce, more generally I treat it as a side dish and dress it with butter and cheese to make it creamy and rich. Every few months I get hungry for polenta with blue cheese, and on those occasions, that and a salad are all I need for dinner.

When I was a kid, my mother used to occasionally make a loaf pan of cornmeal mush, from which she cut slices to fry in butter and serve with maple syrup at breakfast. She acquired that appetite at the table of her Iowa-born mother, and while I liked it well enough, it never became a favorite of mine. But just thinking about it made me want to step into the kitchen to make a batch in my mother's memory.

I have seen tubes of already cooked polenta at the grocery store, and they are pricey. Yet again, making polenta from scratch literally costs pennies instead of dollars, and polenta is so simple to make that I can't see why anyone would buy the manufactured stuff, which I find unpleasantly rubbery. Make regular grits, polenta, and mush all the same way: one-half cup cornmeal to one-half cup cold water; stir together to prevent lumps, then slowly add two cups boiling water and cook over very low heat, stirring almost constantly, until the mixture is thick and bubbly and tastes cooked, usually within twenty minutes (although longer won't hurt it). Add a pinch of salt while it simmers. If it's polenta, top it with pasta sauce or stir in butter and the cheese of your choice and serve it as a side dish. If it's to be mush, pour the hot stuff into a buttered loaf pan and refrigerate, uncovered, until it firms up enough to slice and fry. And if it's going to be grits, serve with butter and sugar or salt and pepper at breakfast, perhaps with a little redeye gravy, if you happen to have it handy.

There's another polenta/mush/grits kind of thing that I like very, very much. Oddly enough, the small Michigan village in which I grew up is home to La Vatra, the U.S. headquarters of the Romanian Orthodox Church. My parents often took us to the annual festival at La Vatra's lovely tree-shaded grounds on Greytower Road outside the village, and I think my mother's hunger for the polenta-like *mamaliga* was the main reason we went. *Mamaliga* is the Romanian national dish, and the ladies' auxiliary at La Vatra always served it in one form or another, with *mamaliga cu branza*, or *mamaliga* baked with cheese and sour cream, the most common offering. Eventually, my mother inveigled some of the women to teach her to make *mamaliga*, and we all learned to love it. Now I had the beginnings of my own *mamaliga cu branza*.

Collecting our goodies, Jim and I called it a day and headed back to the lake. We agreed to meet the next day to set our hard cider to working, and I assured him that I had plenty of yeast and equipment to handle his and my batch both. I snitched a glass of frothy cider from one of my gallons and carried it out to the deck to enjoy as the October day readied itself for bed. The spectacular blushing oranges, reds, and pinks of the sky above the ridgeline to the west told me that the next day would be every bit as fine as that day had been. Jim has a sweet tooth, I remembered; I could make a batch of buttermilk doughnuts tonight, cut them out, and refrigerate them overnight to fry just before he arrived the next morning, so they'd still be warm when he came in.

They would please him, I thought, every bit as much as this day of curiosity and contentment, cider, and cornmeal had pleased me.

Buttermilk Doughnuts with Cider Glaze

Makes 1½ dozen doughnuts

These are cake-style doughnuts, not raised doughnuts leavened with yeast. They are light and fluffy, yet still humble and homey. A cider-sweet glaze seems just right for the season. Use a candy thermometer to monitor the frying oil's temperature; the doughnuts will be greasy if the temperature drops below 375 degrees, and they will burn before they cook through if the temperature goes much higher.

DOUGHNUTS

4 ¼ cups all-purpose flour, plus more for dusting
1 tablespoon baking powder
½ teaspoon baking soda
¾ teaspoon salt
½ teaspoon ground cinnamon
¼ teaspoon ground cloves
¼ teaspoon ground allspice
¼ teaspoon grated nutmeg
2 large eggs, plus 1 large egg yolk
¾ cup granulated sugar
1 teaspoon vanilla extract
1 cup buttermilk (or 1 cup milk soured with 1 tablespoon vinegar)
3 tablespoons salted butter, melted
Neutral vegetable oil, such as canola or soybean, for frying

GLAZE

1 ½ cups confectioners' sugar
2 to 4 tablespoons cider

In a large bowl, combine the flour, baking powder, baking soda, salt, cinnamon, cloves, allspice, and nutmeg. Whisk to lighten and combine well.

In the bowl of a stand mixer, or in a large bowl using a hand mixer, beat the eggs and egg yolk with the granulated sugar and vanilla until light and fluffy, 2 to 3 minutes.

In a large measuring cup, stir together the buttermilk and butter.

Alternately beat the dry ingredients and buttermilk mixture into the egg mixture, one-third at a time, until all of the ingredients are combined and a soft, sticky dough forms.

Fill a deep fryer or a large pot with oil to a depth of at least 3 inches, and heat the oil to 350 degrees over medium-low to medium heat.

Meanwhile, with floured hands, transfer the dough to a generously floured board and gently roll out until the dough is ½ inch thick. Using a 3-inch biscuit cutter, cut the dough into rounds, spacing the rounds as close as possible. Poke a hole in the center of each round with the handle of a wooden spoon, wiggling the spoon to widen the hole. Collect the scraps and roll out to form another batch of doughnuts (Note: the second batch may be a little tougher than the first, as the dough has been worked.) If you have scraps left over after rolling out the dough the second time, discard them.

When the oil is ready, working in batches, place the doughnuts in the oil, being careful not to crowd them. Fry the doughnuts, turning them once, until puffed and golden, 1½ to 2 minutes on each side. Remove the doughnuts and place on a wire rack to drain. Before adding the next batch, give the oil a few minutes to return to frying temperature.

When all the doughnuts are cooked, on the wire rack, and slightly cooled, ice them with cider glaze. To make the cider glaze, in a bowl, combine the confectioners' sugar and 2 tablespoons of the cider. Whisk to blend. Add additional cider as needed to reach a thick glaze consistency. Pour the glaze into a measuring cup and drizzle it over the doughnuts.

Doughnuts are best the day they are made. For longer storage, place the doughnuts on a rimmed baking sheet, freeze until solid, and transfer to zip-top plastic bags before storing in freezer. To serve, warm the frozen doughnuts for a minute or two in the microwave.

The Midwestern Sweet Tooth

To get the essence of Sue Hubbell, you have to hit the road. Highways were (and still are) the Midwest's skeletal system, branching and probing out from southern Missouri's Ozark Mountains, where she ran a commercial beekeeping and honey-producing operation. It was at this time in her life — when she owned and operated the Solarius Honey Farm — that she came up with her rules for finding great pie.

The Great American Pie Expedition

Sue Hubbell

A generation ago in the Ozarks, where I farm, pies also served romance — and an unlikely adjunct, school finance — in what were known as pie suppers. Back in those days of one-room schools in rural areas with a poor tax base, pie suppers were an annual autumn event. Young women would bake the best, the prettiest, the fanciest pies they could and take them to the school in the evening for young men to bid on. The top bidder would earn not only the pie but the right to eat it with its baker. The money from the auction funded the school. The young women would try to mark their pies in such a way that certain young men would recognize them, and the Ozark folklore is full of stories about men who created emotional havoc by bidding — perhaps mistakenly, perhaps not — on the "wrong" pie.

In addition to Pie Rules 1 and 2 (pie is good in 85 percent of the eating establishments that are between two other buildings, and good pie may often be had near places where meadowlarks sing), there is another, which applies to the entire country. Rule 3: never eat pie within one mile of an interstate highway. This rule eliminates pie in most fast-food restaurants and in most truck stops, which are usually also franchises these days. I once violated Rule 3 and had a disappointing piece of gooseberry pie at a much-recommended truck stop just off

---

Sue Hubbell is the author of *A Country Year: Living the Question*, *A Book of Bees*, *Broadsides from Other Orders*, *Shrinking the Cat: Genetic Engineering Before We Knew about Genes*, *On This Hilltop*, and *Waiting for Aphrodite: Journeys into the Time Before Bones*. She lives in Maine.

Interstate 70, between Kansas City and St. Louis. But now I thought I had better check out the small, independent truck stops, so I visited the Wyatt Junction Truck Stop, just west of the Mississippi River, on U.S. 60. A sign on the wall said,

Welcome To
Wyatt Junction Truck Stop
Trucker's Notice
All Coffee Free With
The Purchase Of Diesel Fuel
Thank You For Coming
Have
A
Nice
Day

I ordered the dinner special: chicken-fried steak, fried bread, deep-fried okra, French-fried potatoes, and a tossed salad made almost entirely of fried bacon. A trucker in a black leather jacket came in looking enormously pleased and announced to no one in particular that he'd passed his sweetie about two hundred miles back and left her behind. He hoped she wasn't frosted. He put a quarter in the jukebox:

The last thing I gave her was the bird,
And she returned the favor with a few selected words . . .
Then left two streaks of Firestone smokin' on the street.

Sweetie pulled up and climbed out of her own eighteen-wheeler. She sauntered in. She had a fluffy shock of black hair and was wearing tight jeans, high-heeled red shoes, and a black leather jacket to match his. She glared at him and ordered Royal Crown Cola and apple pie. If she could, I could. I told the waitress to hold the R.C. but lemme have some pie. It was very like that served in the United States Senate Family Dining Room.

I was just a bit bilious by the time that I got to my farm, in southern Missouri, so I spent a couple of days there sucking on soda crackers and letting Tazzie [her dog] visit her favorite places down by the river.

I had heard about Opal Wheeler's Pie Factory, on U.S. 63, south of West Plains, but I'd never been there, and I enlisted the help of my friend Nancy for a pie foray. Nancy is a little bitty skinny woman who runs a healthy-food store and talks a lot about bean sprouts. She is always ready to try something new, however, and is a woman of considerable enthusiasm. We drove down U.S. 63 and found the Pie Factory, a cheery, small, ten-sided building with white walls and red-trimmed windows. It would have been easy to miss, because it sits back from the road and has only a small, hand-painted sign to call attention to itself. Opal Wheeler is a grandmotherly looking woman with a warm smile. She had been in the restaurant business for years before she and her sister drove by the newly constructed building in 1985. Her sister, who understood Opal's love of baking, pointed to it and said, "Opal, wouldn't that make a cute little pie factory?" Opal agreed, rented the place, put up the sign, and set to work. She starts rolling out pie dough on the counter in the center of the building each morning at about five-thirty. She is usually done baking by eleven, and the rest of the day she sells pies — sometimes whole, sometimes by the slice with coffee.

The day Nancy and I were there she had apple, apple-raisin, raisin, pecan, cherry, apricot, blueberry, pineapple cream, peach cream, cherry cream, icebox mixed-fruit, strawberry-rhubarb, gooseberry, lemon meringue, chocolate, coconut, banana, chocolate delight (chocolate, pecans, cream cheese, single crust, whipped topping), lemon delight, pecan delight, and strawberry. I ordered a cup of coffee and told Nancy she could order whatever she wanted if she would talk to me about it. She began with a wedge each of apricot, apple-raisin, cherry, icebox mixed-fruit, and strawberry. And a cup of tea. "Oh, look," she said. "The crusts are sprinkled with sugar and browned. Pretty. . . . This apricot is too mooshy. . . . The apple-raisin is superior, though. I think it's the best one. . . . No, the cherry is the best — tart, lots of cherries, not much gooey filling. . . . No, maybe the mixed-fruit is my favorite. It's got a single crust, then a layer of cream cheese, then cherries with fresh pineapple. And this whipped topping! Wow! Can this lady make pies!"

"Anything else appeal to you?" I asked.

"Well, maybe I'll try a piece of lemon meringue."

I watched in admiration as she ate that, too. Opal Wheeler freshened my coffee. I asked Nancy again which pie was best.

"How can I choose?" she asked. "Each one is a jewel."

"Nancy," I said, "you run a health-food store."

"Yeah, isn't it wonderful? She can make good pies out of stuff like this. I mean, white flour, white sugar, solid shortening? Maybe she could make the crusts out of whole-wheat flour. Oh, well, it just shows you what a talented cook can do."

Nancy left with an entire chocolate delight pie in a box. She was happy, in perfect health, looking not one ounce fatter. And I was happy. I had always hoped that pies were good for us — a hope that had been encouraged by an article in the *Weekly World News* of October 27, 1987. I've long thought that there is a supermarket-tabloid headline designed to sucker every man, woman, or child at least once. Mine was SNICK-ERS AND TWINKIES MAKE YOU HEALTHY, SAYS FOOD EXPERT, touting an article declaring that there was "more nutrition in a Snickers bar or a Twinkie than in an apple." Might I not therefore assume, after watching Nancy tuck into her pies, that apple pie was the healthiest way to eat an apple?

In western Missouri, the good pie places thin out. The town cafés have become Daylight Donut outlets, to the detriment of both pies and doughnuts, but just at the border of Oklahoma I had an unexpectedly dainty and tasty chocolate pie at the Corners Minimart Motel & Café, on U.S. 60. The chocolate filling rested on a flavorful crust and was topped with a perfect, delicate meringue. Outside, prickly pear grew on the sunny south side of the restaurant, where there was a big white box with a sign on it that said,

Caution
Baby Rattlers

Hints of the West.

Once I had crossed the Oklahoma line, I began seeing red-tailed hawks hunting high in the air above the road. It had been a long time since I'd heard a meadowlark sing. In one small town after another, waitresses in the cafés shook their heads when I asked for pie and offered cobbler instead. "And mighty good cobbler it is, too," a customer informed me in the Hot Biscuit Café, in Vinita. But I drove on. There were sandburs at the rest stops, and Tazzie whimpered when she got them in her feet. The sun was warm. Spring had been in Oklahoma for some time. The sky opened up. I could see forever. The road threaded between hills covered with prairie grass, and someplace between Bartlesville and Ponca City I realized that I was in the West. I rolled down all the windows. *Ky-y-y-yr* screamed a red-tail overhead. I leaned out the window and the wind blew and tugged at my hair. "*Ky-r-yr*," I screamed back. Fun. Can't do that on the interstate. The road was empty, and I was in love with driving. Out of nowhere, an Oklahoma trooper came up behind me and pulled me over. He reminded me that the speed limit was still fifty-five off the interstate and gave me a "courtesy" ticket. Nice young man. Troopers know pie, so I asked him where he went to get it. He blushed a little, took off his hat, scratched his head, and thought awhile. Then, by way of explanation, he said, in his slow drawl, "Sorry, Ma'am, but you're in cobbler country now."

As a farm girl growing up in rural Michigan—a place she would later return to in her novels—the author learned that real fudge is not for sale at the cash register. It comes out of somebody's home kitchen in small batches, made with real butter and real vanilla for the people she loves.

The Old Sweetness

Bonnie Jo Campbell

Just after *Good Morning America* named Sleeping Bear Dunes "The Most Beautiful Place in America," my darling Christopher and I were in northern Michigan, admiring the views and visiting the excellent bookstores there. When we took the ferry from St. Ignace to Mackinac Island, we officially became "fudgies," which is what the locals call the tourists. This term dates back to at least the 1960s, as evidenced by a pink pin then given away (now a collector's item) by Ryba's candy store, which reads, "I'm a Mackinac Island Fudgie." On the island there are no cars, so most folks travel by foot, bicycle, or horse-drawn cab, and ready to replenish any burned calories are the fudge shops on every block, where you can watch the candy being rolled and formed on marble slabs. It is said that the humidity of the region slows the oxidation of the candy and makes it creamier. The creation is sold in slices the size of steaks.

As a candy maker, I felt it was important to do a little research, but as a lady nearing fifty with a lust for sweets and a tendency toward weight gain, I knew I had to be careful. In the first shop, I asked if I

Bonnie Jo Campbell is the author of the novel *Once Upon a River* and a 2011 Guggenheim fellow. She was a 2009 National Book Award finalist and National Book Critics Circle Award finalist for her collection of stories, *American Salvage*. Campbell is also author of the novel *Q Road* and the story collection *Women and Other Animals*. She's received the AWP Award for short fiction, a Pushcart Prize, and the Eudora Welty Prize. Campbell lives in Kalamazoo, Michigan, with her husband and in her spare time gardens, cracks black walnuts, and hangs out with her donkeys, Jack and Don Quixote. You can check out her website at www.bonniejocampbell.com.

could purchase a small piece, say, a walnut-size piece, but the gal in the apron with the big forearms like mine shook her head no, said I had to buy a whole half-pound slice. A block farther down the main drag, in the lobby of a hotel, I found a woman in a nineteenth-century frock giving away free samples. Perfect! I helped myself to a chunk, bit it in half, savored the sweetness, and almost committed to buying a whole slab. Then I took a deep breath, slowed myself, and tasted it critically. It was slightly gluey, as though it might contain corn syrup. The sweetness dominated the chocolate flavor. It was a little slow to dissolve, and just slightly greasy.

As a farm kid growing up in Michigan, I was not discriminating about sweets. At the Kalamazoo County Fair, while others bought French fries and marveled at the novelty of putting malt vinegar on them, I spent my babysitting and paper-route money on sweet fried dough dipped in sugar and, whenever possible, filled with custard. As soon as I could stir ingredients, I took 4-H cooking classes and learned to bake all manner of goodies. Sometimes I'd make a pan of brownies and eat the whole thing. Our ingredients at home were not all premium. We had vanillin instead of vanilla. Until we learned to make our own butter, we used lard from our pigs or else the cheapest margarine. As well as government cheese, each month we got a five-pound bag of government sugar.

We didn't take home dried milk from the food bank, though, because we enjoyed the luxury of milk from our cow. This milk even helped me win a blue ribbon for my sour cream chocolate cake at the county fair one year. Of course, I didn't know that sour cream was supposed to be cultured; I made that award-winning cake with bubbling, fizzing, unpasteurized, nonhomogenized cream that had soured in our kitchen.

My mom had a series of mean-tempered milk cows, one of which died from eating livestock feed laced with PBB fire retardant (that's another Michigan story), but after we got our Jersey Bambi from a local pig farmer, I was always willing to give my mom a break from the evening milking chore. It was a soothing, relaxing time, hand-milking into the stainless steel bucket, giving the barn cat an occasional squirt in the mouth. Bambi liked it when I sang, so as I milked I tried out pop tunes and the Joan Baez folk music I'd heard on my mother's records. After returning to the house, I poured the milk through a paper strainer, something like a coffee filter, and put it into glass bottles. Jerseys have always been famous for the high fat content of their milk, and in the refrigerator overnight, the ivory-colored cream rose to the top.

Nobody else in my family took such a keen interest in farm chores, or in sweets, for that matter. My brother Tom loved fish, and one time when he couldn't catch any bluegills or sunfish in the park, he netted, gutted, and fried up a whole pan of minnows. If you gave my mother a box of fine dark chocolates, she'd eat one piece a day with her morning coffee, but show her a prime steak, cooked rare, and she still gets downright misty-eyed. Some in our neighborhood went in a big way for alcohol or pot or stronger drugs (it was the early seventies, after all), but because my craving was always for the next sweet thing, I was able to avoid the trouble caused by those more dangerous cravings.

Dinners at our house consisted of the same fare most everyone we knew ate: midwestern goulash (macaroni, stewed tomatoes, ground meat), midwestern Spanish rice (rice, stewed tomatoes, ground meat), spaghetti (spaghetti noodles, stewed tomatoes, ground meat), or hamburgers. The tomatoes were grown, stewed, and canned by us, of course. The meat was usually beef but might be venison or occasionally bear, elk, or squirrel, if that's what some hunter gave my ma. We had eggs from our chickens. There was always enough for all us kids plus anybody else who showed up, but I couldn't get excited about those savory foods.

I loved Halloween candy, in particular the miniature candy bars, but I especially anticipated Valentine's Day and Easter. My granny Betty, my mom's mom, who lived in Chicago, made fudge candy. Not the sugary bars people sometimes brought around at Christmastime with the popcorn balls and snickerdoodles, but something more akin to the creamy centers of the very best boxed chocolates. Granny sent me blobs of the stuff, sometimes shaped into hearts or Easter eggs. She also sent blobs to my siblings, but they weren't interested, so I could trade or bargain for theirs. I was in heaven, hiding out in my room or in a tree fort or the barn savoring the stuff. When I visited my granny as a little kid I watched her make fudge. Later, when I was in college and lived with my grandparents in Hyde Park on the south side of Chicago, I got to make the candy with her.

The history of fudge is a little murky, but it is generally understood to be an American invention, popularized by college girls occupying themselves late at night in dormitories. I know that Betty's mother, Anne Huff, my great-grandmother, made fudge. As a young woman, Anne Huff almost certainly would have visited the famous candy-making display at the 1893 World's Columbian Exposition in Chicago, and in her own young life she kept a diary, in which she detailed which kinds of candy she made each day and which young men she fed it to. My grandfather talked about his sisters making fudge in the evenings in their apartment on Lake Shore Drive. In the days before packaged candy bars, motorcars, and televisions, fudge-making was apparently an important diversion.

Nowadays candy is for sale cheap at every cash register, but I still want to keep the old-fashioned sweetness of homemade fudge alive. For the last dozen years, at Christmas and sometimes around Valentine's Day, I have been making it and sharing it with people I love.

Sentimentality aside, eating superb fudge is a sensual joy. It is like kissing lips you adore. Fudge rests solidly in your fingers but gives way when your lips and teeth touch it, and then slowly dissolves on your tongue. The texture is velvety, never a bit hard, gluey, chewy, or wet, and real fudge should not have a detectable granule of sugar in it. A few high-end candy makers have figured out how to do this in commercial kitchens, but more often this kind of fudge comes out of somebody's home kitchen in small batches.

As I try to eat a bit less of all sweets, I take even greater enjoyment in the slow, creamy, careful business of making fudge.

PRECIOUS INGREDIENTS

There are fast-food equivalents to fudge, and they contain marshmallow fluff, peanut butter, or other solidifying agents. True fudge is made simply with sugar, chocolate, milk, butter, salt, and vanilla, and the texture comes about through chemistry, through heat and motion.

My grandmother always considered her ingredients to be precious, as though squares of bitter chocolate and brown-glass bottles of vanilla extract were not simply to be gotten at the store but were hard-won prizes, awarded only in modest portions to only the most deserving individuals.

I started with the "Chocolate Fudge" recipe that my granny used, from a book she received as a wedding gift in 1933: *Practical Cookery: A Compilation of Principles of Cookery and Recipes and the Etiquette and Service of the Table*, published in 1927 by the Department of Foods and Nutrition, Kansas State University. If I double the ingredients, that recipe turns out to be pretty much the same as the one for "Fudge Cockaigne" from the old *Joy of Cooking*. The following recipe makes just over a pound of candy.

Fudge

1 cup minus 1 tablespoon rich milk

2 cups sugar

1/8 teaspoon salt

2 ounces grated chocolate

2 to 4 tablespoons butter

1 teaspoon vanilla

1/2 to 1 cup broken nut meats

The choice of pan is important — use the heaviest one you can. My granny used a thick aluminum 1 1/2-quart saucepan. For years, I used an enameled 5-quart pan with handles on the sides, but I've recently purchased a 2-quart Calphalon nonstick pan that I use only for candy, and it's improved things immensely. As well as being heavy, the pan should have a tight-fitting lid.

For the "rich" milk, let me suggest half-and-half, which is about 12 percent cream. That's what my granny used, and that has a butterfat content similar to what I squirted out of my old Jersey milk cow. I tried substituting heavy cream for the milk and found the results greasy, hard to work with, and no better tasting.

Joy suggests grating the bars of unsweetened chocolate, but I don't like to risk my knuckles grating chocolate that way, so I break the chunks up as much as I can with my fingers and stir those into the heated milk until it melts. Then I add the sugar and salt. I used to use just any old baking chocolate, but I've recently discovered the joy of the premium varieties, in particular Scharffen Berger, which a store in Kalamazoo carries. I'm a thrifty gal who saves string, shells her own black walnuts, and pulls nails out of old lumber for reuse, so trust me when I say the finished product is worth the much-higher cost.

If I'm not mistaken, Granny added a little bit of cream of tartar at this time to discourage sugaring, maybe a quarter teaspoon, but I like the idea of keeping the recipe as basic as possible. Anyway, I can never find the cream of tartar in my disorganized cupboard — and I can't very well buy more if I already have some.

(Note: In the new *Joy of Cooking*, the recipe has been very much changed to include corn syrup and bittersweet chocolate, but I'm sticking to the old recipe.)

THE SOFT-BALL STAGE

If you've tasted some of the mixture you are cooking, you might not be impressed. That's because there's more to fudge than ingredients — temperature plays an important role. Start by bringing your mixture to a boil and then immediately turn down the heat and let it simmer with the lid on for a couple of minutes. This gives the mixture a kind of kick start, and the captured steam should wash most of the sugar crystals off the sides of the pan. Then take off the lid and prepare to wait. Fudge will become fudge when it is good and ready. Depending on the humidity, the altitude, the slight variations in amounts of your ingredients, and the alignment of the planets, your fudge will have to simmer somewhere between ten and forty minutes. Now is the time that you will put your candy thermometer in the pan, should you decide to use one. Granny always used one, but I no longer do, because I have found them unreliable and I prefer using my instincts and the soft-ball test.

Thermometer or no, you must leave this mixture alone while it barely bubbles, and please don't stir it. I know this is difficult, but resist. Well, okay, I can't always resist either, fearing that if that stuff on the bottom of the pan all sticks I will be wasting precious ingredients. If you must move the mixture, do it very gently, with a silicone spatula, in very slow motion. But don't scrape the sides at all.

Joy explains, "When we were inexperienced, we were constantly baffled by the tendency of smooth, promising candy sirups to turn with lightning speed into grainy masses. We did not realize that one clue to our failure was stirring down the sugar crystals which formed on the sides of the pan into crystals of quite different structure in the candy mass."

If you notice a lot of the mixture sticking to the bottom, then turn down the heat. I cook on an electric stove, so I have to be more careful changing the heat than the lucky souls who cook on gas flames.

One Easter, back when I was still using a thermometer, my grandpa wanted me to get the fudge off the stove so I could start making our supper. He always liked to eat exactly at 5:30, but my candy was not cooperating. He said, "It's not going to get up to 238 degrees. It's not going to get any hotter than 212," which is, of course, the boiling temperature of water. My grandpa, an engineer and mathematician who graduated from the University of Chicago, is rarely wrong, but he didn't realize how candy making involves serious chemistry. Sure, at first, when the sugar, milk, and chocolate begin to boil, they do so at 212 degrees. But as the ingredients heat and mingle, chemical changes take place, so that the boiling temperature of the mixture gradually rises. The longer you let it boil, the higher the boiling temperature will become, and the harder the finished product will be. If you boil this mixture way too long, you will end up with chocolate rock candy.

Fudge is made by taking the mixture to the soft-ball stage. You discover whether you've reached this stage by dribbling a bit of your syrup into a cup of ice water and then reaching in and trying to shape it into a ball with your fingertips. Or else get a little syrup on the spoon and hold the spoon under ice water and pull the stuff off to test it. Test often, using a clean, dry spoon or spatula each time, and don't let any extra syrup drip back into the cooking mixture, for one drop of that air-cooled stuff (or a single drop of water, for that matter) can screw up your whole batch, causing sugar to crystallize in the pan. In fudge, crystallization is a place from which the mixture cannot usually return.

If the syrup won't form a ball or disintegrates into the water, you have not yet reached the soft-ball stage. If the syrup hardens solid, you have gone too far and it's time to consider chocolate taffy instead of fudge. You want to form a mushy ball, which, according to *Joy*, "does not disintegrate but flattens out of its own accord when picked up with fingers."

Even within the soft-ball range you will get a variety of textures. The higher the temperature, the firmer the final product will be. For candies that I plan to send in the mail, which might be at risk of melting, I sometimes push the envelope, cooking until I get something that's almost a firm ball, but if I push it too far, the texture will lose its creaminess. After many batches of candy, I can now guess pretty well when I've reached the soft-ball stage, by observing the bubbling on the surface, by noting a kind of double bubbling of small bubbles within a mosaic pattern on the surface of the chocolate mixture. Between your attempts at forming balls in cups of ice water, occupy yourself by getting out a deep oblong platter, something like a smallish turkey platter. Measure out four tablespoons of unsalted butter and set them aside. (The recipe in *Joy* says two to four tablespoons, and so I always use four.)

THE COOLING, THE BEATING

When your syrup has cooked enough, get it off the heat immediately. You are going to pour the mixture onto the platter with as little jostling as possible. Do not scrape the pan — in fact, put the spatula away so you won't be tempted, since that would almost assure that the sugar would crystallize. Like my granny and me, you will lament the wasting of the precious ingredients that stick to the pan, but just count your losses and consider using a thicker pan and lower heat next time.

Cut up your butter on top of the mixture and let it melt over the top.

If you taste the stuff that is stuck to the bottom of your pan before running water into it in the sink, you will find that it still tastes like nothing special. That is because fudge is about more than the right ingredients and the right application of heat; fudge finally becomes fudge as a result of well-timed motion.

You now want the mixture to sit and cool to about 110 degrees, or "lukewarm," which I think of as just a little hotter than my darling Christopher's forehead when he comes home from work at the paper company where he operates machinery that turns paper into muffin cups. I usually rest the whole platter on a couple of plastic ice-cube trays to hasten the process, and it takes twenty minutes or so. So put the platter where nobody will mess with it and where no bugs will crawl into it. Granny used to set her platter out to cool on her third-story back porch, until the time the neighbor's dog climbed the stairs and put his nose into it.

While you're cooling the mixture, measure a teaspoon of vanilla (or maybe two, if you're feeling rich) and put it in a shot glass so it's handy — also, it'll make your kitchen smell great while you're waiting. Be sure to have handy a wooden spoon as well as a metal teaspoon and lay out wax paper on a couple of cookie sheets.

If you're going to add walnuts or pecans to the fudge, measure out between a half and a full cup, depending upon how nutty you are. Christopher is a nut lover, but he has recently decided that for him nuts actually compromise the texture of perfect fudge, and he now prefers it nutless. Children seem to prefer it without nuts as well, so you might consider making some of each.

If you are going to mix the nuts into the fudge, you will want to chop them a bit. However, consider this variation that will lessen your work: rather than putting the nuts in the fudge mixture, press one perfect half pecan or half walnut into the top of the piece of candy as the last step in the process.

When the temperature reaches lukewarm, it's time to start beating with your wooden spoon. Fold in the butter that has melted on the top. Turn it and fold it and beat it and keep your arm moving. At first the thick chocolate mixture will resist incorporating the butter, but persevere. When the butter is all mixed in, add the vanilla and mix that in — again, you will have to overcome the resistance of the mixture. Now keep beating. Your arm is already tired? Your midwestern ancestors cleared and plowed acres of land with mules, went deep into copper and iron mines, worked in deadly hot steel mills and auto plants, so be strong like them and keep beating. As long as that fudge is glossy, keep it moving. This may be five minutes or twenty or even more. My grandfather remembers his sister Mae beating fudge in their Lake Shore Drive apartment, demanding everyone look at how her arm had swollen visibly as she was working, but still she kept on. In the last few years, this beating stage has become easier because I've built up the right arm muscles, one of which is the same muscle I developed by milking our cow as a kid.

Just when you may be thinking that you can't go on, that the whole enterprise is a disaster (even after hundreds of batches, I still have this fear), suddenly the mixture will lose some of its gloss. At this magic gloss-losing moment, add your chopped nuts if you are going that route.

Not to scare you, but one time after the fudge lost its gloss, I retrieved the premeasured chopped walnuts from across my very small kitchen and, as I poured them, they bounced off the fudge mixture onto the table. The stuff had hardened in an instant. This told me, too late, that I had cooked it a little too long. In that case, you'll leave the fudge on the platter and have slightly crumbly slices instead of creamy little blobs. The texture will be off, but the flavor will still be great.

Other times I've had the opposite experience. Once my darling Christopher came home at midnight from his second-shift job and found me beating a platter of liquid fudge, tears pouring out of my eyes because of the frustration and the ache in my arm after an hour of beating. He pitched in and took over the work for a while, giving me time to pour a glass of wine. We switched off until both of us had to admit that the batch was a failure. In this case, you can put the stuff in a jar in the fridge and use it as the best imaginable frosting or fudge topping for ice cream.

But let's assume everything is going well. Once the gloss has left the fudge, you are in a race against time. Grab your metal spoon and hurriedly scoop up one spoonful after another, pushing each drop off the spoon with your finger onto the wax paper. If you've heated and timed this just right, you will be able to scoop and drop every bit of the fudge mixture.

I used to favor big dollops of fudge because it was easier, but now I try to make small pieces because they seem more elegant, but making small pieces means more spooning and puts me at risk of not getting the candy off the platter on time.

Once you've finished creating the individual candies, you or a helpful friend or spouse may press a walnut or pecan half into the tops of the candy (if you're going that route).

Now you can collapse in a chair and take a deep breath!

I usually sample the candy at this time by scraping the platter, and while I'm licking the spoon I sometimes have a crazy, selfish idea that I will just eat the entire batch myself and not share it with anyone.

After the fudge has spent a night cooling on the counter or in a cool oven, I usually melt some bittersweet chocolate and drizzle it over the top of each piece. Then I let it cool in the refrigerator for an hour or so before packing it into little boxes for my favorite people. Turns out that, like love, this sweetness has to be shared.

Two Jewish women living in Minneapolis in the forties longed for the moist, heavy cakes of their native Europe. They asked Minnesota-based Nordic Ware owner H. David Dalquist to make a pan that could help them reproduce the longed-for *kugelhopf*.

The Little Cake Pan That Could

Bonny Wolf

Want is the mistress of invention
SUSANNA CENTILEVRE

When H. David Dalquist died in 2005, many people remembered that somewhere in the house they had one of the classic pieces of bakeware that he'd invented — a long-unused Bundt pan.

Why did we stop making Bundt cakes? They were so easy and so beautiful. The cakes were perfectly shaped, evenly browned, and consistently moist. You could make anything with a Bundt pan, a cake mix, and some instant pudding. More than forty-five million Bundt pans have been sold, making it the top-selling cake pan in the world.

Sometime after the Bundt pan heyday in the 1970s, we became food snobs. No more casseroles with cream of mushroom soup. No more

---

National Public Radio commentator **Bonny Wolf** grew up in Minnesota and has been a journalist for more than thirty years. She contributes a monthly food essay to NPR's award-winning *Weekend Edition Sunday* and is editor of Kitchen Window, NPR's web-only, weekly food column. She taught journalism at Texas A&M University, where she encouraged her student Lyle Lovett to give up music and get a real job. Wolf gives better advice about cooking and eating. She was also chief speechwriter to Secretaries of Agriculture Mike Espy and Dan Glickman.

Bonny lives, cooks, and eats in a nineteenth-century row house in Washington DC's historic Capitol Hill district. Her home is across the street from the Eastern Market, a public food market, and she is there several times a day. She lives with her husband, Michael, a professor and legislative consultant, and her dog, Clio. They will both eat anything.

Bundt cakes with instant pudding mixes. We put our Bundt pans out of reach on the top shelf.

For my mother's ninetieth birthday party, I took mine down. I had made plum tarts and pear *tatins*, and I decided to throw in the chocolate pistachio Bundt cake she used to make to rave reviews. It calls for cake mix, instant pistachio pudding mix, and chocolate syrup. After the party, that was the recipe all my guests wanted.

Mr. Dalquist's death definitely touched a culinary nerve. Newspapers published stories about the Bundt pan phenomenon and the Internet was lit up with Bundt pan exchanges. I did an essay for National Public Radio on the Bundt pan, and the people who track these things told me 1,125 people e-mailed the piece to someone else.

NPR also got a lot of letters such as the one from Jan Frank in Bloomfield, Minnesota. The recipe for the chocolate pistachio cake mentioned in the radio essay was also the one Jan had eaten as a child. It had appeared in the 1975 Leonhard Elementary School's PTA cookbook. "It remains the most worn, most ingredient-soaked page of that cookbook," she wrote. "That cake never failed to satisfy. Sunday afternoon my twelve-year-old son and I dragged out the cookbook and the Bundt pan and started a new generation of pistachio-cake lovers."

That recipe was a particular favorite of my mother and her best friend, Leah. You could be pretty sure if you ate at their houses, there would be a chocolate pistachio Bundt cake for dessert. It was the dessert I made when I was newly married. Our friend Wayne would come from New York to our New Jersey apartment — what he called a trip to the country — just for a piece of that Bundt cake.

The existence of the Bundt pan is the happy result of a Judeo-Scandinavian cultural exchange.

Dave Dalquist and his wife, Dotty, invested $500 in a basement business in their Minneapolis home in 1946. They produced rosette irons, *ebelskiver* pans, *krumkake* irons, and other Scandinavian bakeware. Nordic Ware has been in business ever since.

After they had been open for four years, the Dalquists received a visit from the ladies of the local chapter of Hadassah, the national women's Zionist organization. The chapter president had a ceramic *kugelhopf* pan in which her German grandmother had made a dense cake filled with raisins, fruits, and nuts. She wanted one in metal. So Mr. Dalquist, a metallurgical engineer, made his first Bundt pan in cast aluminum, with fluted sides and a center tube, like a *kugelhopf* pan.

The pan's name comes from the German word *bund*, for "gathering," a cake suitable for a gathering. Mr. Dalquist added a *t*, trademarked the name, and the Bundt pan was born.

Things were pretty slow in the Bundt pan business until 1966, when Ella Helfrich of Texas won second place in the seventeenth annual Pillsbury Bake-Off for her Tunnel of Fudge Cake, made in a Bundt pan. (First place went to a Nevada woman for a recipe for snack bread using processed cheese spread and dry onion soup mix.)

Bakers went nuts. Pillsbury got more than two hundred thousand letters from people wanting to know where they could get a Bundt pan. The Dalquist factory ramped up production and the Bundt cake era began. Home cooks had found a way to bake the perfect cake — simple, sculpted, and evenly cooked. As a bonus, frosting was optional. Bundt cakes are so pretty, they don't need more than a sift of powdered sugar or a drizzle of simple syrup.

For a while, everyone made Bundt cakes — blueberry cream cheese, walnut rum, even one with 7-Up. The Harvey Wallbanger Bundt cake — the first fancy dessert I learned to make — used yellow cake mix, vanilla pudding mix, eggs, oil, orange juice, vodka, and Galliano liqueur, just like its namesake cocktail. The margarita cake involved margarita mix, orange liqueur, and tequila.

In 1971 Pillsbury launched a line of Bundt cake mixes, and Dorothy Dalquist wrote a cookbook called *Over 300 Delicious Ways to Use Your Bundt Brand Fluted Tube Pan*. It included recipes for cakes and other desserts, breads, entrées, and salads. The Bundt pan was originally used for pound cakes, so there are many of those in Mrs. Dalquist's book. There are cakes made from scratch and cakes made from mixes. Bread recipes call for ingredients such as beer, cheese, and saffron. A recipe for Bean Bread uses a can of pork and beans and a package of hot-roll mix. Entrées include Elegant Pressed Chicken (in aspic), Frosty Lime Seafood Salad (with lime and apple gelatin, a can of tuna or crab, and

French dressing), and various meat rings with mushroom soup, peanut butter, or canned pineapple.

In 2004 Nordic Ware published a new book called *Bundt Entertaining* with one hundred recipes "for all meals of the day and for all times of the year," a sign that the Bundt pan was back.

I have gone to five weddings recently for which the bride and groom have registered for Bundt pans as gifts. Besides the classic original, Bundt pans now come in more than thirty shapes and sizes. There are flower pans wrought as daisies, roses, sunflowers, wildflowers, and chrysanthemums. Others come in the form of hearts, stars, fleur-de-lis, and Christmas trees. There's even one shaped like a Gothic cathedral. Bundtlette pans make six muffins and mini-Bundts make tiny individual Bundt cakes. Cupcake, loaf, pound cake, popover, and shortbread pans have all joined the classic Bundt pan, available in two sizes.

I hadn't thought about a Bundt pan in years until I saw the movie *My Big Fat Greek Wedding* in 2002. In one hilarious scene, the groom's mother brings a Bundt cake to a party given by the bride's mother. The Greek woman stares in bewilderment at the "cake with a hole in it." She solves the problem by putting a potted geranium in the center. With a Bundt, you can do anything.

Chocolate Pistachio Cake

Makes 12 to 14 servings

1 (18 ¼ ounce) box white or yellow cake mix
1 (3 ½ ounce) box pistachio instant pudding mix
½ cup orange juice
½ cup water
4 large eggs
½ cup oil
1 teaspoon almond extract
¾ cup chocolate syrup
Confectioner's sugar (optional)

Preheat the oven to 350 degrees. Grease and flour a 12-cup Bundt pan (or a 10-inch tube pan).

In a mixing bowl, combine the cake mix, pudding mix, orange juice, water, eggs, oil, and almond extract. With an electric mixer, blend at low speed until moist. Beat for an additional 3 minutes at medium speed, scraping the bowl occasionally, until well blended.

Pour about two-thirds of the batter into the pan. Add the chocolate syrup to the remaining one-third of the batter. Mix well. Pour over the batter in the pan.

Bake for 1 hour. Allow the cake to cool in the pan for 15 minutes. Loosen cake with a blunt knife and turn onto a cake plate. Sprinkle with confectioner's sugar, if desired.

Ella Helfrich's Tunnel of Fudge Cake

Makes 16 servings

CAKE

1 3/4 cups sugar
1 3/4 cups margarine or butter, softened
6 eggs
2 cups powdered sugar
2 1/4 cups Pillsbury BEST® All Purpose or Unbleached Flour
3/4 cup unsweetened cocoa
2 cups chopped walnuts

GLAZE

3/4 cup powdered sugar
1/4 cup unsweetened cocoa
4 to 6 teaspoons milk

Preheat the oven to 350 degrees. Grease and flour a 12-cup fluted tube cake pan or 10-inch tube pan. In a large bowl, combine sugar and margarine; beat until light and fluffy. Add eggs one at a time, beating well after each addition. Gradually add 2 cups powdered sugar; blend well. By hand, stir in flour and remaining cake ingredients until well blended. Spoon batter into greased and floured pan; spread evenly.

Bake for 45 to 50 minutes or until top is set and edges are beginning to pull away from sides of pan. Cool upright in pan on wire rack 1 1/2 hours. Invert onto serving plate; cool at least 2 hours.

In small bowl, combine all glaze ingredients, adding enough milk for desired drizzling consistency. Spoon over top of cake, allowing some to run down sides. Store tightly covered.

Note: Nuts are essential to the success of this recipe; since this cake has a soft filling, an ordinary doneness test cannot be used. Accurate oven temperature and baking times are essential.

In the low-ceilinged room beneath a church sanctuary, the author enters a church-basement supper and it touches a culinary nerve. The quality homemade foods are straight-forward and honest, a spread of choices so ordinary they represent nothing but themselves.

When a Pie Is More Than a Pie

Jeremy Jackson

When I was a boy, my father's side of the family was peopled so densely with devout Baptists that they could have started their own church without having to hire anyone. My grandfather was a deacon, my grandmother a church organist and Sunday school teacher. Uncle Kent, my father's only sibling, was an ordained minister of music, his wife an accomplished pianist. And my grandfather's sister Clarice had more or less devoted her life to the Baptist church and would have surely signed up for the Baptist nunnery if there had been such a thing.

But my parents, despite having once been promising junior officers in God's Baptist army, were basically heathens. This was worse than being Catholic and put my sisters and me in the always mildly uncomfortable and sometimes extremely unpleasant situation of being nonbelievers at my grandparents' church during major Jesus holidays. I spent many

---

Jeremy Jackson writes fiction and cookbooks in the magical land of Iowa. He was raised on a farm in central Missouri, where his family raised cattle and had a garden just slightly smaller than Texas. Other animals on the farm included horses, a pig, sheep, chickens, ducks, and a pony. They ate many of these animals, but not the pony. Jeremy is a graduate of the Iowa Writers' Workshop and the author of seven books, including *Desserts That Have Killed Better Men Than Me* and *The Cornbread Book*, which was nominated for a James Beard Award. His novels include *Life at These Speeds* and *Hot Lunch* (written as Alex Bradley), which follows the adventures of two high school girls who are given the task of running their school's kitchen. Though usually conspicuously underemployed, Jeremy has taught English and creative writing at Vassar College and Grinnell College. Jeremy's memoir, *I Will Not Leave You Comfortless*, was published in 2012.

hours as a boy sitting in the pews, listening to sermons that made it quite clear that I was a pretty darn bad person. It was enough to make a boy feel very icky. And it made me question all kinds of my own behaviors. Did picking one's nose decrease one's chances of going to heaven, for example? Was it wrong to use the church's stubby half pencils intended for filling out donation envelopes to instead draw pictures of skirmishing space vessels on the back of the church program? Did the inclusion of explosions in such pictures make them even more sinful?

Theirs was a small-town church in western Missouri, a big, boxy brick affair with a white classical pediment supported by four imposing Doric columns that revealed themselves to be hollow if you rapped your knuckles on them. The sanctuary itself was composed of three elements: light, air, and red. And beneath it was a simple low-ceilinged basement. It was there, in the basement, that potluck meals were frequently served: after Wednesday evening services and for special events like revival, or old-persons' social club, or church choir jamboree, or the celebration of Jeremy Jackson's Grandmother's Twenty-Five Years of Church Organ-Playing and Sunday School Teaching and Excellent Grooming. There on long tables the food was arranged in the typical first-stuff, middle-stuff, sweet-stuff fashion. An average spread might include meatloaf, fried chicken, ham, roast beef; a flotilla of casseroles — zucchini, green bean, something-something-noodle; a small flock of salads combining Jell-O with surprising elements such as cottage cheese or finely grated carrots; home-canned green beans, home-grown corn, sliced tomatoes in summer, three-bean salad, potato salad, baked beans, more baked beans, and also baked beans; coleslaw, at least four different choices of deviled eggs, fruit salad, bread, iced tea, coffee, lemonade.

You loaded your paper plate as you wished. Even if you were a child. Even if your mother was a whole-grain and raw-milk and brown-egg fanatic. You moved along the table, taking what you wanted, always mindful of the particularly tricky loading characteristics of the thin paper plates of the 1970s. And then . . . And then!

Then you came to the land of desserts.

In my memory, the acreage covered by the desserts was equal to or greater than that occupied by the nondesserts. And what desserts!

This was farm country, after all, and though in those days the fuel that ran the farms was gasoline, the fuel that ran the farmers was still — as it long had been — protein and sugar. Here in the church basement, bathed in the holy fluorescent light, was a veritable promised land of desserts, a congregation of calories, a tabernacle of yum.

There were cakes aplenty. The Bundt and the marble and the chocolate sheet. The angel food, the devil's food, the sponge, and the chiffon. Here was seven-minute frosting, there was lemon glaze, and yonder stood the butter icing. The usual pies were lemon meringue, chocolate cream, apple, and cherry. Maybe a strawberry rhubarb in season. Pumpkin in the fall and winter. You could also count on there being a plate of chocolate chip cookies, and perhaps brownies, too. Maybe some sandies or sugar cookies. Fudge did oft appear, as well as the thematically appropriate white nougat called "divinity."

So you ate a little first stuff, a smattering of second stuff, and plenty of dessert. And the people were nice. They joked about how much meatloaf Charles Who-and-Who ate. They praised your grandmother's pie. They ruffled your hair. They did not mention Jesus.

If the feeling that I got upstairs was that I was not a member of the club, the feeling that I got downstairs was that in fact I was part of a more important club: my family. And an important member. A member who could eat more dessert if he darn well wanted to.

In my opinion, from my viewpoint of some thirty years later, the implicit messages about food and family and community that were at the literal foundation of the church were more powerful and important than any amount of moralizing or ceremony or slipshod interpretation of a huge and complicated and difficult to translate book by dozens of writers who didn't know each other and who did not have good editors from thousands of years ago ever could be.

But back to the pie. Though my grandmother contributed all manner of food to hundreds of potlucks over her fifty-plus-year membership in the church, she was — at least during my childhood — most likely to bring her lemon meringue pie. It was perfection. That is not hyperbole. That is established fact. Her pie had a billowy meringue that *did not weep*. It had a lemon custard that *did not slump*. It had flaky crust that *did not sog*. It was, as I have written elsewhere, cut into eight pieces that the first eight people in line took. All the people who did not get a piece of that pie spent the rest of the day with a shadow upon their hearts. A shadow the shape and size of a piece of Mrs. Jackson's lemon meringue pie.

And though we have the recipe, and though my mother and I are both accomplished and capable bakers, and though my mother had in fact on more than one occasion witnessed my grandmother's making of the lemon meringue pie and taken mental notes as to the particular techniques employed, neither she nor I can make the lemon meringue pie so that it matches the quality of Grandma's pie.

Our pies weep, even if just a little bit. They sog slightly. The custard slumps. They taste very good, mind you, even extremely good, and they would generally put any truck stop lemon meringue pie to shame. But they are not hers.

Sometimes I wonder if there is a quantity of what I suppose could be called magic to cooking. The cook takes various elements from the natural world — wheat, fruit, milk, eggs, etcetera — and combines them in a specific way that is set forth in a spellbook (or one's memory), and applies transformative forces such as heat and air, and creates something that did not exist before and would not exist without the skills of the cook, and which contains more goodness and deliciousness than the sum of its parts. That is magical.

I don't intend to conflate *magic* and *religion* here. I'm simply suggesting that there is something miraculous about what a good cook can do with good ingredients. (On a side note, though, let me suggest that I do think that the Bible would have done well to include more recipes.) And when the cook then serves the result of her efforts to people she cares for, it seems to me that the magical essence of the food — the result of a collaboration between the natural world and the human world — then reinforces the bond between the cook and the diner.

What I'm getting at, I suppose, is that my grandmother's pie was more than just a pie. It was — like all handmade, good food that is shared with others — a symbolic and literal token of connection between people and the land, between members of the community, between family members, and if you so believe, between people and their maker.

To extend my argument, let me point out that Grandma did not just cook and bake for church and family. She took food to people who were sick or bereft or just lonely. She would take food to the nursing home. She would contribute to the meals served before or after funerals and drop off dishes for those who were recently widowed. She gave treats to her piano students.

And she was not an anomaly. She was following the customs of her era and her home. There were dozens of women — and perhaps a few men — who did the same thing in her small town. And if I think about the home-cooked food that they were constantly making and distributing, it awes me. It was a network. A network of food that bound people together.

Out of respect for the rest of the family's religiosity, and as a sort of nod toward my parents' own nature-centric kind of secular humanism, when the Jackson side of my family gathered at our house for meals, we did say grace before eating. But it was not the kind of "Jesus, thank you for being Jesus," kind of prayer that my grandfather said at his own house; instead, it was a simple song that went like this:

> We thank the Lord,
> for giving us the things we need,
> the sun and the rain and the apple seeds.
> We thank the Lord.

It was, I have learned, a variation on a song that Johnny Appleseed supposedly sang as he traveled, but I really don't care if that's true or not. What I like about the prayer is how it celebrates the centrality of food in our lives. Food, I think it is saying, is at the root of the root. The basement.

Three years ago, at that point in August when in Iowa there had just commenced the tug of war between the-beginning-of-the-end-of-summer and the-beginning-of-the-beginning-of-autumn, I received a phone call early one morning. It was my parents — both of them on the line — and they delivered the news that my uncle Kent had killed himself at dawn.

As my wife, my six-month-old daughter, and I drove down the length of Illinois later that week on our way to the funeral in Kentucky, we left the Upper Midwest almost-autumn and returned fully to the province of summer. The ripening cornfields fanning past our windows had almost completed their transformation from green to that particular kind of field corn tan that reminds me of the dust that used to cling to the bumpers of our cars on the farm where I grew up. So seasonally we were traveling backward, and by the clock of the corn harvest we were moving forward — for the fields in Iowa had been planted later in the spring and still held great reservoirs of a glossy and jungle-dense green — but this divergence, this sensation of time moving forward and backward simultaneously, amounted to little more than ripples traveling away from the spot where the stone had been dropped in the water. Kent had died. He had died, and harvest was still coming, as it did every year, and summer was ending, as it did every year, and the rich soil of Illinois gave us only field corn and soybeans, neither of which were actual food.

The day of the funeral was difficult. We had our little baby in tow, and we had a poor breakfast without coffee, and we came to the doors of the church so late that we were ushered — by people we had never met, but who were waiting for us, watching for us — quickly through a side door into the enormous sanctuary, where as soon as we sat down next to my parents and sisters, the service began. It was a cavernous Baptist church, of recent vintage, with parking lots that covered acres, and though the funeral service clearly honored my uncle's life, it did not speak to my values, and it made almost no mention of the one person in the church who had known Kent through Kent's entire life: my father.

When we finally made it back to the church from the cemetery it was late afternoon, and my wife and I were, to put it plainly, depleted, and we walked what seemed liked hundreds of yards through the church building to get to the meal that has always been, as far as I know, a feature of Baptist funerals. And there, in a charmlessly functional cafeteria, we were offered fried chicken and ham and green beans and salads and iced tea and cornbread and rolls and coffee and a variety of cakes. The food, to a large extent, was homemade, and it was straightforward and honest fare, and of a style of midcentury cookery that would have pleased any hungry farmhand. We ate and were nourished in such a deep and satisfying way that the entire aspect of the day was altered. We were comforted. And we were reminded of the goodness of life, and the goodness of the land, and the goodness of family. It was, in my reckoning, as fitting a response to Kent's death as anything I had witnessed all day.

We were sorrowful, and you fed us. We were distraught, and you nourished us. We were worn down, and you gave us drink.

In the months following Kent's death, my family tried to make some sense of it. He had been a garrulous and jocular man. A loud talker with a southern accent that he picked up from living in Texas, Louisiana, and Tennessee. He was a man of faith, a doting grandfather, an avid outdoorsman. He dressed neatly, stood straight, sang in a clear tenor voice, and didn't seem to be the kind of person who ever doubted himself. Only in his last several months of life did he have a serious problem with anxiety.

I personally found myself wondering what could have changed the way Kent left us. I regretted not having had the chance to introduce him to my daughter. She was only six months old when he died, but I felt that if I had made the effort — if I had known how bad he was feeling — and he had met her, she would have lit up his life the same way she had lit up mine the moment she was born. She could have saved him, right?

It is a simplistic fantasy, but it is impossible for me to dismiss outright.

Or to carry the point further, what if his family all still lived near each other? What if his son weren't three states away, his brother in central Missouri, his nieces and nephews scattered throughout the Midwest? What if we met every week for Sunday "dinner" — religious beliefs or no — and celebrated birthdays together and graduations and went fishing and played softball and mowed lawns and sang and complained about the weather and cheered on the St. Louis Cardinals?

But that, too, is just a fantasy, and he did, after all, have a wonderful wife, and his daughter and her children and husband lived minutes away and were a large part of his life, and he lived in a town where he was known and loved.

Okay. But what if — *what if* — he had been able to taste his mother's lemon meringue pie one more time?

Food and family and community can sustain us and connect us, but they can also buoy us, and sometimes transform us. They can save us from ourselves. Can't they?

Mildred Jackson's Lemon-y Cream Pie

Makes 8 servings

1 cup sugar
1/4 cup plus 1 tablespoon cornstarch
1/4 teaspoon salt
2 cups milk
3 egg yolks (whites reserved)
1 teaspoon lemon zest
1/3 cup lemon juice, about 3 lemons
3 tablespoons butter
9-inch pie crust, prebaked

MERINGUE

3 to 4 egg whites
1/4 teaspoon cream of tartar
6 tablespoons sugar

Preheat the oven to 350 degrees. Mix the sugar, cornstarch, and salt in a saucepan. Add the milk slowly, stirring until the mixture is smooth. Cook over low heat, stirring constantly, until the mixture is thick. Remove from stove.

In a mixing bowl, whisk the egg yolks briefly, then add a little of the hot custard while continuing to stir. Then stir the yolk mixture into the custard. Return the custard to the stove and cook over low heat for 5 more minutes, stirring constantly. Remove the custard from the heat and stir in the lemon zest, lemon juice, and butter.

For the meringue, beat the egg whites with the cream of tartar until the mixture is frothy. Beat in the sugar gradually, and continue beating until the mixture is stiff and shiny.

Pour the custard into the prebaked pie crust and put the meringue on top, spreading it onto the edge of the crust so that it seals in the custard. Bake the pie for 12 to 15 minutes, until the meringue is golden. Serve at room temperature or chilled.

Source Acknowledgments

"In the Midwest, It's Meatloaf," by Elizabeth Berg, previously appeared in *Special Reports* magazine. © Elizabeth Berg.

"Field Trips," by Stuart Dybek, previously appeared in *Harper's*, February 2000. Reprinted with permission of the author.

"Easter Island Noodles Almondine," by Thom Jones, was originally published in *Granta*. © 2009 by Thom Jones, reprinted with permission of The Wylie Agency LLC.

"Let Them Eat Pâté," by Peter Sagal, previously appeared in *Saveur* 105. Copyright © by Wrights Media. All rights reserved. Reprinted by permission.

"Le Dog, Ann Arbor, Michigan," by Jules Van Dyck-Dobos, is reprinted from *Gastronomica* 6, no. 1 (2006), 93–94, © The Regents of the University of California. Used by permission. All rights reserved.

Recipes in "The Door County Fish Boil," by Peggy Wolff, are reprinted with permission from The White Gull Inn and appear in *The White Gull Inn Centennial Cookbook — More Favorite Recipes from Our Kitchen*.

"Thrill Food," by John Markus, is reprinted from *Gastronomica* 3, no. 3 (2003), © The Regents of the University of California. Used by permission. All rights reserved.

"Tomorrowland," by Peter Meehan, is reprinted from *Saveur* 105. Copyright © by Wrights Media. All rights reserved. Reproduced by permission.

"On Cider, Cornmeal, and Comfort," by Robin Mather, is reprinted from the memoir *The Feast Nearby: How I Lost My Job, Buried a Marriage, and Found My Way by Keeping Chickens, Foraging, Preserving, Bartering, and Eating Locally (All on $40 a Week)*. Reprinted with permission from Ten Speed Press and the author.

To order or obtain more information on these or other University of Nebraska Press titles, visit www.nebraskapress.unl.edu.